The Coming Age of Direct Democracy

The Coming Age of Direct Democracy

California's Recall and Beyond

Mark Baldassare
and
Cheryl Katz

ROWMAN & LITTLEFIELD PUBLISHERS, INC.
Lanham • Boulder • New York • Toronto • Plymouth, UK

ROWMAN & LITTLEFIELD PUBLISHERS, INC.

Published in the United States of America
by Rowman & Littlefield Publishers, Inc.
A wholly owned subsidary of The Rowman & Littlefield Publishing Group, Inc.
4501 Forbes Boulevard, Suite 200, Lanham, Maryland 20706
www.rowmanlittlefield.com

Estover Road, Plymouth PL6 7PY, United Kingdom

British Library Cataloguing in Publication Information Available

Library of Congress Cataloging-in-Publication Data

Baldassare, Mark.
  The coming age of direct democracy : California's recall and beyond / Mark Baldassare
and Cheryl Katz.
    p. cm.
  Includes bibliographical references and index.
  ISBN-13: 978-0-7425-3871-9 (cloth : alk. paper)
  ISBN-10: 0-7425-3871-0 (cloth : alk. paper)
  ISBN-13: 978-0-7425-3872-6 (pbk. : alk. paper)
  ISBN-10: 0-7425-3872-9 (pbk. : alk. paper)
  1. Direct democracy—California. 2. California—Politics and government—21st
century. 3. Governors—California—Election. 4. Recall—California. 5. Elections—
California. 6. Political campaigns—California. I. Katz, Cheryl. II. Title.
  JK8789.B35 2008
  324.9794'054—dc22

                                                              2007006408

Printed in the United States of America

♾ ™ The paper used in this publication meets the minimum requirements of American
National Standard for Information Sciences—Permanence of Paper for Printed Library
Materials, ANSI/NISO Z39.48-1992.

Contents

Preface

California has long been in the forefront of direct democracy, having been one of the first states to adopt the tools of citizen-initiated legislation early in the twentieth century. In recent years, California's experiment with direct democracy took a new and dramatic turn with the recall of its governor. *The Coming Age of Direct Democracy* examines this extraordinary era in political history, when California voters went to the polls to vote in statewide elections five times in five years. This experience was transforming, representing both the best of times and the worst of times for a governance system whose roots stretch back to the Populist era.

Over the course of a few years, the balance of political power in California shifted significantly and perhaps permanently from the state's elected officials to a dwindling number of voters making public policy at the ballot box. Led by political neophyte Arnold Schwarzenegger, who tapped into Californians' long-standing populism and distrust of representative government, a new, hybrid form of democracy emerged. The resulting blend of the legislative and citizens' initiative processes illuminates a path that could be followed in many other states and perhaps even at the national level.

What has enabled this changing system of state governance? In the *Coming Age of Direct Democracy*, we hypothesize that four factors have driven the Golden State farther away from its elected representatives and closer to the initiative process in setting public policy. We define these factors as: populism, partisanship, special interests, and voter distrust. While none of these is unique to the political environment of the past few years, their combined presence is amplified by the turbulent demographic and economic transition underway in this mega-state of 37 million residents.

The collective effects of decades of growing voter distrust, increasing partisanship by the major political parties, and the rising influence of special interests first surfaced during the California gubernatorial election of 2002. It was a campaign season best remembered for negative ads that soured the electorate on both the challenger and the incumbent, resulting in the lowest voter turnout in state history. Voters' confidence in their governor and state legislature imploded when a multibillion dollar budget deficit was announced soon after the election. Less than a year later, Californians made history by turning to a rarely used provision of direct democracy—the recall—to vent their frustration with their state government.

Voters made good on their threats in 2003 when they collected enough signatures to qualify a special election to recall governor Gray Davis and replace him with one of 135 challengers. Ironically, this recall election featured a populist candidate whose political debut had been an initiative campaign the previous year. While the Democratic governor was locked in a nasty battle with his Republican challenger during the 2002 gubernatorial campaign, Arnold Schwarzenegger was conducting a folksy effort to champion a highly popular, nonpartisan initiative, Proposition 49, which was designed to earmark existing state funds for after-school programs for schoolchildren. One year later, Schwarzenegger was able to parlay this populist approach into success during the recall election by reinforcing voters' fears that their state government was in the grip of special interests and partisans and portraying his lack of political credentials as the antidote.

In the year after Schwarzenegger's election, Californians of all political stripes enjoyed a new era of bipartisanship and a cooperative spirit in 2004. In recent years, the state legislature had become highly polarized along party lines and business, labor unions, and other special interests created a stalemate on most major policy decisions. Now, led by their charismatic, politically independent, and highly popular new governor, Californians had hope that the partisan gridlock would end. Having inherited a huge budget deficit, Schwarzenegger coaxed the divided legislature into submitting a recovery bond for voter approval, and voters in turn showed their support for his fiscal package. The new governor was a masterful negotiator, bringing both Democratic and Republican leaders into his tent, and ordering them to work together to produce legislation on contentious issues such as workers' compensation reform or face the prospects of having him go directly to the voters and pass his policies through the initiative process.

But, seemingly as in a Greek tragedy, things soon reverted to form. By early 2005, Schwarzenegger had fallen under the sway of business leaders and conservatives, who were his main source of financial support, and went on the attack against groups he characterized as "special interests"—including school teachers, nurses, and public employee unions. His agenda in the "Year of Reform" included an effort to redraw the political boundaries of legislative seats, empower the governor to limit state spending without legislative approval, change the public employee pension system, redefine teacher tenure, and restrict the political contributions of unions. In stark contrast to the unifying themes of his gubernatorial bid, his efforts in 2005 seemed designed to splinter the electorate and bolster special interests. When Democratic legislators refused to comply with his reform agenda, Schwarzenegger called a special election and placed the package on the ballot as initiatives. His strategists hoped to win by convincing all but the most loyal Republicans to stay at home on election day. The plan backfired badly. All his initiatives were defeated, his ability to work with Democrats was destroyed, and the threat of taking his policies directly to the voters if the legislature failed to act was now toothless. In the wake of Schwarzenegger's faulty efforts, Californians' approval of their elected representatives and trust in their state government plunged once again.

But, in a turn of events highly unusual in contemporary American politics, there was a reversal of political fortunes in 2006. The governor repeatedly apologized for taking voters through an unwanted special election and promised to work with the legislature in finding bipartisan solutions before approaching voters again. What followed was an election year with surprisingly little tension between the Republican governor and a legislature that was controlled by Democrats. Abandoning his divisive themes of the previous year, Schwarzenegger turned to an ambitious, nonpartisan agenda of rebuilding the state's dilapidated infrastructure. The legislature cooperated and enacted a $37 billion bond measure, which was placed on the November ballot for voter approval. In a rare show of political harmony, a state budget was passed on time. The governor and legislature agreed to a package of popular laws including a minimum wage increase, restrictions on greenhouse gas emissions, and prescription drug discounts. During the fall election campaign, the Democratic candidate for governor sought to tap into voters' partisan loyalties and rally special interests against Schwarzenegger, but with little success. In a year in which the Democrats experienced significant gains on the national scene, GOP Governor Schwarzenegger was reelected by a substantial margin in a "blue" state with significant support outside of his party and voters endorsed his entire package of infrastructure bonds. The "Year of Recovery" ended on a hopeful note for California's distrustful electorate, which had rejected efforts to use direct democracy for partisan and special interest purposes in favor of the promise of progress through a combined system of legislative actions and the initiative process.

California's recent experience illuminates the flaws of direct democracy—the limited checks and balances by other branches of government, its vulnerability to manipulation by well-funded partisan and special interests, and the emergence of a political industry feeding the wallets of scores of signature-gatherers, pollsters, campaign strategists, advertisers, and others seeking to profit from promoting or fighting measures on the ballot. Despite this, Californians have not changed their views about the overall value of the initiative system. They do complain about the clutter and confusion on the ballot, the fact that measures appear before the legislature has had a chance to weigh in, and especially about the influence of money and special interests. They also support a number of changes that they believe would make the initiative system function better.

The California experience also shows the merits of a process that energizes voters and rededicates them to the political system—taking the reins of power into their own hands. In today's society, citizens want and need the ability to create their own laws and the political system needs a fourth branch to circumvent gridlocked legislatures, hidebound political parties, and sometimes-corrupt politicians. But the process also needs safeguards to make certain that direct democracy really is "for the people." A hybrid democracy, which preserves the current system of electing representatives to carry out the duties of governance but incorporates increased amounts of citizen input and oversight, may be the answer to the public's desire for populism and the solution to the partisan divisions, special interest influence, and voter distrust that currently plague America's political process.

Acknowledgments

We could not have completed this massive project without the support and help of others. We are indebted to the Public Policy Institute of California (PPIC) for the dedication of resources to pursue this study of direct democracy. The institute has been providing detailed information on the intersection of public opinion and public policy since founding the PPIC Statewide Survey in 1998. Over this period, there have been more than seventy large-scale surveys of at least two thousand adults each that allow us to intensively analyze the opinions of more than 150,000 Californians on political issues, public policy preferences, and ballot choices. Much of this survey work was supported from the endowment of the institute. For this support, we owe special gratitude to PPIC; its board of directors; the gift from William Hewlett to fund the institute; and Arjay and Frances Fearing Miller for their gift of an endowed chair.

In addition, many of the PPIC Statewide Surveys that are mentioned in this book were made possible with generous funding from other foundations with interests in political participation, the well-being of residents, and the public policy-making process in California, including the William and Flora Hewlett Foundation, the James Irvine Foundation, the David and Lucile Packard Foundation, the California Endowment, and the Pew Charitable Trusts. We would like to thank Paul Brest, James Canales, Carol Larson, Amy Dominguez Arms, Hal Harvey, Kristi Kimball, Barbara Masters, and Robert Ross for their support.

We benefited from the expertise and writings of colleagues at PPIC. We would like to acknowledge the research of Hans Johnson, Paul Lewis, Max Neiman, Karthick Ramakrishnan, Deborah Reed, Belinda Reyes, Fred Silva, and Michael Teitz. Others who have worked with the PPIC Statewide Survey in the past include D. L. Apollonio, Ana Maria Arumi, Jon Cohen, Renatta DeFever, Chris Hoene, Eliana Kaimowitz Rodriguez, Eric McGhee, Kristy Michaud, Douglas Strand, and Mina Yaroslavsky. We also benefited from discussions with other institute colleagues, including Abby Cook, David Lyon, Joyce Peterson, and Gary Bjork. We appreciate the contributions of the PPIC Statewide Survey project team in recent years, including Dean Bonner, Jennifer Paluch, and Sonja Petek. The views expressed in this book are those of the authors and do not reflect the views of PPIC.

We received many useful ideas about elections and initiatives from members of the PPIC Statewide Survey Advisory Committee, including Angela Blackwell, William Hauck, Dennis Hunt, Sherry Bebitch Jeffe, Monica Lozano, Donna Lucas, Dan Rosenheim, and Cathy Taylor. We have also received good feedback on a regular basis from Nick Bollman, Corey Brown, David Lesher, Michael Mantell, Noel Perry, Tony Quinn, Jaime Regalado, Jean Ross, Robert Stern, Steve Weiner, and Tracy Westin.

There are many scholars, authors, and columnists whose works influenced our thinking about the themes of this book. These individuals include Shaun Bowler, David Broder, Bruce Cain, Lou Cannon, Jack Citrin, Todd Donovan, Elisabeth Gerber, Larry Gerston, Thad Kousser, David Magleby, Joe Mathews, John Matsusaka, David McCuan, Jack Peltason, Susan Rasky, David Schmidt, Peter Schrag, George Skelton, Daniel Smith, Ray Sonenshein, Caroline Tolbert, Dan Walters, M. Dane Waters, and Dan Weintraub.

We are grateful for the contributions of others involved in nonpartisan, independent public opinion surveys on elections and public policy, including Mollyann Brodie, Jon Cohen, Mark DiCamillo, Scott Keeter, Andrew Kohut, and Susan Pincus.

We have learned a great deal in discussions and from the writings of California journalists including Mark Barabak, Amy Chance, Evan Halper, Peter Nicholas, John Marelius, Carla Marinucci, John Myers, Warren Olney, Scott Shafer, Robert Salladay, John Wildermuth, and others cited in the bibliography. We gained insights from those with a working knowledge of political campaigns, including Gale Kaufman, Steve Kinney, Steve Maviglio, Julie Buckner Levy, Donna Lucas, Sal Russo, Dan Schnur, Garry South, and Larry Thomas.

We would like to express our appreciation for the patience and wisdom of our editors at Rowman & Littlefield during the lengthy process of this book project, including Niels Aaboe, Jennifer Knerr, and Renee Legatt. We also thank the two anonymous reviewers of earlier draft manuscripts for their thoughtful comments and suggestions that helped to improve this book.

Lastly, we wish to acknowledge the contributions of our two children, Benjamin and Daniel, whose developing interests in California's political scene from the Davis recall in 2003 to the Schwarzenegger reelection in 2006 provided an inspiration and an audience for ideas. We hope this book will be useful to students in their generation, as well as others today and far into the future who seek to better understand the dynamics and consequences of this path-breaking time in California and its implications for the national political scene.

1

Introduction:
A New Era in Direct Democracy?

A flurry of political events and related trends in public opinion have ushered in a new era in direct democracy in California. The centerpiece of this sea change was the recall of governor Gray Davis in 2003 and his replacement by movie actor Arnold Schwarzenegger. Yet the political movement toward ballot-box decision making had its roots in the election season a year earlier—the 2002 Davis reelection campaign that sowed the seeds of voter discontent and the Schwarzenegger initiative campaign that energized and inspired voters. The course of that election stirred up voters' distrust of government and fueled their perception that elected leaders were in the grip of partisans and special interests. In response, voters turned to the populist tools of direct democracy—and put them to a new use in recalling their governor. But the factors that enabled the recall remain in effect today, pointing to the increasing appeal of populism and growing use of the ballot box for policy making. In the wake of the recall, an overwhelming majority of California voters support setting state policy at the ballot box and the use of ballot measures in policy making has reached unprecedented levels.

Fundamental changes are underway in the relationships between the people, their elected representatives, the ballot box, and the government. As the balance of power between voters and legislators is now dramatically altered, California's experience serves as an example of "hybrid democracy" that could spread to other states.

This chapter offers an overview of the history of the direct democracy movement in the United States over the past century and the developments in California in recent decades. We present four enabling conditions for the emergence of a new and more prominent role for direct democracy in recent years: the rise of populism, partisanship, special interests, and voter distrust.

1

While these themes were present in earlier eras, they have grown and reached a new level of influence on the California political scene since 2002.

We review the trends in public opinion on the initiative process and elected representatives by studying a large-scale survey series conducted since 1998. We also discuss the social, political, and economic trends that have implications for direct democracy use and the lessons to learn from California's recent experience. This introduction ends with an overview of the book—chapters that follow provide explanation of and evidence for the factors that have created a new political reality, marked by an enhanced role for direct democracy in California governance since 2002. We conclude with a chapter on the future of direct democracy and potential reforms to improve the workings of a hybrid democracy.

AN EXPANDING ROLE FOR DIRECT DEMOCRACY

The California gubernatorial recall in 2003 signals a groundbreaking move into a new age of direct democracy—citizens grabbing the wheel from their elected representatives and insisting on driving—which has long been building. Certainly, there were unique contextual factors driving the downfall of Gray Davis and special personal qualities leading up to Arnold Schwarzenegger's emergence as a winning candidate in California. But the surprising outcome of having a Republican actor with no political experience become the head of this large, Democratic state simply could not have occurred without the public being predisposed toward a populist campaign: one that appeared to avoid divisive partisanship and the influence of special interests, at a time when a distrustful electorate was seeking a new way to express its growing misgivings about representative democracy.

In his eleven-week journey from action-movie hero to governor of the state that is home to one in eight Americans, Arnold Schwarzenegger stunned the nation by convincing voters to recall their governor and choose him as the replacement from a long list of candidates. By toppling a veteran member of the political establishment, and parading his "take it to the people" approach to governance before a raptly watching world, this Austrian-born bodybuilder became a modern-day Samson, pulling down a pillar of the nation's foundation of representative democracy and shifting the balance toward a new political order built on the uncertainty of direct voter intervention.

"This election was not about replacing one man; it was not replacing one party. It was about changing the entire political climate of our state," Schwarzenegger proclaimed on November 17, 2003, at his inauguration as governor of California. "The election was the people's veto for politics as usual." Politics as usual had been under attack for some time in the state that was the first in the nation to dust off the tools of direct democracy created during the Progressive era nearly seventy years earlier and put them to modern use. California's historic deployment of the initiative process that brought about the Proposition 13 tax revolt in 1978 triggered a spate of imitations among the twenty-four states with citizens' initiative provisions.

Fueled by plunging confidence in the judgment of their elected leaders, frustration over legislative gridlock, and a large dose of antitax sentiment, citizens' initiatives quickly became a mainstay of legislation in most of the states that allow them. Today, statewide initiatives are used an average of more than seventy times per election cycle. The majority of initiatives do not pass, but their existence changes the dynamics between the voters and their elected representatives, and many of the state ballot measures that have been enacted have had powerful effects on the political system (see Waters 2003).

Among the significant uses of the initiative provision—where legislation is enacted by voters directly at the ballot box, rather than by legislators in the statehouse—and its related measure, the referendum—where voters vote to remove laws from the books—have been the legalization of physician-assisted suicide in Oregon, the creation of the Taxpayers' Bill of Rights in Colorado, and numerous efforts to curtail the power of politicians. Legislators have been further constrained by term limits, which have been passed in most of the states that allow citizens to place initiatives directly on the ballot. In California, initiatives and referenda have appeared on the state ballot more than two hundred times in the past twenty-five years. While historically fewer than half of the initiatives on state ballots have passed, the results have still been dramatic for policy making, with past outcomes such as capping property tax increases, mandating life sentences for third-time offenders, denying public benefits to illegal immigrants, and dictating how the state budget should be spent (see Allswang 2000; California Commission on Campaign Financing 1992; Waters 2003).

But in the new century, these citizens' initiatives alone were not sufficient to mollify California's dissatisfied voters. With confidence in their leaders at an all-time low amid a faltering economy, a deepening budget crisis, an aloof governor, and general insecurity in the wake of the 2001 terrorist attacks, California voters were no longer content with merely writing new laws or revoking existing legislation. The 2002 gubernatorial campaign had been short on substance and long on acrimony, spurring the voters' belief that their elected representatives didn't care much about the needs of people like themselves. Charges of political cronyism lobbed during the campaign inflamed Californians' long-standing suspicion that the state government was under the influence of special interests. Meanwhile, political partisanship had gridlocked the legislature. Public anger had reached such a level that when veteran antitax activist Ted Costa dipped back into the bag of 1911 provisions and came up with a third tool of direct democracy—the recall—more than a million voters signed petitions to put this old instrument to a new and dramatic use.

What followed was a media frenzy, as reporters from around the world converged on California to cover the "circus"—a Hollywood star cruising up and down the state in campaign buses with names like "Predator One" and "Running Man"—titles from some of his action-hero movies. Not to miss out on the fun, Californians from all elements of the state's huge and diverse populace rushed to join the carnival. In addition to reporting Schwarzenegger's every move, the bloated campaign press corps delighted in covering the antics of the multitude of other governor wannabes, ranging from a porn film actress to a former child movie star to the lieutenant governor of the state. The world was transfixed as allegations circulated of Schwarzenegger groping women on his movie sets.

An audience that was previously unimaginable for public affairs programming watched the gubernatorial candidates debate. Round-the-clock press coverage brought the campaign into a larger number of homes than ever before by any race for any office. On that overcast Sacramento morning in November 2003, California was the talk of the nation as governor Gray Davis stepped down from office less than a year after he was reelected for a second term and was replaced by the Terminator.

But the impact of the California recall reached far beyond the spectacle of that summer and fall. For as voters throughout the nation were entertained by the outlandish events on the West Coast, they were also witnessing a phenomenon that touched them on a personal level—people like themselves ceasing to put up with the feelings of political alienation, mistrust, and helplessness that they knew all too well. A heady message lay under the goings-on in the Golden State: people should have the power to reject a system they feel has failed them. Not only did Californians oust their governor in the fall of 2003, they also turned against the entrenched partisanship that had ossified state government and forged a nonpartisan coalition supporting a political outsider. Having crossed the threshold with the recall, the use of direct democracy continued to rise in its aftermath, occupying a steadily increasing role in Californian governance. Distrust of government continued and public disdain for the role of partisanship and special interests seemed to feed off of this historic event. Direct democracy had come of age, transforming the nature of elections and policy making in the state's largest political arena.

THE 2003 RECALL: MAKING HISTORY
AND CHANGING ELECTIONS

In some ways, the 2003 recall could be seen as the result of a "perfect storm"—a series of unconnected events that happened to coincide and create the ideal situation for the recall to take place (see Gerston and Christensen 2004). The end-of-the-century boom economy that Californians had enjoyed during Governor Davis's first two years in office began to collapse after the hyperinflated dot-com industry started leaking air in mid-2000. That same year, the state was hit by rolling blackouts and spiraling electricity costs as the result of a flawed energy deregulation plan and price manipulation by unscrupulous traders. Then the terrorist attacks of September 11, 2001, shook the confidence of the nation and especially California, where the hijacked planes had been headed. By the end of the year, the state had lost thousands of Internet and technology-related jobs and the state budget was headed for a deficit. With little positive to focus on, the 2002 gubernatorial election had been nasty, and many voters had been turned off. Davis had squeaked by to a five-point victory in November, but his image had suffered mightily in the process.

All these events put Californians in an ugly mood when Ted Costa, a frequent user of the state's initiative provision, announced the launch of a recall effort against Davis on February 5, 2003. The events that followed, including Davis's initial arrogant response to the threat and reality of a recall campaign, the spread of the recall message via the Internet and talk radio, and the eleventh-hour cash infusion by a would-be candidate that turned "partisan mischief" into a serious threat, also seemed at least part serendipity.

But when the recall effort qualified for the ballot on July 23, 2003, with 1.3 million valid signatures—more than 400,000 over the number required—the world began to take notice. The movement was further propelled by the entry of Schwarzenegger into the race in early August, triggering an avalanche of media coverage. By late September, when an estimated 2.4 million households tuned in to the candidates' debate—more than had watched any of the presidential debates the previous year (*Los Angeles Times*, September 26, 2003)—the recall was unstoppable. On October 7, 2003, in a two-part ballot that asked voters first to approve or reject the recall and second to select a replacement candidate (even if they voted no on the recall), Californians voted 55 percent to 45 percent to recall Governor Davis. Arnold Schwarzenegger was elected governor with 49 percent of the vote, easily beating out the closest contender, Democratic lieutenant governor Cruz Bustamante (32%).

Moreover, in the aftermath of the recall, direct democracy has become a growing force in California politics. The use of this provision, which had been steadily rising since the 1970s, exploded under the new administration (see table 1.1). Governor Schwarzenegger has relied more on the initiative process to enact his agenda than any other governor in the nation's history. In his first year in office, virtually all of his major accomplishments were instituted through ballot measures—either those actually placed on the ballot or those used as a threat to get recalcitrant lawmakers to go along with his plans. In his second year, Schwarzenegger's "take it to the people" approach

Table 1.1: **State Propositions on the Ballot**

	Number on Ballot	Number Approved
1912–1919	30	8
1920–1929	33	10
1930–1939	37	10
1940–1949	20	6
1950–1959	12	2
1960–1969	10	3
1970–1979	24	7
1980–1989	44	21
1990–1999	69	32
2000–2006	86	46

Sources: Baldassare 2000; Lee 1997; California Secretary of State March 2000, November 2000, March 2002, November 2002, October 2003, March 2004, November 2004, November 2005, June 2006, November 2006.

continued, although he failed to achieve the changes he wanted in a special election in November 2005. In a highly partisan election with big money from special interests on prominent display, all his reform proposals were defeated. Despite their rejection of Schwarzenegger's measures, however, voters remained committed to the state's provisions for direct democracy—and deeply distrustful of government and their elected representatives. By 2006, the governor was back with a new agenda, rebuilding the state's aging infrastructure, and was again appealing to voters' populist desires. His new agenda was an attempt to cut across the deep partisan divide that had once again surfaced in state politics. As usual, the voters had a part to play at the ballot box, and they complied, passing the largest bond package in the state's history. With Schwarzenegger's sweeping victory in the fall of 2006, both in the success of his political agenda and his reelection as governor, the age of direct democracy was all but certain to continue.

But the experiences of the California recall and its aftermath had also made voters aware of the need for reform of their system of democracy and several efforts began to get underway. There were ongoing discussions about how to improve representative democracy in the state—including efforts to expand the size and diversity of the voting population, redraw legislative boundaries to offer more partisan competition in state and federal races, extend term limits to create a more experienced legislature, and manage the flow of campaign cash from dominant special interest groups. Meanwhile, under the lens of recent heavy use, the state's direct democracy tools were seen as popular, yet flawed. There were increased calls to better manage the process by which initiatives qualified for the ballot. Some called for requiring legislative review of citizens' initiatives before they could appear on the ballot, in hopes of reaching a compromise or at least avoiding legal and drafting errors. Others sought to curb the expanding role that special interest groups and big money were playing in a process that had been designed to be the people's tool when elected representatives failed them. With a hybrid democracy taking root and seemingly here to stay, the focus of public policy discourse turned from discouraging the use of ballot box legislation to making the adjustments necessary to provide for the best functioning of a new system of governance.

WHAT IS DIRECT DEMOCRACY?

For California and most other American states that have constitutional mechanisms for direct democracy, the roots go back to the end of the nineteenth and beginning of the twentieth century. The desire to reform the legislative system and free it from the influence of powerful corporations and corrupt politicians led to provisions for direct democracy being written into the constitutions of twenty-two states between 1898 and 1918 (see Cronin 1999).

Although the tools of direct democracy were first put to statewide use during the Progressive era of the early twentieth century, their origins are found in the end of the previous century and the short-lived political movement known as populism, or the People's Party. Born from the deep distrust of the political system by farmers, along with laborers, miners, and other political outsiders who were left behind by the industrial revolution, direct democracy was seen as a way to rescue government from the control of wealthy industrialists, and give power to "the people" (Cain and Miller 2001; Cronin 1999; Hofstadter 1955; Kazin 1995). Populists hoped to return the nation to a preindustrial time, when they felt that conditions were more favorable for them. As Cronin (1999, 44) describes, "Although their problems were mainly the result of overproduction, farmers believed that certain greedy influences—bankers, railroaders, land speculators and the tax structure—were at work like thieves, robbing farmers of their fair share."

Populism's main tenets were the desire for restraints on the ability of special interests to profit at the expense of the people and the belief that government should be controlled by the majority will of ordinary citizens. At the People's Party's first national convention in 1892, resolutions calling for legislative reforms included adopting the initiative and the referendum and enacting limits of a single term for the president and vice president (see Cronin 1999). Populism was fleeting, however, failing to draw widespread public support. The movement fizzled after the presidential election of 1896, in which the ideas of populist activist William Jennings Bryan, a congressman from Nebraska, were adopted by the Democratic Party, which nominated him as their presidential candidate. This usurpation of their spokesman and platform left the People's Party with little recourse but to "merge" with the Democrats. Bryan's subsequent loss to Republican William McKinley that

year exposed irreconcilable differences within the People's Party and it soon
went into demise (see Brinkley 2004). But the spirit of populism has remained a perennial force in American politics, emerging a century later as an
abiding distrust of government and a renewed effort to reshape it by placing
political power in the hands of common people (Kazin 1995).

After the collapse of the populist movement, the concept of direct democracy became embraced by the newly formed Progressive Party, a somewhat
discordant collection of political philosophies that agreed on the goal of a
professional government guided by an informed, enlightened citizenry. The
movement essentially began as a response to articles written by "muckrak-
ers"—journalists who exposed scandal and corruption, especially in politics
and corporations. The writings of reporters such as Lincoln Steffens, who
profiled machine politics and boss rule in cities, spurred a group of largely
urban "progressives" to attempt to curb the power of the political machines
(see Brinkley 2004).

Like Populists, Progressives saw the government as co-opted by corrupt
leaders and powerful corporate interests. Unlike the Populists, they did not
want government to be controlled by the plebeian masses, but rather by
educated professionals like themselves, who would reform the system and
make it work toward creating a better society (Hofstadter 1955). Believing
that corrupt elected leaders and selfish corporate interests were conspiring to
use government to hold back social progress, party activists called for a spate
of measures aimed at restructuring the political system, including campaign
finance and election reform, and the initiative, referendum, and recall.

Spurred by a national thirst for reform and fueled by the societal changes
of the industrial age, the push for direct democracy gathered steam. The first
state to give its residents the ability to pass legislation through the citizen's
initiative was South Dakota, which adopted the process in 1898, followed
by Utah in 1900 and Oregon in 1902 (Cronin 1999). However it was not
until 1904 that the first initiatives appeared on a statewide ballot—in Oregon—giving voters the right to elect state legislators in primary elections
(rather than party conventions) and giving counties the right to ban liquor
sales. Both measures passed, showing the rest of the nation that the initiative
process worked.

Two years later, Oregon citizens' petitions placed ten measures on the
state ballot and voters passed seven of them. Included among these was an
amendment to the state constitution giving all municipalities the ability to
use initiatives and referenda and another establishing provisions making it
difficult for the legislature to prevent citizens from using these measures.
This set the ball rolling for reformers across the nation to call for allowing
citizens to write and pass legislation, with four states (Montana, Oklahoma,
Maine, and Michigan) and numerous cities adopting initiatives and referenda

in the next two years (Schmidt 1989). By 1910, ten states had enacted direct democracy provisions.

Direct democracy came to California in 1911. Led by then-governor Hiram Johnson, a group of Republican reformers known as the "Progressives" placed three direct democracy provisions—the initiative, the referendum, and the recall—into the California Constitution. The goal of these provisions was to limit the power of corrupt politicians and the influence of big businesses, most notably the Southern Pacific Railroad, on state politics. Since the 1870s, the railroad had gained enormous influence over California politics, bribing legislators and judges and "holding Democrats and Republicans alike in receivership" (Starr 1985, 200). It was a series of scandals involving the inappropriate relationships between the railroad and other large corporations and the state's legislature and courts that catapulted Johnson and the Progressives to power (Schrag 1998).

The new governor made giving voters the powers of direct democracy a central platform, declaring in his inaugural speech that, "While I do not by any means believe the initiative, the referendum, and the recall are the panacea for all our political ills, yet they do give to the electorate the power of action when desired, and they do place in the hands of the people the means by which they may protect themselves" (Johnson, January 3, 1911).

In a special election on October 10, 1911, all three measures were passed into state law. Now California voters would be able to create new legislation, repeal actions passed by the legislature, and use petitions to recall judges and other elected officials.

Shortly after bringing direct democracy to California, Johnson left to spread it to the nation, joining the newly formed Progressive Party as the running mate to presidential candidate Theodore Roosevelt in 1912. Although the Progressive ticket lost to Democrats Woodrow Wilson and Thomas Marshall, the public attention the campaign focused on direct democracy helped spur its adoption. By 1914, a total of eighteen states had passed initiative and referendum provisions (Schmidt 1989). By appealing to the educated, urban middle class, the Progressives succeeded in instilling an amount of direct democracy into the political system that the Populists could only dream of. In contrast to its predecessor, however, the progressive movement intended these tools to be used to strengthen government, rather than supplant it (Cronin 1999).

Citizens' Initiatives

Today, twenty-four states give their citizens the right to enact legislation through a citizens' initiative.[1] Others, such as Minnesota (2004), Alabama (1998), and Rhode Island (1996) have seen recent, but so far unsuccessful, efforts to add initiatives and referenda to their state constitutions (Initiative and Referendum Institute 2007). In New York, governor George Pataki called for the creation of a statewide initiative and referendum throughout his administration, including as recently as his 2005 State of the State Address (*Post-Standard*, January 6, 2005). In 2002, the New York Senate endorsed an amendment to the state constitution allowing voter-sponsored initiatives, but the House refused to put the matter up for consideration. All together, seventeen noninitiative states considered legislation creating an initiative provision between 1999 and 2002, although none passed (National Conference of State Legislatures 2002). The most recent adoption of a statewide initiative provision was by Mississippi, in 1992, which allows for citizen-sponsored amendments to the state's constitution. In addition, citizens' groups in California and Virginia, sponsored by former Alaska senator Mike Gravel, are trying to pass an amendment to the U.S. Constitution that provides for national initiatives.

Initiative measures can reach the ballot through two different methods: direct and indirect. Direct initiatives go directly on the ballot when they have achieved the required number of signatures from registered voters and the signatures have been verified by a state elections official. Generally, proposed direct initiatives must be reviewed by the state attorney general before they are approved for circulation. Signature requirements, specific procedures, and timetables vary from state to state.

In states with the indirect process, sponsors of a ballot measure submit it to the state legislature, which reviews it and decides whether or not to place it on the ballot. The legislature may also generate its own competing measure. In some states, the initiative goes on the ballot if the legislature refuses or takes no action. California had both types of initiatives until 1966, when the indirect process was repealed by voters who were unhappy with the fact that the legislative review requirement meant petitions had to begin circulating at least two and a half years before the election.

Each initiative state is unique in its requirements for qualifying initiatives. Signature requirements range from a low of 2 percent of the state's population (North Dakota) to a high of 15 percent of total votes cast in the last general election (Wyoming). Most states are in the range of 5 to 8 percent of voters participating in the last gubernatorial election; however, there is considerable variability even on this point, with Colorado requiring 5 percent of votes cast for secretary of state, Idaho requiring 6 percent of eligible voters in the last election, and Oklahoma requiring 8 percent of votes cast for the office that received the highest number of votes in the most recent state election. And Montana requires initiative petitions to be signed by 5 percent of the state's registered voters. In some states, signature requirements vary depending on whether the proposed initiative is a statutory measure (creating or changing laws) or a constitutional measure (amending the state's constitution). In addition, some states require a specific geographical distribution of signatures, ensuring that voters in all regions of the state are represented.

The Referendum

The referendum allows citizens to approve or reject legislation placed on the ballot by their elected representatives. Today, all states but Delaware require citizen approval for amendments to the state constitution. In addition, twenty-four states give citizens the opportunity to vote on laws and bond measures enacted by the legislature.[2] Although the referendum is an important tool of direct democracy, its role is limited to a reactive one. Its effects have generally not been as far-reaching as the initiative, which gives citizens the ability to write and enact legislation, or the recall, which allows them to remove an official from office.

The Recall

Eighteen states currently have a provision for citizens to recall elected officials before the end of their term.[3] Most uses of the recall have been to remove local officials, such as city council or school board members, from office. Before the recall of California governor Gray Davis, there had been only one successful recall of a governor, with the removal of North Dakota governor Lynn Frazier, as well as that state's attorney general and commissioner of agriculture, in 1921. Arizona voters gathered enough signatures to qualify a recall election against governor Evan Meacham in 1988, but he was impeached by that state's legislature before the election was held. In California, there were thirty-two recall efforts to recall sitting governors between 1911 and 2003, but none qualified for a ballot before the Davis recall (National Conference of State Legislatures 2006).

Recall requirements vary from state to state. Alaska, Georgia, Kansas, Minnesota, Montana, Rhode Island, and Washington need special grounds, such as incompetence or conviction of a felony, to initiate a recall, while other states do not have a specific requirement. The number of signatures required to qualify a recall petition are higher than for an initiative petition, ranging from 10 percent of voters who were eligible to vote in the last election in Montana to 40 percent of the votes cast in the last election for the official being recalled in Kansas. California, which requires petitioners to gather signatures from 12 percent of the voters casting ballots in the last election for the official they are attempting to recall, has one of the lowest signature requirements. A low voter turnout in the 2002 gubernatorial election made the recall signature goal much easier to reach. California recall petitions circulate for a maximum of 160 days, while other states range from 60 days (Colorado, Idaho, Nevada, Wisconsin) to 320 days (New Jersey) (National Conference of State Legislatures 2006). Prior to the Davis recall, there had been numerous threats to start petition drives to remove state elected officials. But Californians had recalled just two state senators (1913 and 1914), and two state assembly members (1995).

LIMITED USE AFTER THE DAWN OF DIRECT DEMOCRACY

Direct democracy experienced a heyday between 1910 and 1920, when a total of 276 citizens' initiatives were placed on state ballots (Matsusaka 2004). By 1920, however, the public's attention had moved elsewhere. In the aftermath of World War I, people were tired of the responsibility and self-sacrifice the effort had required and were ready to shed the yoke of leadership. Initiative measures continued to appear on state ballots, but the earlier enthusiasm for direct legislation had subsided.

The number of measures hovered at around 200 to 250 in the 1930s and 1940s, then dropped to under 150 during the World War II years. In the heady postwar years, people's desire to control the legislative process waned even further, and by the 1960s, the use of ballot propositions had fallen to a low of eighty-eight throughout the decade (Matsusaka 2004). It looked like the era of direct democracy was over.

GROWING USE AFTER THE REDISCOVERY OF INITIATIVES

But the call for direct democracy began to be heard again in the 1970s, when national malaise and increasing public skepticism toward elected leaders reawakened interest in initiatives and referenda as a way to advance political goals. Emerging issues, such as tax reform, environmental protection, and homosexual rights drew citizen attempts to shape policy through direct legislation. One of the most far-reaching pieces of legislation to be created through this process was California's Proposition 20, the coastal conservation initiative. The initiative, which was created partly in response to a catastrophic oil spill in the ocean off Santa Barbara, was placed on the November 1972 ballot by a grassroots coalition of citizens hoping to block what they envisioned as a future of shoulder-to-shoulder fast-food restaurants and high-rise condominium projects along the state's shoreline. The measure passed with a 55 percent majority, creating the California Coastal Commission—known as the toughest government environmental agency in the United States.[4]

In 1978, California shook the nation with the passage of the tax-limiting measure Proposition 13. The voters' revolt arose from scandals involving property tax assessors who gave tax breaks to business friends, big property tax hikes fueled by fast-rising home values, and from legislative gridlock over efforts to ameliorate the property tax crisis. Proposition 13 triggered a nationwide wave of tax revolts and opened the floodgates for direct democracy. More than 800 initiatives have appeared on state ballots across the nation in the years since Proposition 13. The initiative process has now become a virtual "fourth and new branch of state government" in California (California Commission on Campaign Financing 1992, 2) and several of the twenty-four other states that allow it.

As direct democracy has become an increasingly prevalent force in state policy making, it has shifted power away from elected representatives and toward the "parallel legislature" of governing by initiative (McCuan and Stambough 2005). Initiatives have shaped public policy in a broad range of areas, from campaign finance reform to hunting rights, including issues such as affirmative action, environmental protection, abortion, law and order, and definition of marriage. They have been used repeatedly in the past quarter century to address what voters consider the failures of representative democracy (see Baldassare, Cain, Apollonio, and Cohen 2004). The solution voters have seized on time and again is to limit the powers of elected officials through passage of measures such as legislative and executive branch term limits, caps on taxes and government spending, supermajority vote requirements for new taxes or tax increases, and budget mandates designating what proportion of the state budget should be allocated to specific issues, such as public education. The cumulative effect of these direct democracy efforts over the years has transformed the political environment in California and elsewhere.

One of the broadest-reaching uses of the initiative process has been the enactment of tight term limits for elected officials, which passed in Colorado, California, and Oklahoma in 1990 and quickly spread to other states. By the end of the 1990s, eighteen states had placed term limits on their legislatures, primarily through initiatives. Although term limits were repealed in some of the states that originally passed them, fifteen states today continue to limit the time their legislators can stay in office.[5]

The effect of this legislation in many states has been the replacement of experienced political leaders with a revolving cast of newcomers. Legislators limited to two four-year terms in office find themselves unable to carry out long-range plans. The constant churn in statehouses with term limits means that a good portion of the legislative body is always trying to learn its way around the building. The passage of term limits has severely curtailed the power of elected leaders in these states. As political analyst Peter Schrag

(1998, 244) describes the effect in California, "What it did do was to send a new generation of politicians to Sacramento, many of whom were long on partisanship and painfully short on both legislative experience and policy background—and, worse, seemed not much to care." A recent study of the impact of California's 1990 term limit law (Proposition 140) found that the number of women and minorities in the state legislature did increase as a result of term limits. But it also found that limiting legislators' time in office made for less experienced, less effective leaders who were less able to manage the state's budget. Frequent changes in legislative committees, as experienced members and leaders were "termed-out" and replaced with newcomers, lowered the level of expertise in key policy areas. This led to fewer bad bills being weeded out, and the need for more rewriting down the line. The lack of experience also reduced legislators' capacity for oversight of state agencies (Cain and Kousser 2004). Nationwide, term limits have damaged legislatures' ability to compromise and work together, because members have less time to build relationships and trust (National Conference of State Legislatures, "Joint Project on Term Limits," 2006). Thus, the use of direct democracy to impose term limits appears to have made state legislatures function less effectively and its unintended consequence is the rising influence of political parties in replacing officeholders and of special interests in framing the policy debate, as the political power and influence of elected representatives have been weakened with a shortened time in office. As a consequence, public confidence in the representative system has eroded, increasing the appeal of direct democracy.

Another far-reaching use of the initiative provision is tax and spending limits. Within a year of the 1978 passage of Proposition 13, tax-limiting measures appeared on the ballots in seventeen states and all but five passed. By the 1990s, twenty-one states had enacted tax and spending limits (see Tolbert 1998). In 1992, Colorado passed an initiative imposing on their state the strictest spending limits in the nation. Known as the "Taxpayer's Bill of Rights," or TABOR, the measure wrote into the state constitution a tight formula calculating how much state spending could increase each year based on population growth and inflation. The passage of TABOR triggered a new era of direct democracy in Colorado, with eighteen state ballot measures winning voter approval in the next twelve years—the same as the number enacted in the previous thirty-eight years. Although as of this writing Colorado is currently the only state with a TABOR in effect and its voters in 2005 moved to suspend the strict cap on legislative spending, citizens in several others states, including California, Maine, Michigan, Ohio, Oregon, and Oklahoma, have recently been attempting to promote similar tax-limiting ballot measures.

In a study of the impact of tax and spending initiatives between 1970 and 2000, Matsusaka (2004) concludes that states with the initiative provision spent and taxed less than states without it. He also found that initiative states decentralized their spending, shifting some control from state to local governments, and raised more money from user fees and less from taxes than did noninitiative states.

In California, debate over the merits of Proposition 13 and subsequent tax and spending initiatives is probably the most acrimonious political issue in the state. Proposition 13 has often been referred to as the "third rail" of California politics (touch it and you die). But it is certain that these measures will dictate California's fiscal policy making for years to come: curtailing state revenues, making it nearly impossible to raise taxes and contributing to chronic budget shortfalls.

One of the consequences of tax limitations is that elected officials can find themselves powerless in one of their key functions as representatives of the people—managing the flow of revenues and expenditures to cover the basic requirements of state and local government services. If an economic downturn triggers a sudden and unexpected decline in tax revenues, legislators can find themselves stripped of the tools to respond to such a crisis and dependent on voters with little background in public finance to approve their fiscal recovery plans. In one famous example, Orange County voters refused to raise their local sales tax to bail their local governments out of bankruptcy, citing a philosophical opposition to new taxes and an unwillingness to pay for the mistakes of elected officials as the justification for their fiscal choice (Baldassare 1998).

California also gave rise to another creative and highly significant use of the initiative process with ballot-box budgeting. The use of citizen's initiatives to guarantee, rather than restrict, funding began with the passage of Proposition 98 in November 1988. This measure dedicated a minimum of 40 percent of the state's annual general fund revenues to Californian public schools and community colleges. The initiative, sponsored by the powerful California Teacher's Association, was drafted in response to the failure earlier that year of Proposition 71, which sought to loosen the spending limits imposed by Proposition 13 and subsequent measures. Proponents of Proposition 98 successfully argued that school funding levels should be determined by the voters, rather than left up to legislators to allocate in their annual state budget.

Proposition 98's success opened the door to the most sweeping use of direct democracy yet, by giving citizens direct control over the state's budgeting process. Now citizens could not just limit the amount they paid in taxes—they could dictate how those funds were spent. In the decades that followed, California voters enacted citizen-sponsored legislation that mandated funding for the state's prisons (a by-product of initiatives directing criminal sentencing laws), stipulated that the sales tax on gasoline must be used only for transportation projects, earmarked state funds for preschool and after-school programs, and raised income taxes on millionaires to fund mental health programs, among other things. The California Budget Project concludes that approximately 77 percent of the state's general fund is now beyond the legislature's control (Riches 2003); others have put the amount as high as 90 percent (California Commission on Campaign Financing 1992). The result has made it more difficult for legislators to find ways to balance the budget and allocate state spending, leading to protracted battles and late budgets in many recent years. By restricting legislators' fiscal options, ballot-box budgeting has had the opposite effect from what its proponents intended— making government less responsive and accountable to the public while still vulnerable to the influence of powerful special interests (Citrin 1996).

More recently, the initiative process has also played a significant role in the civil liberties debate in many states, spilling over into national politics. The most notable issue currently being defined at the ballot box is same-sex marriages, sparked by the Massachusetts Supreme Court ruling in November 2003, which ruled that it was unconstitutional to prohibit same-sex couples from having the right to legal marriage. The ruling triggered a flurry of state ballot measures aimed at outlawing same-sex marriage, primarily by defining marriage as the union between a man and a woman.

The November 2004 general election saw eleven statewide ballot measures banning same-sex marriage, including Arkansas, Georgia, Kentucky, Michigan, Mississippi, Montana, North Dakota, Ohio, Oklahoma, Oregon, and Utah. All passed handily, with margins ranging from 59 percent in Michigan and Oregon to 86 percent in Mississippi. This came on the heels of Louisiana and Missouri having passed similar measures in state primary elections earlier in the year.

The same-sex marriage issue was credited as a key force in president George Bush's reelection that year, drawing conservative voters to the polls in the "make or break" state of Ohio to vote on definition of marriage initiatives. State Issue 1, amending the Ohio Constitution to stipulate that the only marriages valid in that state are "between one man and one woman," passed with 62 percent approval on November 2, 2004, the same day Bush eked out a 51 percent victory to claim the state's twenty electoral votes. It was enough to put him over the edge in the tight election and many believed that the gay marriage issue, fueled by a media blitz when San Francisco mayor Gavin Newsom responded to the Massachusetts decision by issuing marriage licenses to hundreds of couples in California, galvanized "values voters" to back the Republican president. As senator Dianne Feinstein, a California Democrat, expressed after Bush's reelection, the nationally broadcast images of gay and lesbian couples in tuxedos and wedding gowns at San Francisco City Hall "did energize a very conservative vote. It gave them something to rally around" (*San Francisco Chronicle*, November 4, 2004).

California has been the center of the resurgence of the direct democracy movement in recent decades. In the years between Proposition 13 (1978) and the recall (2003), large numbers of initiatives appeared on the California ballot. In twelve election years, 123 initiatives qualified—an average of ten per year (see table 1.1). Moreover, in half of the election years, the number of initiatives that had qualified was in the double digits.

Since the turn of the twenty-first century, the use of direct democracy in California has soared. Between 2000 and 2006, eighty-six propositions have appeared on the state ballot, including fifty-eight from the watershed year of 2002 on. This approaches the sixty-nine statewide propositions during the entire decade of the 1990s. Moreover, the rate of passage is increasing—from an average of 35 percent throughout the last century (Waters 2003) to 53 percent from 2000 to 2006. As our examination of the events leading up to the recall, the event itself, and its aftermath will show, the resurgence of populism, rise of voter distrust, a government stalemated by political partisanship and subject to the influence of special interests—much of which came about as the result of initiatives directed at reform of representative democracy—have propelled direct democracy into a new and growing role in the governance of California.

"INITIATIVE INDUSTRY" BECOMES AN ACTIVE FORCE

One cannot consider the growth of direct democracy in the modern era without acknowledging the extent to which the initiative process has spawned its own industry. Despite the populist appeal as lawmaking by and for ordinary citizens, efforts to enact legislation through direct democracy generally involve a large number of professional campaign consultants and a considerable amount of advertising—adding up to sizeable sums of money. Virtually since their inception, initiative campaigns have employed legal experts to write the ballot language, signature-gatherers to qualify the measures for the ballot, and marketing experts to generate publicity, develop messages, and promote the measures through advertising. Today, most of those who are involved with initiatives—relying on donations from average citizens, special interests, and partisan groups—turn at least part of the campaign over to paid professionals whose task is to persuade voters to join in their cause (Bowler and Cain 2006; Bowler, Donovan, and Tolbert 1998; Broder 2000; Gerber 1998, 1999; Magleby 1984; Magleby and Patterson 2000; McCuan 2005; McCuan and Stambough 2005; Sabato, Ernst, and Larson 2001).

Even the earliest efforts spent large amounts on mass mailings, posting of handbills, and billboard advertising.[6] For instance, backers of a proposal to create a state water and power commission that could issue bonds to expand facilities put up initiatives on the 1922, 1924, and 1926 ballots, spending as much as $150,000 (more than $1 million in 1995 dollars) each time.[7]

Indeed, the campaign consulting industry was essentially born in California, when the husband-and-wife team of Clem Whitaker and Leone Baxter, both journalists, founded Campaigns, Inc. in 1930. The firm's first statewide project was to defeat a referendum put up by the Pacific Gas and Electric Company, which sought to repeal the 1933 Central Valley Water Project Act. Whitaker and Baxter used their media expertise to insinuate their campaign materials into newspapers and radio stations throughout the state. Their efforts succeeded and the referendum was defeated (Magleby and Patterson 2000). Since then, campaign consulting has grown to become a highly lucrative industry throughout the nation and especially in California, where initiatives routinely appear on the ballot every election. For instance, in the November 1998 general election, proponents and opponents of the twelve measures appearing on that ballot spent a grand total of $193 million. Much of that ($92 million) was spent on a single initiative—Proposition 5, an Indian casino measure sponsored by California tribes (California Secretary of State 1999).

Another industry created by direct legislation is professional signature-gathering. The use of paid workers going door to door with petitions to qualify a measure for the ballot began nearly as soon as states adopted provisions for initiatives and referenda (Broder 2000). The first professional signature-gathering firm in California was established in the late 1930s by Joe Robinson (California Commission on Campaign Financing 1992). In the late 1960s, the practice was revolutionized by Sacramento car salesman Ed Koupal, who developed "tabling," where one worker intercepts passersby and directs them to a table where another worker has petitions set out. This method, which was quickly adopted in direct democracy states nationwide, greatly increased the rate at which signatures could be gathered (Schmidt 1989). Koupal and his wife, Joyce, funneled their signature-gathering expertise into a political action committee they founded, called the People's Lobby, which was a key player in environmental protection and political reform campaigns for much of the next decade. Others, meanwhile, were using the technique and its variations for profit. By the late 1970s, several signature-gathering businesses had sprung up in California, with teams of circulators soliciting people outside of malls, movies, and other gathering places. Reliance on volunteers alone to circulate petitions had become a thing of the past. The advent of targeted direct mail petition circulation by the Newport Beach–based firm of Butcher-Forde in 1978 further increased the profitability of professional signature-gathering enterprises—with some campaigns in the 1980s and 1990s paying more than $2 million per initiative in direct mail costs (California Commission on Campaign Financing 1992).

The initiative industry also created a market for numerous other campaign professionals. California's initiative industry has become a potent force in the state, paying the salaries of scores of legal experts, media consultants, pollsters, advertising consultants, political strategists, accountants, telephone call-center workers, canvassers, signature-gatherers, public relations experts, and a host of others whose jobs are linked to efforts to convince voters to accept or reject a piece of citizens' legislation. By the 1980s, at least ninety professional consultants or firms were working full time on initiative campaigns in California (McCuan et al. 1998) and the industry has undoubtedly grown in initiative states since then (Donovan, Bowler, and McCuan 2001).

REINVENTING DIRECT DEMOCRACY
IN THE TWENTY-FIRST CENTURY

The recent era ushered in by Schwarzenegger's election in 2003 represents a "new millennium" for direct democracy. Not only was it just the second time in U.S. history that a governor had gained office through the recall provision (and eighty-two years since the first one), but also never before had a sitting governor used initiatives as his primary means of advancing his legislative agenda.

By the end of his first year in office, Schwarzenegger had successfully used the initiative process to pass his plans for reducing the state's budget deficit—Proposition 57, a $15 billion bond measure, and Proposition 58, the so-called Balanced Budget Amendment. Both won handily in March 2004, emboldening the governor and spurring him to take positions on a slate of fifteen propositions on the November ballot that year. Again, he was fortified by the results, with voters following his lead on all but four of the measures. In between the primary and general election, Schwarzenegger used direct democracy as a threat whenever the legislature failed to move quickly enough in supporting his plans, saying he would put them up as propositions and "let the voters decide." Remarkably, the legislators reached agreement on a workers' compensation reform bill that had been stalled as a result of partisan and special interest gridlock for many years. The governor's sky-high approval ratings and voters' penchant for making policy decisions on their own made the legislature take note of these calls for action in 2004.

By the middle of his second year, Schwarzenegger had made good on his threats to bypass the legislature and launched a special election to take his stalled package of government reforms directly to the voters. He supported four initiatives that attracted big money from partisans and special interests—school reform, campaign finance reform, state budget reform, and legislative redistricting reform. Four other initiatives also qualified for the special election ballot—requiring parental notification for minors seeking an abortion, two measures on prescription drug discounts, and an electricity industry regulation proposal. The November 2005 special election set a new record for initiative spending in California, with campaigns for the eight ballot measures shelling out more than $300 million (*Sacramento Bee*, February 4, 2006). But voters, angry at the overt partisanship and special interest involvement displayed during the election, rejected the entire ballot.

Heading into his third year, stung by his defeat in the special election and plagued by low approval ratings among voters who supported him earlier, the governor expressed remorse about overusing the tools of direct democracy. The outcome, he said at a November 10 press conference, taught him that "the people want us to take care of the job right here in this building [the state legislature], and not to go to them if things don't work out" (Schwarzenegger, "Press Conference," 2005). He turned his focus in 2006 to rebuilding the state's outdated infrastructure—hoping to repair his damaged relationship with the voters and the legislature in the process—with a package of four propositions on the November ballot. This time he succeeded, gaining passage of a record $37 billion in bonds to finance public works projects, and handily winning reelection to a second term as governor in the process.

Schwarzenegger's experience with legislating by initiatives portrays a range of stages in direct democracy: from enacting measures forged in bipartisan cooperation to using his influence to advance a spate of citizen's initiatives, to boxing himself into a conservative corner with only extreme partisans and special interests willing to support his agenda, to rebuilding a bipartisan relationship with the legislature and placing the responsibility for governing jointly in elected leaders' and voters' hands. Through this rapid evolution in governance since the 2003 recall, we see the promises and the pitfalls of citizens acting as legislators and the transformation in the role of representative government as we witness the emergence of a new, hybrid form of democracy.

Led by the Golden State, the era of direct democracy is now taking shape. With this type of fundamental changing of the political guard, we face an uncertain future in which voters at the ballot box supplant the power of a forum of elected representatives in deciding public policy. Will there be a new era of citizen involvement and truly democratic decision making, or a system ruled by self-interested mobs and tyrannical minority groups? Will we have more responsive and responsible elected leadership, or will special interests—and their money—play an increasing role in the workings of government through both the legislative and initiative systems?

With voter participation uneven and declining, will an increasing number of public decisions be made by a relatively small and increasingly unrepresentative populace of affluent, aging, white voters who bother to go to the polls? Alternatively, will the opportunity to make important policy decisions lure a large and broad spectrum of the public to reengage in the political process and make it truly democratic? Close observation of California's latest political experiment will provide critical guidance for the nation.

ENABLING FACTORS FOR DIRECT DEMOCRACY

Four key factors led up to the recall and determined that fateful election. These factors—populism, partisanship, the influence of special interests, and voter distrust—are the focus of recent trends. Each of these factors is a compelling influence in the relationship between direct democracy and representative government in American politics today. Their convergence in California created the conditions that gave rise to this unprecedented use of direct democracy. And as examination of public opinion throughout the course of this historic event shows, they remain dominant in its aftermath, signaling that direct democracy will continue to be a powerful force in California's—and America's—politics in the years ahead.

Populism

While the Populist era of the 1890s was relatively brief, the spirit of the movement, characterized by championing the rights of the "common man" against the perceived tyranny of wealthy and powerful special interests, has remained a vital force in American politics. As discussed earlier in this chapter, the populist philosophy espoused by the People's Party in the late nineteenth century held that the "real" Americans were ordinary, hard-working people who were being cheated and robbed by the upper echelons of society. The movement fostered a suspicion of politicians, intellectuals, and the wealthy, who were seen as manipulating national affairs to benefit their own interests. Populists held that the will of the majority should be the dominant force in deciding public issues, even if it meant sacrificing the rights of citizens who are in the minority. Although the People's Party had disappeared by the beginning of the twentieth century, many of its ideas found a home in the Progressive era that followed. It was this movement that gave rise to the tools of direct democracy in many states, enabling citizens to overrule their legislators through the use of initiatives, referenda, and recalls.

As the events that unfolded in California a century later demonstrate, populist ideas are still a major influence among voters. One key area in which the effects of populism have influenced California politics is the dominance of the new fiscal populists—leaders who capitalize on voters' belief that government needs to be more efficient with public money (Clark and Ferguson 1983; Clark 1994). For many years, both in California and the nation, new fiscal populists had influenced policy and gained elected office by appealing to the public's perceptions that their tax money was being wasted and that government was run in an inefficient manner (Baldassare 1998). The belief that profligate bureaucrats were squandering public money also led to numerous uses of initiatives attempting to set limits on taxes and bring state and local government spending under control—most notably California's Proposition 13 and its progeny. Californians' belief that they were better at making decisions about government spending than their elected representatives also led to a series of ballot measures dictating how public funds were to be spent, eliminating much of the legislature's control over the state budget.

The populist objection to big government has resulted in numerous efforts to weaken the power of legislatures throughout the nation with the passage of measures such as term limits. Voters' goal in placing such constraints on elected officials is to make themselves the primary lawmakers. By using the initiative process to undermine the legislature's ability to set policy and make decisions that take a variety of concerns into account, voters have expressed the populist belief that government must yield to the majoritarian will (Cain and Miller 2001). Sometimes this position prevails at the expense of minority rights, which lose the protection afforded by the checks and balances inherent in the legislative process. While research on the overall effect of initiatives on minority rights has been mixed (see, for example, Gamble [1997] and Donovan and Bowler [1998]), recent years have seen the passage of citizen-initiated measures such as California's Proposition 63 (1986), which declared English to be the state's official language; Proposition 187 (1994), which denied public benefits to illegal immigrants; Proposition 209 (1996), which outlawed affirmative action in awarding government contracts, in public college admissions, and other programs; and Proposition 227 (1998), which limited bilingual education.

On the national scene, numerous politicians in recent years have attempted to drape themselves in the populist mantle. Notable efforts include Ross Perot's third-party presidential campaigns in 1992 and 1996, Jesse Ventura's iconoclastic turn as governor of Minnesota (1998–2002), the Internet-driven, grassroots campaign of Howard Dean for the Democratic presidential nomination in 2004, and Ralph Nader's crusade against both major political parties in 1996, 2000, and 2004.

Ironically, it was an Austrian immigrant, a multimillionaire movie actor who gained international fame playing larger-than-life heroes, who most adroitly invoked the populist spirit in 2003. Schwarzenegger's folksy approach and talent for connecting with ordinary people made voters feel they were participating in a grassroots movement—a populist revolt—with citizens tossing out their leaders and seizing control of the government.

Table 1.2: Support for Direct Democracy

"In general, do you think it is a good thing or a bad thing that a majority of voters can make laws and change public policies by passing initiatives?"

	October 2000	August 2006
Good thing	68%	74%
Bad thing	24	21
Other/don't know	8	5

"Overall, do you think public policy decisions made through the initiative process by California voters are probably better or probably worse than public policy decisions made by the governor and state legislature?"

	October 2000	August 2006
Better	53%	60%
Worse	25	24
Same (volunteered)	7	6
Don't know	15	10

Sources: PPIC Statewide Surveys, October 2000 and August 2006. Likely voters.

Moreover, populist feelings have been on the increase in California, as shown in our comparisons of public opinion surveys between 2000 and 2006. During this time, voter support for setting public policy with initiatives and their preference for voters over elected officials in making policy decisions actually gained in strength—even after the process had been put to the test often and in controversial arenas such as the 2003 recall and the 2005 special election (see table 1.2).

Partisanship

California politics had been close to impasse for much of the past decade because of entrenched partisanship dominating the state legislature. Two conditions created by citizens' initiatives—term limits and the supermajority vote requirement for passage of tax increases—contributed to the partisan impasse. A third factor, partisan redistricting by the members of the legislature after the 2000 Census, had worsened the situation by allowing the parties' elected representatives to become even more polarized as party primary voters were given what amounted to the final say in determining these elections.

Term limits, passed by initiative in California in 1990, capped the time a legislator could serve in the same state office at six years in the Assembly and eight in the Senate. While research has found no direct link between term limits and increased partisanship in the California legislature (Cain and Kousser 2004), some political observers maintain that it has this effect by putting legislators into a constant state of campaigning (see Broder 2000; Schrag 2006). From nearly their first day in office, members of California's

Senate and Assembly are looking toward their next political move. This increases legislators' dependence on their parties for campaign support and all but eliminates the possibility that they will go against partisan positions. In addition, term limits mean that about one-third of the legislature is termed out of office every two years, ensuring a constant stream of neophytes who lack the backbone to go against their party.

California's requirement for a two-thirds majority in each house to pass state budgets and fiscal measures was written into the state constitution in 1933. Only two other states (Rhode Island and Arkansas) have such a high bar. The requirement was expanded to include state tax increases as part of Proposition 13. As a result, the minority political party has the power to stalemate any budget bill, which has made the process extremely contentious and led to the state starting its new fiscal year without a spending plan in place twenty times over the last three decades (see Schrag 2006). In 2002, under Governor Davis, partisan standoff delayed the state budget a record sixty-seven days.

The parties increased their clout in 2001, with a highly partisan redistricting plan that guaranteed virtually no seats would change party in a general election. This was accomplished through state law allowing legislators to redraw the boundaries of the state's 173 legislative and congressional districts every ten years, after the decennial U.S. Census. The 2001 redistricting resulted in a convoluted scheme, with districts shaped like hourglasses, question marks, and pizza slices—all with the purpose of guaranteeing a party victory by aggregating like-minded voters and excluding opponents. The scheme worked, strengthening both parties' grip on their districts. The lack of bipartisan contests increased the role of the party primaries, with nominations often going to the parties' most extreme, activist members. Moderates were pushed out, and the parties became more ideological—Democrats more liberal and Republicans more conservative—with successful candidates showing little interest in compromise or finding common ground (see Gerston and Christensen 2004; Surrusco, Goldin-Dubois, and Davis 2005).

Yet while their elected leaders were moving toward the extreme ends of their political parties, California's voters were becoming increasingly nonpartisan. The biggest growth in voter registration in recent years had been among those declining to choose a party. Between 1990 and 2006, the number of voters registered as independents has more than doubled, growing from 9 percent to 18.7 percent (see table 1.3). In the summer of 2003, 16 percent of voters were registered as independents, up two points since the turn of the century—and the number of independent voters has grown even more since the recall (California Secretary of State, "Report of Registration," 2003, April and October 2006).

Indeed, California voters had opted for an "open primary" system when they passed a citizens' initiative in 1996 that allowed voters to vote for their favorite primary candidate for each office irrespective of the party designation. California voters flexed their new political muscle in the 1998 primary, when they had the option of crossing party lines in selecting candidates for state and national offices. In response to legal challenges by both of the major parties, the open primary was ruled unconstitutional by the U.S. Supreme Court and the partisan system was back in time for the March 2002 primary. But disappointed voters would have an opportunity to choose their replacement governor a year later on a recall ballot that in some ways resembled an open primary.[8]

As the recall gathered steam, Californians were tired of partisan leadership that seemed long on rhetoric and short on action. Into this walked Schwarzenegger—nominally Republican but politically independent and ideologically moderate—with a bona fide claim to be the people's choice without the partisan mantle of a GOP primary nomination. He was able to persuade Republicans and Democrats alike to cross party boundaries, joining independents searching for a middle ground in what they saw as a new "People's Party."

This legacy has continued, with voters increasingly turning away from the major parties in search of a new blend of politics that they feel better reflects their needs. Today, only one in three California voters think the Republican and Democratic parties do an adequate job of representing the American people, while the majority (56%) says a new, third party is needed (see table 1.3). The rise of the independent voter should not have been an unexpected trend—disaffiliation with the major parties was another enduring theme from the Populist era. But its recent, rapid acceleration is one more indicator that a new political environment has emerged.

Table 1.3: Declining Significance of Major Parties

	Party Registration			
	Democrats	*Republicans*	*Independents*	*Other*
1990	49.5%	39.2%	9.0%	2.3%
1994	49.0	37.2	10.3	3.5
1998	46.7	35.5	12.7	5.1
2002	44.6	35.2	15.2	5.0
2006	42.5	34.3	18.7	4.5

Source: California Secretary of State, October 2002 and October 2006.

"In your view, do the Republican and Democratic parties do an adequate job of representing the American people or do they do such a poor job that a third major party is needed?"

	September 2004	*October 2006*
Adequate job	48%	34%
Third party needed	46	56
Don't know	6	10

Sources: PPIC Statewide Survey, September 2004 and October 2006. Likely voters.

Special Interests

Another Populist era holdover is the widespread belief that the government is being manipulated by powerful special interests. During the 1890s and early 1900s, "Citizens were increasingly convinced that powerful, organized, self-seeking interests shaped legislative outcomes at the expense of the public interest" (Cronin 1999, 54). It was this concern that led California to adopt the tools of direct democracy in 1911, in an effort to break the grip of the Southern Pacific Railroad on the state legislature.

The perception that government was being manipulated by special interests has been a persistent force in politics, both in California and nationwide. Since 1970, according to the American National Election Studies conducted by the University of Michigan, Americans have generally been more inclined to believe that the government is run by "a few big interests looking out for themselves" than to say it is run "for the benefit of all the people." The sole exception to this trend is the year 2002, when Americans rallied around their government in the wake of the 2001 attacks on the World Trade Center and the Pentagon. But by 2004, the belief that the government was controlled by special interests had again risen to 56 percent nationwide (American National Election Studies 2004).

Concern about special interests wielding undue influence on state politics played a powerful role in the events surrounding the Davis recall. Heading into the gubernatorial election, in a January 2002 survey a majority of Californians said they thought state government was being run by a few big interests, with agreement across political groups. Californians' concerns about special interests can be seen as especially high in the context of the post–September 11 surge in confidence in government seen nationwide.

The Davis administration had done nothing to assuage the public's fear about the influence of special interests—in fact, it had exacerbated it. This became a major theme in the 2002 reelection campaign. One of the most prolific fund-raisers in state history, Davis was accused by his GOP challenger of running a "pay-to-play" administration and only making time for those who came armed with campaign contributions. He was accused of being overly beholden to labor unions, especially the California Teacher's Association and the state's prison guards, as well as casino-owning Indian tribes (a charge also levied against his lieutenant governor, Cruz Bustamante) and other groups that made major campaign contributions. Voters were angered by revelations that the governor was busy raising money even as the state battled an energy crisis and slid into a budget deficit. The result was declining approval of Davis and confidence in state government.

Schwarzenegger capitalized on the public's perception of undue influence by the powerful elite while average citizens were ignored. He adopted this

Table 1.4:   Perceived Influence of Special Interests

"Would you say the state government is pretty much run by a few big interests looking out for themselves or that it is run for the benefit of all of the people?"

	January 2001	August 2006
Few big interests	60%	73%
Benefit of all of the people	31	20
Other/don't know	9	7

Sources: PPIC Statewide Surveys, January 2001 and August 2006. Likely voters.

as a major theme of his recall crusade, castigating Davis for his fund-raising and touring the state pledging to "terminate" the special interests in Sacramento. With millions of dollars of his own money to finance his campaign, Schwarzenegger promised voters that he would never take money from special interests. As he announced on CNN television on August 8, 2003, "I am rich enough that I don't have to take anyone's money."

By his constant references to special interests in his omnipresent television advertising and widely publicized campaign appearances, Schwarzenegger tapped into Californians' long-standing suspicions and elevated them to the forefront in voters' minds. The six in ten who perceived state government as being run for the benefit of "a few big interests" before the recall got underway had risen to nearly seven in ten when Schwarzenegger began his term in 2004. And once released, the issue showed no signs of going away. In 2006, nearly three in four voters said state government was being run mainly for special interests—a thirteen-point increase since 2001 (see table 1.4).

Voter Distrust

Another factor that set the stage for the California recall and increasing use of direct democracy in its wake also harks back to the Populists—voter distrust of government. As Cronin (1999, 10) notes, "A populist impulse, incorporating notions of 'power to the people' and skepticism about the system has always existed in America." The notion that citizens should be independent-minded, self-determining, and dubious about the establishment is an intrinsic part of American philosophy—especially in the western states. Distrust of government had been a prevailing mood in California politics since the voters' passage of the Proposition 13 property tax limits—roughly the time that Americans began to question their confidence in the federal government in the wake of the Vietnam War, Watergate scandal, and the resignation of president Richard Nixon.[9]

The public's mistrust of their leaders has been strengthened and reinforced by politicians themselves over the years. In 1966, Ronald Reagan propelled himself into the governorship of California with an antigovernment message, refusing to even identify himself as a politician (Cannon 2003). Following that mold, populist rhetoric, extolling the virtues of "working men and women" and disparaging the competence of government, became a regular part of stump speeches throughout the nation. By the 1992 presidential election, the theme of "the people" rising up against the politicians was central to nearly all campaigns (Kazin 1995).

Antipolitical sentiments and voter distrust of government have been on the rise nationwide, with polls showing significant growth in beliefs that the government is ineffective, wasteful, and not trustworthy (Citrin 1996). But the unsavory campaigns and distressing events taking place in California in 2002 kicked voter distrust into high gear. Between 2001 and 2002, the number of voters saying they trusted the government in Sacramento to do what is right "just about always or most of the time" fell from 46 percent to 33 percent. Heading into the fall 2002 election, two in three voters said they trusted state leaders "only some, or none of the time."

This widespread mistrust of government provided fertile ground for the recall the following year. By September 2003, only 21 percent of voters expressed even moderate trust in state government, while three in four were confident only occasionally or never. Within this context, voters were inclined to see Davis, a "professional politician," as the source of all the state's problems. Replacement candidates, such as lieutenant governor Cruz Bustamante and state senator Tom McClintock, were similarly hampered by their association with government. Schwarzenegger's ability to portray himself as a political outsider, coupled with his exceptional skills at playing on the emotions of a dubious public that had grown tired of the political status quo, convinced voters that he was the antidote to a corrupt and incompetent government.

After rising up against state government during the recall, voters have remained highly skeptical about the institution. Despite electing Schwarzenegger to a second term as governor and passing all the infrastructure bond measures put on the ballot by the legislature in 2006, only one in four voters that year said they trusted their state government all or most of the time. This

Table 1.5: Trust in State Government

"How much of the time do you think you can trust the government in Sacramento to do what is right?"

	January 2001	August 2006
Always/most of the time	46%	23%
Only some of the time	50	72
None of the time (volunteered)	2	5
Don't know	2	—

Sources: PPIC Statewide Surveys, January 2001 and August 2006. Likely voters.

Table 1.6: Legislature's Approval Ratings

"Do you approve or disapprove of the way that the California Legislature is handling its job?"

	January 2001	October 2006
Approve	56%	26%
Disapprove	31	61
Don't know	13	13

Sources: PPIC Statewide Survey, January 2001 and October 2006. Likely voters.

represents a twenty-three-point drop since 2001, with confidence levels half what they were before the recall (see table 1.5).

Voters' trust in the legislative process has taken a similar plunge. While 56 percent approved of the job the legislature was doing at the beginning of 2001, that number had dropped to 40 percent by the middle of the following year. Confidence in California's representative system of governance has fallen even further in the wake of the recall, with only a quarter of voters in 2006 approving of the legislature's performance (see table 1.6). Once again, voters' skepticism of state government institutions is ongoing—attesting to the emergence of a new political reality centered on direct democracy.

A SPECIAL ROLE FOR PUBLIC OPINION

Public opinion goes hand in hand with the study of direct democracy. Citizens' perceptions of initiatives and other tools of direct legislation are important in determining their interest in using this process and in participating in voting. Public attitudes about specific policies and policy choices help shape their decisions at the ballot box. Similarly, opinions about elected officials and the decisions and workings of representative democracy have a significant role in voters' choice to rely on initiatives for making public policy. Moreover, understanding the roles that populism, partisanship, special interests, and voter distrust play in shaping the current trends in direct democracy requires a careful examination of the climate of opinion. For this reason, in studies of the initiative process—including this one—a great deal of attention has been devoted to public opinion, including general perceptions, specific attitudes, knowledge and information sources, and how and why the voters make their ballot choices (Abrams 2002; Allswang 2000; Baldassare 2000, 2002; Bowler et al. 1998; Bowler and Donovan 2000; Cronin 1999; McCuan and Stambough 2005; Magleby 1984; Schrag 1998, 2006; Smith and Tolbert 2004).

The public opinion data in this introductory section and in the chapters that follow are derived from the Public Policy Institute of California (PPIC) Statewide Survey, directed by Mark Baldassare.[10] The PPIC Statewide Surveys have been conducted by telephone several times a year since 1998, and at the time of this writing, included interviews with more than 150,000 adult residents of California. The PPIC Statewide Surveys are designed to uncover the political, social, and economic attitudes that are shaping policy preferences and ballot choices in the state. As such, these large-scale surveys have delved deeply into residents' opinions about direct democracy and attitudes toward representative government.

A similar methodology was used in each of the more than seventy surveys that have been conducted at PPIC. Respondents were selected at random from a computer-generated sample of listed and unlisted telephone numbers. Interviewing was conducted by professional telephone survey research firms and respondent interviews took about twenty minutes to complete. A minimum of two thousand adults was included in each survey, allowing for large and representative subsamples across the state's varied regions, political parties, and racial/ethnic and demographic groups. For all surveys, interviews were conducted in English or Spanish according to the respondent's preference.

For most surveys, respondents were divided into groups of likely voters, all registered voters, and those who are not registered to vote. Some of the questions in the surveys were repeated from national surveys, to allow comparisons between California and the nation. These national survey questions are derived from nonpartisan sources, such as ABC News/*Washington Post*, CBS/*New York Times*, the *Los Angeles Times* Poll, the Gallup Poll, and the Pew Research Center. Many questions were repeated over time to allow analysis of time trends, such as before, during, and after the 2003 recall. With questions repeated on a regular basis, including voter distrust, perceptions of partisanship and special interests, attitudes toward the initiative process, and support for political and governance reforms, we can examine trends in the public's views on direct democracy and representative government over time.

Postelection surveys with two thousand voters were also conducted in the days after each of the 2004, 2005, and 2006 November elections. In each survey, voters were asked about their ballot choices and election experiences and how voting in the election shaped their broader attitudes about government, elected representatives, partisanship, special interests, the initiative process, and governance reforms.

In designing all of the survey questions, valuable information was gained on Californians' opinions and perceptions through a series of focus group discussions conducted with selected groups of registered voters in regions around the state, including Los Angeles, Orange County, Sacramento, Concord, Walnut Creek, San Francisco, San Jose, Fresno, and San Diego. The help of a politically diverse group of state government experts was also enlisted in "brainstorming sessions" on questions prior to the surveys.

In the following section, we briefly provide the recent climate of public opinion on direct democracy and representative government in California. Later in the book, we reexamine these general attitudes in the context of specific elections and political events.

ATTITUDES TOWARD DIRECT DEMOCRACY

Do Californians' attitudes toward direct democracy reflect populist attitudes? Since the days of its inception, a large proportion of residents are reported to have perceived of the initiative process as an improvement on the representative system of state government; thwarting special interests and expanding democracy by raising it to the morally superior (and decidedly populist) ideal of rule by "the people" (Allswang 2000). This sentiment is echoed in a national survey in 1999 (see Waters 2003) and in every PPIC Statewide Survey that we have conducted in California since 1998. For instance, table 1.2 shows the overwhelming support for the initiative process and greater confidence in the decisions of voters than elected officials that existed before the recall and are rising in its wake.

Just as it did during the Populist era, citizens' ability to propose their own legislation continues to be seen today as a defense against an elitist and unresponsive government. Three in four Californians, in a survey we conducted in September 2005, agreed that "citizens' initiatives bring up important public policy issues that the governor and state legislature have not adequately addressed." Among likely voters, this belief rises to 79 percent. The view is strongly held by Democrats (75%), Republicans (78%), and independents (80%), and across all regions and demographic groups. Nearly two in three Californians in the same survey expressed the populist view that citizens' initiatives usually reflect the concerns of average residents.

All together, about seven in ten Californians (72%) and likely voters (71%) in an August 2006 survey said they were satisfied with the way the initiative process is working in California today. This is consistent with all of the earlier surveys. Solid majorities across party lines and demographic groups express favorable views about the initiative process.

Still, residents are not so enamored with this direct democracy provision that they do not see its less-than-perfect elements. Only one in ten in an August 2006 survey were "very satisfied" with the way the initiative process is working and nearly four in ten, in a survey conducted a month later, said the system is in need of major changes. Among the complaints voiced by residents in surveys are that the process is subject to too much influence by special interest groups, that too much money is spent on campaigns, that ballots are crowded with too many measures, and that voters are confused over the ballot language. In all, though, the positive features of direct democracy far outweigh the negative elements of the representative form of government in most Californians' minds.

ATTITUDES TOWARD REPRESENTATIVE DEMOCRACY

One of the reasons Californians are so supportive of direct democracy is their view that governance by elected representatives has serious limitations. Like many Americans responding to recent national surveys, Californians seem to have reached the conclusion that the two major parties do an inadequate job of representing the people. A majority now says a major third party is needed. As we also noted earlier in table 1.3, many California voters are opting for "decline to state" registration, rather than choosing the Democratic or Republican party as their political identity. While this voter registration trend has been underway for two decades in California, the desertion of the major parties for independent status has accelerated in the wake of the 2003 recall.

Negative perceptions about representative government are not just confined to the dysfunctional qualities of the major political parties. Most Californians believe their state government is run by a few big interests rather than for the benefit of all of the people. This public perception is strongly held across all political groups and, as indicated in table 1.4, seems to be on the rise. Californians are similarly suspicious of the federal government, the PPIC Surveys find. This belief that special interests manipulate representative government gives voters all the more reason to favor a system of direct democracy.

Echoing the populist complaint that politicians do not have the good of ordinary people at heart, only one in five residents and 18 percent of voters in a September 2005 survey rated the state legislature as excellent or good at working for the best interests of people like themselves. Fully three in ten adults—and 37 percent of voters—rated their state government as poor. Democrats, Republicans, and independents all gave the legislature low ratings on this dimension, and approval ratings were similarly low across regions, racial/ethnic, and demographic groups.

The general distrust of government, shown by a variety of measures, means that a large percentage of the public has serious doubts about its elected representatives. Distrust has been a major political theme for decades in California. Voters of all political stripes today are dubious that their state and federal governments can do the right thing most of the time. Moreover, job approval ratings for the state legislature and U.S. Congress have been low, indicating displeasure with the performance of lawmakers. This lack of trust in government has helped fuel support for policy making by initiative. Tables 1.5 and 1.6 earlier in this chapter demonstrate the growing distrust in state government and the legislative process, as voters increasingly turned to the ballot box for lawmaking.

Californians also see their state government as inefficient, as well as ineffective and unresponsive. More than nine in ten Californians in an August 2006 survey said that the state government wastes at least some of the money it gets in taxes, with 58 percent of adults and 61 percent of likely voters saying it wastes "a lot." This populist attitude, once again, reinforces residents' belief in the need for public policy intervention through direct democracy. Moreover, perceptions of government inefficiency are growing over time. Between January 2001 and August 2006, the percentage of Californians saying that the state wasted "a lot" of taxpayer money climbed eleven points. The belief that state government is wasteful is widely held in all parties, regions, and demographic groups.

CALIFORNIA MEGATRENDS AND DIRECT DEMOCRACY

At the same time that California has seen an increasing role for legislation at the ballot box, the face of the California people has been undergoing a dramatic transformation. These population trends are the backdrop for the growing use of the initiative process and have important implications for the future use of direct democracy.

In 1910, when the push for direct democracy in the state was getting underway, California had 2.4 million residents, according to the U.S. Census Bureau. By 1980, when initiatives began to gain their place as the legislature's fourth branch, the state's population had grown by a factor of ten, reaching 24.7 million (Baldassare 2000). As of 2006, the population had climbed to 37.2 million (California Department of Finance, "Population Estimates," May 2006). Can direct democracy operate effectively in such a populous state?

The first requirement of direct democracy is a healthy level of voter participation. But the level of political engagement in California has failed to keep pace with its recent population growth. While the state's adult population has surged by 25 percent, voter registration rolls have increased by just

Table 1.7: Trends in Voter Registration

	1990		2006	
	Millions	*% of Adults*	*Millions*	*% of Adults*
Adults 18+	22.0	—	27.7	—
Eligible to vote	19.2	87	22.6	82
Registered to vote	13.5	61	15.6	56
Major party voters	12.0	55	12.0	43

Sources: California Department of Finance (May 2004a, May 2004b, and April 2006); California Secretary of State (November 2004 and April 2006).

15 percent. Between 1990 and 2006, 5.7 million adults have been added to the state's population, 3.4 million of whom are eligible to vote. However, the number of registered voters has only grown by 2.1 million. As a result, just over half of California adults are able to participate in the state's elections (see table 1.7).

In recent years, the percentage of adults who are registered to vote went from 61 percent in 1990 to a high point of 65 percent in 1994, down to 56 percent in 2006. Some of the decline in the proportion of registered voters may be related to the immigration-fueled increase in the number of noncitizens. Among the state's 12 million nonvoters today, 7 million are eligible to vote and 5 million are not. But even among eligible adults, the proportion that is registered to vote has declined during this active era of direct democracy (Baldassare 2006).

Another important trend is the lack of growth in party membership, which we referred to earlier in this chapter in our discussion of partisanship. In 2006, 12 million California voters were registered as Democrats and Republicans, the same as in 1990. Since then, the percentage of adults who are major party voters has declined (55% to 43%), marking the first time in modern California history in which the majority of adults do not belong to one of the major parties that dominate the candidate choices in elections (Baldassare 2006).

Independent voters, by their very definition, do not fit into traditional "liberal" or "conservative" pigeonholes. They make choices on an issue-by-issue basis, rather than following the advice of partisan leaders, interest groups, or their elected representatives. They follow liberal positions on social issues and the environment but are conservative on most fiscal matters, perceiving their government as too large and their legislators as wasteful with tax money. As the modern-day embodiments of populism, independents are skeptical of their elected representatives. Their distrust, coupled with policy choices that are often at odds with political leaders, contributes to independents' perception that elected officials do not represent them. The rise of independents is a significant factor in the move to direct democracy (Baldassare 2002).

California's voter turnout has been low by historical standards in recent elections, reflecting a counterintuitive political trend for a state that is increasingly using the initiative process to make policies. Since 1990, fewer than half of eligible adults voted in the five statewide elections that included the selection of governor and other executive branch offices, federal and state legislators, and many state propositions (see table 1.8). Importantly for the evaluation of the direct democracy process, special elections for the 2003 recall and the initiative-only ballot in 2005 included fewer than half of adults who were eligible to vote. Indeed, despite the state's rapid growth in total population, number of adults, and the number eligible to vote—about the

Table 1.8: Voter Turnout in Nonpresidential General Elections

	Percent of Registered Voters	Percent of Eligible Adults	Millions
1990	58.6	41.1	7.9
1994	60.5	47.0	8.9
1998	57.6	41.4	8.6
2002	50.6	36.1	7.7
2003 (special)	61.2	43.1	9.4
2005 (special)	50.1	35.4	8.0
2006	56.2	39.3	8.9

Source: California Secretary of State, "Statement of the Vote," November 2006.

same number of ballots were cast in the gubernatorial election in 2006 as in 1994. The largest turnout in a recent nonpresidential year was for the 2003 recall. While the declining voter participation is neither a cause nor an effect of direct democracy, it is a cause for concern about fairness, as more and more policy decisions are being made by a dwindling proportion of the public.

Moreover, in examining the context of the increasing role of voters making policy decisions at the ballot box, it is important to note that the state's population mix today is vastly different from what it was in the past. In the 1910 U.S. Census, 95 percent of Californians were classified as "white." The state was still overwhelmingly white in 1980, around the time that the Proposition 13 property tax limits passed, when seven in ten Californians were non-Hispanic whites. But today, less than half of the state's residents are non-Hispanic whites, while one in three adults were born outside of the United States (see table 1.9). No racial or ethnic group now makes up a majority of the state's population. Latinos and Asians account for the bulk of the new population growth and are changing the racial and ethnic composition of the population (Baldassare 2006). Latinos are widely expected to become California's single largest racial and ethnic group in a few years and to constitute a majority by midcentury (Baldassare 2002; Johnson 2005). Are the views of new residents and the different perspectives in this increasingly diverse state reflected in the policy choices made at the ballot box through direct democracy?

An electorate shrunken by low voter turnout can still reflect the overall makeup of the adult population—or it can be a selective and biased subgroup. The relatively small percentage of adults who frequently vote in state elections is indeed an unrepresentative slice of the population (see table 1.9). While no ethnic or racial group is in the majority in California today and many are immigrants, voters do not currently reflect the diversity of the state population. Nearly three in four of the Californians who frequently turn out to vote are white and nine in ten are U.S.-born. In addition, likely voters are more likely than the overall California adult population to be forty-five or

Table 1.9:   Demographics of California Voter Groups

	Likely Voters	Not Registered to Vote	All Adults
White	72%	24%	46%
Latino	14	63	32
Black	5	3	6
Asian/other	6	8	16
Homeowners	77	34	57
45 and older	62	24	47
College graduates	53	17	24
$60,000 or more	56	18	39

Source: Baldassare (2006) from PPIC Statewide Surveys, May 2005 to May 2006.

older, college graduates and homeowners, and have incomes of $60,000 or more (Baldassare 2000, 2006).

Moreover, there are stark differences between the large number of nonvoters and those whose ballot preferences are likely to be recorded on election day. Nonvoters are mostly Latino, two in three are born outside the United States, and most are renters, are under forty-five years of age, have low income, and have not been to college (Baldassare 2006). The preferences of this vast and different group are left out of election results (see table 1.9).

California's changing demographic face has greatly increased the complexity of its residents' wants and needs. Latinos and immigrants lag well behind the state's white and U.S.-born residents in income, education, and homeownership, and they are younger and more likely to have children in their homes. Compared to whites and native-born residents, Latinos and immigrants are considerably more likely to use government programs such as public health and schools. In polling, Latinos and immigrants favor a larger role and more services from state government, while whites and U.S.-born residents favor a smaller role and fewer services (Baldassare 2006). Though the number of Latino elected representatives in the state legislature has grown in recent years,[11] Latinos' rate of voter participation is still far behind that of whites, raising doubts about how well the direct democracy process reflects public preferences (Baldassare 2002).

As in the Populist era, when a backlash against a changing economy triggered the desire for direct democracy, fears of a changing society may be another significant factor behind the use of direct democracy today. Although residents are more likely to say they consider immigrants a benefit to California because of their hard work and job skills than see them as a burden to the state, Californians are keenly aware that the immigrant population has been increasing (Baldassare 2002). The state's likely voters—who are disproportionately white, long-term residents, older, more affluent, and homeowners—may also be less likely to see themselves as the direct beneficiaries of state spending for public services. This may diminish their support for funding these services. Some propose that this voter disconnect—an older and affluent electorate confronted with a growing number of younger and less well-to-do nonvoters—has been a motivation behind recent initiative efforts such as the tax revolt, limiting legislative power, and measures aimed at doing away with bilingual education, affirmative action, and public services for illegal immigrants (see Schrag 2006). In this way, the growing use of the initiative process could be a means for voters to take control of not only the legislative process, but also a demographic process that has changed the demands on government.

In addition to its shifting demographic makeup, California has also become a place of extreme political fragmentation, leading many to question whether the state is even governable. Its sheer size—home to more than 37 million residents in 2006 and stretching over 164,000 square miles—is a challenge for direct or representative democracy. Regions divide the population: residents of the two major metropolitan areas—Los Angeles and the San Francisco Bay Area—are largely Democratic and liberal, while those in the fast-growing Central Valley and Inland Empire (San Bernardino and Riverside counties) and the South Coast (Orange and San Diego counties) are much more Republican and conservative. With a divided electorate, both citizens' initiatives and elected officials have a difficult task of making policy choices that benefit all of the people.

IS CALIFORNIA A TRENDSETTER?

California is not the only state with a rich history of direct democracy. The tools that were put in place in California and many other states during the Progressive era were created primarily as cautionary procedures, intended more as a threat than a reality. They were designed to bolster representative government by creating more responsible leaders (Cronin 1999). Early advocates of direct legislation throughout the nation also hoped that having citizens' initiatives on the ballot would help educate the public about political issues and increase voter turnout (Smith and Tolbert 2004).

As Hiram Johnson described them in his 1911 inaugural address in California, the initiative and referendum were meant to be a means to prevent the "misuse of the power temporarily centralized in the legislature" and the recall was to be a "precautionary measure . . . the existence of which will prevent the necessity for its use."

Today, fueled by recent developments such as the Internet, a frenzied twenty-four-hour news cycle, a pumped-up communications network allowing activists to reach millions of people in an instant, and a lucrative initiative industry, these provisions have acquired a power never imagined by their creators. These new trends can be found in many states, although California's size, wealth, and history place it at the political forefront.

In the past thirty years, the number of initiatives appearing on statewide ballots throughout the nation has more than quadrupled, from a low point of eighty-seven during the decade of 1961 to 1970 to a peak of 389 from 1991 to 2000. So far, the new millennium looks to be keeping pace, with 220 initiatives on state ballots nationwide between 2001 and 2006 (Waters 2003; National Conference of State Legislatures, "Ballot Measures Database," 2006). Initiatives have thus become a major force for creating public policy not only in California, but also in many of the other states with direct democracy provisions.

The Pacific Coast states lead the pack in initiative use. Between 1990 and 2004, Californians considered a total of ninety-one initiatives on their statewide ballots, followed closely by Oregon, with eighty-seven. Other states coming closest to this frequency of use were Colorado (fifty-six) and Washington (forty-five). At the other end of the spectrum, Illinois did not use its initiative process once during that time and Mississippi did so only twice (National Conference of State Legislatures, "Ballot Measures Database," 2006).

With the use of the direct democracy provision to remove Governor Davis from office and the increasing use of initiatives to make policy since the state's historic recall, direct democracy has crossed a new threshold in California. Will other states follow? We argue that the factors enabling this trend in California—populism, partisanship, special interests, and voter distrust—are persistent and common features today and can all be found elsewhere in the nation. Moreover, the state's struggles with accommodating a growing use of direct democracy, at the same time that its changing population raises issues about political participation, are evident in other states. California is once again the testing ground for a grand political experiment. The outcome is well worth watching.

CONCLUSION

In this introductory chapter, we lay out a framework for understanding the new era of direct democracy ushered in by the 2003 recall in California. We describe the tools of direct democracy and trace its history and evolution in the United States and California, tying this movement to the nation's abiding populist spirit. We offer evidence that recent events have led to political trends and increasing public support for a permanent change in the balance of power between representative government and direct democracy.

We describe the four forces that are enabling the recent expansion of the role of direct democracy in California policy making—populism, partisanship, special interests, and voter distrust. These four factors serve as organizing principles for understanding the chain of events leading up to the recall, determining its outcome, and continuing to shape policy in the most populous state. We find evidence for their growing role in elections and voter preferences that are moving California toward a new, hybrid democracy.

We look at the role of public opinion, which includes high praise for the initiative process and deep concerns about the current workings of representative democracy. The bonds of trust and understanding between the people and their government appear to be further unraveling, as more voters have lost faith in campaigns, major parties, elections, and elected officials, thus driving up disillusionment with representative government. The decline in confidence in elected leaders coincides with growing restrictions on their abilities to govern enacted by citizens' initiatives, such as term limits, tax and spending caps, and ballot-box budgeting. Concerns about gerrymandering of legislative seats and the effects of campaign donations by special interest groups have also taken a toll on elected leaders' credibility. Such opinions are increasing voters' desires to directly intervene at the ballot box.

We examine the social context of this new era of direct democracy in California, pointing to population and voting trends that raise questions about the frequent and broad use of the ballot box for making policy. Can the people's views be represented by direct democracy in such a large and diverse state? One of the challenges in California today is lagging political participation amid population growth. As troubling is the fact that the electorate is mostly white, older, and affluent, and that the views of younger, less affluent, and nonwhite residents are not adequately represented in voting on ballot measures. An unrepresentative electorate creates the possibility of a minority of voters imposing their political will on the majority of the population, with the needs of the general population being ignored in the policies that result.

We argue for the study of the California experience in light of the Golden State's long history of serving as a starting point for change. While California is unique in many ways, other states also have provisions for direct democracy and have expanded its use following the passage of Proposition 13. In addition, conditions that led California to the path of increased use in the early twenty-first century—populism, partisanship, special interests, and voter distrust—are also major elements on the national political scene.

Subsequent chapters examine the events in the 2002 election leading up to the recall (chapter 2), the recall in 2003 (chapter 3), the major developments of Schwarzenegger's tenure in the efforts for fiscal recovery in 2004 (chapter 4), the attempts at government reform in 2005 (chapter 5), and the emphasis on rebuilding in 2006 (chapter 6). In each chapter, we consider the political events, public opinion trends, and election results, and show how the growing use of direct democracy is explained by the enabling factors of populism, partisanship, special interests, and voter distrust—all in evidence and on the rise in this history-making era of governance change.

In a final section (chapter 7), we discuss the implications of California's most recent experiment with direct democracy. In many ways, representative democracy has suffered a setback with the use of the recall and increasing reliance on initiatives to make public policy. But the flaws in the direct democracy system are also more apparent, and voters are now more aware of the limitations and possible misuses of citizens' initiatives to benefit partisan and special interest goals. We predict a growing trend of direct democracy in California and other states. Recognizing that direct and representative democracy must find a way to coexist in the future, we offer recommendations for governance reforms to improve policy making in a hybrid democracy.

NOTES

1. For a list of states with the initiative provision and a description of the process in each, see M. Dane Waters, *Initiative and Referendum Almanac* (Durham, N.C.: Carolina Academic Press, 2003), 12–29.

2. For a more detailed description of the popular referendum process and a list of states with this provision, see Waters, *Initiative and Referendum Almanac*, 11–12.

3. For a list of states with recall provisions, and a description of the process in each, see the National Conference of State Legislatures website, "Recall of State Officials," March 21, 2006, www.ncsl.org/programs/legismgt/elect/recallprovision.htm (April 1, 2006).

4. A lively and detailed account of the Coastal Conservation Initiative campaign can be found in David D. Schmidt, *Citizen Lawmakers: The Ballot Initiative Revolution* (Philadelphia: Temple University Press, 1989), 44–51.

5. For a list of states with term limits, see National Conference of State Legislatures website, "Term-Limited States," February 2006, www.ncsl.org/programs/legismgt/about/states.htm (April 1, 2006).

6. See discussion in Shaun Bowler and Todd Donovan, *Demanding Choices: Opinion, Voting and Direct Democracy* (Ann Arbor: University of Michigan Press, 2000), 14–17.

7. Described in John M. Allswang, *The Initiative and Referendum in California, 1898–1998* (Stanford, Calif.: Stanford University Press, 2000), 39.

8. Most notably, Schwarzenegger was not selected as his party's candidate in a GOP primary and voters chose from a ballot that included more than one Republican, in addition to Democrats, independents, and several other parties.

9. For reviews of the literature on trust in government and opinion trends over time, see Mark Baldassare, *California in the New Millennium: The Changing Social and Political Landscape* (Berkeley: University of California Press, 2000); Mark Baldassare, *A California State of Mind: The Conflicted Voter in a Changing World* (Berkeley: University of California Press, 2002); Bernard Barber, *The Logic and Limits of Trust* (New Brunswick, N.J.: Rutgers University Press, 1983); Jack Citrin, "The Political Relevance of Trust in Government," *American Political Science Re-*

view 68 (1974): 973–88; Jack Citrin and Christopher Muste, "Trust in Government," in *Measure of Political Attitudes*, ed. John Robinson (New York: Academic Press, 1999), 465–532; Terry Clark and Ronald Inglehart, "The New Political Culture," in *The New Political Culture*, ed. Terry Clark and Vincent Hoffman-Martinot (Boulder, Colo.: Westview Press, 1998), 9–72; Margaret Levi and Laura Stoker, "Political Trust and Trustworthiness," *Annual Review of Political Science* 3 (2000): 475–507; Seymour Martin Lipset and William Schneider, *The Confidence Gap: Business, Labor and Government in the Public Mind* (New York: Free Press, 1983); Arthur Miller, "Political Issues and Trust in Government," *American Political Science Review* 68, no. 3 (1974): 951–72; Daniel Yankelovich, *New Rules: Searching for Self-fulfillment in a World Turned Upside-Down* (New York: Random House, 1981).

10. Questionnaires and results for all the PPIC Statewide Surveys can be accessed on the Public Policy Institute of California website: www.ppic.org.

11. In 2005, 29 of the 120 members of the state's Assembly and Senate were Latino. In addition, mayors of two of the state's largest cities—Los Angeles and San Jose—were Latino.

2

Political Change Takes Root: The 2002 Elections

Parallel events in the 2002 election cycle that illuminate the public's growing disenchantment with representative democracy and the increasing appeal of direct democracy are the focus of this chapter. Gray Davis's reelection bid, in the context of his aloof style of leadership, the gridlock of state government in the midst of economic and fiscal problems, and allegations of his running a "pay-to-play" administration fueled California voters' populist spirit, perceptions of government in the grip of partisanship and special interests, and distrust. The Davis campaign's manipulation of the Republican primary election for governor in March, which succeeded in derailing the candidacy of the moderate Richard Riordan and created the opportunity to run against the conservative Bill Simon, further stoked voters' cynicism and anger at their elected representatives.

Voters reaffirmed their desire to constrain the power of their elected officials through the solid defeat of Proposition 45 in the same March primary. This was a citizens' initiative placed on the ballot by partisans and interest groups that sought to bend the rules of Proposition 140 (legislative term limits), enacted by voters in 1990, and give termed-out legislators the chance to gain another four years in office.

At the same time, Arnold Schwarzenegger was launching his political career though California's system of direct democracy, stumping for Proposition 49. This was a citizens' initiative that would earmark state funding for before- and after-school programs for school-age children. Schwarzenegger sought to attract voters from across the political and ideological spectrum and, thanks to his effort to build a populist and bipartisan base of support, his successful direct democracy campaign provided a stark contrast to the negative and divisive race for the governor's seat.

Davis won reelection with a narrow 47 percent of the vote, while on the same November ballot 57 percent of voters supported the Schwarzenegger initiative. While both men achieved victory in the 2002 elections, Davis's was to be short-lived. We detail the trends in public opinion, highlight the election results, and describe some of the key events throughout this year that show the importance of the 2002 elections in setting the stage for the 2003 recall and subsequent developments in direct democracy.

A BOOM-TO-BUST ECONOMY

While governor Gray Davis was launching his 2002 reelection bid, the roots of the movement for political change that would ultimately unseat him were already beginning to spread across the California landscape. Davis faced a very different political environment in early 2002 than the one that had delivered him a landslide victory four years earlier. The sizzling dot-com economy had turned out to be mostly smoke, triggering a stock market tumble, widespread job losses, and a fulminating state budget deficit. On top of that, the attempt at energy deregulation enacted in 1996 during the administration of governor Pete Wilson was fundamentally flawed—and manipulated by out-of-state energy traders for their profits—resulting in skyrocketing costs and electricity shortages for which Davis initially took the heat. Even though he had not been involved in creating the deregulation legislation, Davis was widely perceived as mismanaging a state crisis.

As a result, the Democratic governor's popularity had sagged to 52 percent in a January 2002 Statewide Survey—ten points lower than it had been a year earlier and fourteen points below the 66 percent approval rating measured in a September 2000 survey.

National events of the previous two years had also helped spread voter disillusionment with their system of representative democracy. Al Gore was the top vote-getter in the 2000 presidential race, but was denied a victory by what many California Democrats saw as an illegitimate election. The mood shifted to somber and worried after the September 11 terrorist attacks in 2001. Citizens rallied around their flag and the president. But their patriotism didn't trickle down to the state level, where people grew ever more angry and cynical with their leaders as economic slowdowns, job losses, and budget deficits became the order of the day. While fully eight in ten in the January 2002 survey said they approved of the job George Bush was doing as president, just over half of Californians gave Davis a positive performance rating (52%). Nonetheless, the public remained wary of all levels of government in the wake of terrorist attacks—fewer than half in the same survey felt they could trust the government in either Washington, D.C., (46%) or Sacramento (47%) to "do what is right" always or most of the time.

In California, the public's disillusionment began with the collapse of the so-called dot-com industry about halfway through Davis's first term in office. The extravagant spending by young "techies" flush with venture capital funds and the proceeds of blockbuster IPOs had supersized the economy and made Californians giddy with visions of limitless wealth and abundance. In this ebullient mood, voters had handed Davis a twenty-point victory over Republican challenger Dan Lungren in 1998. The governor basked in the heat of a blazing economy during his first eighteen months in office, doling out surplus budget funds to the public's favorite programs such as schools and transportation. All seemed well in the Golden State. Voters were happy with their leaders, giving the governor a respectable 51 percent job approval rating in a September 1999 poll, while 61 percent said they thought the state was heading in the "right direction." Davis's approval rating had climbed to 66 percent by September 2000, and even the California legislature received a positive job evaluation from 56 percent of the public.

THE ELECTRICITY CRISIS

But looming on the horizon was an electricity crisis that would eventually become one of the arrows shooting Davis down. The crisis was the result of a utility-industry deregulation law enacted in 1996 under Davis's predecessor, Republican governor Pete Wilson. Until that time, most of the state's electricity was produced and sold to consumers by three major utility companies. The 1996 deregulation bill sought to lower energy prices by breaking up the utilities and creating competition among new energy service providers that would be allowed to enter the market. The bill also imposed price ceilings on California power companies. However, a flaw in the legislation, coupled with a shortage of electricity-generating capacity and increased demand, allowed wholesale energy distributors based outside the state to charge wildly inflated prices to California companies.[1] The results were sky-high electricity bills and energy shortages for California homes and businesses.

The crisis became apparent in the spring of 2000, when the price of electricity suddenly shot up precipitously. That summer and fall saw a series of "rolling blackouts"—where electricity was turned off to customers on a rotating basis whenever the power supply fell below demand. Consumers began to see their energy bills double and triple. But price caps did not allow California power companies to recoup the exorbitant prices they were paying to purchase electricity from out-of-state wholesalers. By January 2001, the California utilities had amassed enormous debts and lost their creditworthiness, forcing the state to become the purchaser of last resort and take on huge amounts of debts itself. The total costs of the electricity crisis have been estimated at $40 billion to $45 billion—around 3.5 percent of the state's total yearly economic output (Weare 2003).

The energy crisis hit Californians hard and they took it out on their elected leaders. By October 2000, half of Californians expected that the climbing energy prices would hurt the state's economy "a great deal" in the coming year, according to the PPIC Statewide Survey. Yet Davis and the legislature were slow to take action on an issue that was spreading across the state and would come to hit voters squarely in the pocketbook.

By January 2001, three in four Californians in the PPIC Statewide Survey were calling the cost and supply of energy "a big problem" and 62 percent disapproved of the way the governor was handling the issue. By May 2001, the electricity crisis was rated as the top problem facing California and 67 percent of residents said that it made them less confident in the state's ability to plan for the future. In July 2001, eight in ten Californians believed that the electricity problem would hurt the state's economy over the next few years, 45 percent had very little or no confidence in the state legislature when it came to passing new state laws to solve the problem, and 65 percent said they preferred that voters intervene and set policy through initiatives on the state ballot.

Although the electricity crisis would resolve itself in the coming year through a combination of increased supply, conservation, and renewed regulatory efforts,[2] Californians' confidence in their governor and state government was severely damaged. At the start of 2002, only 39 percent of Californians approved of the way that Davis was handling the state's electricity situation. His approval on this issue was even lower among likely voters (32%), including fewer than half of Democrats (46%) and independents (42%), and 24 percent of Republicans. The electricity crisis had become a symbol to Californians that their elected leaders were failing them.

THE BUDGET SHORTFALL

Meanwhile, the state's economy was tanking. The inflated dot-com economy began seriously leaking air in the spring of 2000, when Internet enterprises started to collapse in on themselves. First, the wildly overvalued Internet stocks began to slide. Then, the young techies who had reveled in luxurious offices, dined regularly on the priciest haute cuisine, and pumped up the state's economy with their profligate spending, suddenly found themselves unemployed. What followed was a domino effect of massive layoffs, office vacancies, business collapses, and bankruptcies, beginning in the summer of 2000 and continuing through 2001—culminating in a huge drop in state and local tax revenues. The economic picture was further darkened by plummeting consumer confidence in the wake of the September 11 terrorist attacks. By November 2001, the state's unemployment rate had risen to a three-year high of 6 percent, and the California Economic Development Department reported the loss of 53,400 jobs in that month alone—the biggest one-month job loss in a decade (*Los Angeles Times*, December 16, 2001).

It was a stark contrast from the first half of Davis's term, when a flood of income taxes collected on capital gains and stock options during the dotcom boom swelled state coffers by tens of billions of dollars (see Baldassare 2002). As state legislators pondered what to do with the unexpected bonus, Davis urged them to put the funds toward the state's reserves, or limit their use to one-time spending. Committing the budget surplus to permanent spending or tax cuts, Davis cautioned, could lead to deficits in future years if the windfall failed to reappear.

But Davis had been unable to resist the pressure from Republicans, who demanded the surplus be used to cut taxes, and Democrats, who insisted on increasing funding for state programs. During negotiations on his revised 2000 to 2001 budget, which included a $12 billion bonus in income tax collections, Davis yielded to groups such as the California Teachers Association, granting an extra $1.8 billion from the general fund to schools, as well as raising transportation funding by $2 billion, dedicating $43 million for construction of a new University of California campus at Merced, and increasing funding for state parks and health care. To appease the conservatives, the revised budget Davis approved cut taxes by $1.5 billion and sent out rebates on the state's car registration fee. In all, the $99.4 billion budget passed in June 2000 was nearly 18 percent higher than the previous year (Legislative Analyst's Office 2000).

History repeated itself in 2001. Despite signs that the economy was cooling, the legislature attempted to increase funding for a number of state programs. After a fight that delayed passage of the budget by nearly a month, Davis signed a $103 billion spending plan that included substantial increases for schools and health care for low-income children, as well as tax breaks for farmers, ranchers, and senior citizens. The budget was immediately predicted to create a nearly $4 billion deficit, as spending exceeded the now-diminished revenues (Legislative Analyst's Office 2001).

True to Davis's worst fears, the economy's decline accelerated into a nosedive in the last half of 2001, leaving the state with the tab for the tax cuts and funding hikes—and not enough funds to cover it. By November, Davis had put a freeze on state hiring, and was looking for ways to trim

$2 billion from the budget he signed four months earlier. More than half of Californians in a December 2001 survey were expecting bad financial times in the next twelve months.

The budget situation was exacerbated by Proposition 98, a citizens' initiative passed by voters in 1988, which set funding for public schools at a minimum outlay based on the previous year's budget. Under the dictates of this ballot-box budgeting measure, the increased amount of money granted to schools during the boom times would have to be matched in future budgets despite the decrease in tax revenues—further widening the budget gap. The year 2001 closed with analysts forecasting a $14 billion budget deficit for 2002.

Between January 2000 and January 2002, the proportion of Californians who disapproved of the way that Davis was handling the state budget had doubled in PPIC surveys (23% to 46%). Among likely voters, disapproval of Davis's fiscal performance rose to 52 percent overall, including 36 percent of Democrats, 50 percent of independents, and seven in ten Republicans. With the large surplus gone and multibillion dollar deficits on the rise, voters had lost confidence in their state elected officials' ability to handle the worsening budget situation.

PUBLIC PRIORITIES

As 2002 got underway, Californians continued to place public schools at the top of the list of issues they wanted the governor and state legislature to work on in the year ahead, with 20 percent of adults calling this the most important issue. Schools had been residents' top priority since a January 1999 survey (36%), which was conducted shortly after Davis, who campaigned as the "education governor," took office. But the number mentioning this issue had declined since then, while concerns about jobs and the economy had nearly tripled over that time (from 5% in 1999 to 14% in 2002). Another 14 percent in the January 2002 survey cited electricity prices and deregulation as the most important issue for the upcoming legislative session—still high, but down significantly from a year earlier (25%). Fourth on the list was the state budget and taxes, mentioned as the most important issue by 7 percent in 2002, similar to previous years.

As further evidence of California's diverse needs and interests, the public's priorities for their state government varied by racial and ethnic group, with Latinos placing greater emphasis than whites on jobs and the economy (18% to 12%), while whites were more likely than Latinos to consider the energy crisis as the more important issue for the governor and legislature's attention (17% to 10%).

THE MARCH PRIMARY:
GOP CANDIDATES FOR GOVERNOR

Davis, meanwhile, turned his attention to his reelection campaign. He faced a cool audience. Among likely voters in the January 2002 survey, fewer than half approved of the way he was handling their top four issues: the state's public schools (34%), the electricity situation (32%), jobs and the economy (43%), and the budget (39%).

From the start, the GOP candidates for their party's nomination for governor—California secretary of state Bill Jones, former Los Angeles mayor Richard Riordan, and multimillionaire businessman Bill Simon—were united in their campaign efforts to place the blame for California's troubles squarely on Davis. Their themes resonated with voters, with more than two in three (69%) in the January survey saying they blamed Davis for the state's electricity problems "a lot" or "some," and 71 percent saying the governor was at least to some degree at fault for the state's budget deficit (see table 2.1). While Republicans were overwhelmingly likely to blame Davis at least somewhat for the energy crisis (84%), majorities of Democrats (56%) and independents (69%) also agreed. Similarly, while nearly nine in ten Republicans (87%) said they blamed Davis a lot or some for the state budget deficit, more than half of Democrats (58%) and independents (74%) also held him responsible for this problem.

Clearly, the governor's record was a tough sell as his reelection campaign got underway. Instead of a positive focus on Davis's accomplishments, his campaign strategists opted to hammer on the opponent they deemed to pose the biggest threat in a November matchup. In a virtually unprecedented move in California gubernatorial elections, the Davis campaign focused its money and efforts in the early days of his reelection bid not on wooing his fellow

Table 2.1: Governor Davis and the State's Problems

"How much do you blame Governor Davis for . . . ?"

	Likely Voters	Democrats	Republicans	Independents
Electricity Problems				
A lot	38%	22%	57%	40%
Some	31	34	27	29
Very little/none	29	41	15	30
Don't know	2	3	1	1
State Budget Deficit				
A lot	28%	13%	47%	31%
Some	43	45	40	43
Very little/none	27	39	12	24
Don't know	2	3	1	2

Source: PPIC Statewide Survey, January 2002.

Democrats, but on influencing Republican voters as they contemplated their choices in their party's March primary.

The target was Richard Riordan, the popular two-term mayor of Los Angeles. A successful businessman and political moderate, Riordan was considered by most to be the front-runner for the Republican gubernatorial nomination. The January 2002 survey showed Riordan with a sizeable lead among likely GOP primary voters, drawing 41 percent to Jones's 13 percent and Simon's 4 percent. The least conservative of the three, Riordan had more support than Jones and Simon combined among moderate, somewhat conservative, and very conservative Republicans alike. Riordan also was the only candidate to edge out Davis (41% to 37%) in a potential November match-up, while Davis handily beat both Jones (42% to 31%) and Simon (42% to 29%) among likely November voters (see table 2.2). Riordan's strength came from his more moderate positions, which attracted a significant number of voters outside of his party—one in six Democrats and four in ten independents. Jones and Simon, by contrast, had the support of fewer than one in ten Democrats and about one in four independents. Moreover, Riordan had strong support in the GOP base. These early trends raised questions in the Davis camp about how the incumbent governor would be able to win in the fall election.

Starting in January 2002, the Davis campaign began airing television advertisements attacking Riordan. Unleashing a $10 million barrage of commercials on Republican voters in the three months before their March primary, the Davis team attempted to portray the moderate Riordan as someone who flip-flopped on issues such as abortion and call his character and

Table 2.2: Early Trends in Gubernatorial Race

"If these were the candidates in the November 2002 governor's election, would you vote for . . . "

	Likely Voters	Democrats	Republicans	Independents
Davis-Riordan matchup				
Richard Riordan	41%	17%	73%	41%
Gray Davis	37	63	9	37
Don't know	22	20	18	22
Davis-Jones matchup				
Gray Davis	42%	66%	15%	35%
Bill Jones	31	8	64	26
Don't know	27	26	21	39
Davis-Simon matchup				
Gray Davis	42%	68%	15%	32%
Bill Simon	29	6	61	27
Don't know	29	26	24	41

Source: PPIC Statewide Survey, January 2002.

integrity into question. The goal was to knock Riordan, who was seen as the stronger challenger, off the Republican ticket, and get him replaced with a more conservative nominee who would be a weaker foe in November.

The strategy paid off. Davis's campaign of attack ads, later dubbed "puke politics"[3] by California attorney general Bill Lockyer, a Democrat, had a decided effect on the GOP primary. In early February 2002, after a month of Davis's negative advertising, a PPIC survey found Riordan with stagnant support among likely GOP primary voters (41%). Bill Simon, however, had gained twenty points since January (4% to 24%), while Bill Jones trailed well behind (9%). Among all voters, Riordan continued to beat Davis in a potential November matchup (46% to 40%), while Davis topped both Simon (44% to 40%) and Jones (44% to 39%). Of the three in four voters who said they noticed advertising by the candidates, two in three mentioned the source of the political commercials as Davis (32%) and Riordan (33%) while just one in ten mentioned Simon, Jones, or others.

One month later, after a continued assault of Davis's campaign ads succeeded in alienating Republican moderates and conservatives, Riordan's lead had vanished. He ended up losing the Republican nomination to Simon by a wide eighteen-point margin (49% to 31%) in the party's March 5, 2002, primary (see table 2.3). According to the Los Angeles Times Exit Poll (March 5, 2002), more GOP primary voters had an unfavorable than a favorable image of Richard Riordan (53% to 47%). After weeks of negative advertising, the two GOP candidates who were not under attack by the Davis campaign were viewed favorably by solid majorities of GOP primary voters.

Davis's gambit got him the adversary he preferred to face, but it did nothing to win voters to his cause. In fact, it served to turn voters off—the March 2002 voter turnout of 34.6 percent was the lowest in California primary history up to that date (California Secretary of State, March 2002)—and alienated voters would become an even bigger factor in the November election and the subsequent recall. In the February survey before the primary, a majority of likely voters (53%) said they disapproved of Davis's performance

Table 2.3: March 2002 Primary: Governor and Term Limits

Republican Candidate for Governor	
Bill Simon	49.5%
Richard Riordan	31.4
Bill Jones	17.0
Other candidates	2.1
Proposition 45: Term Limits Extension	
Yes	42.3%
No	57.7
Registered voter turnout	34.6%

Source: California Secretary of State, "Statement of the Vote," March 2002.

as governor. By comparison, majorities were in approval of President Bush (71%) and Senators Feinstein (58%) and Boxer (53%). Davis's approval was below 50 percent in all state regions and among men and women alike.

PROPOSITION 45:
TERM LIMIT EXTENSION INITIATIVE

As they selected gubernatorial candidates in the March 2002 primary election, voters also expressed their continued desire to keep elected leaders in check, by rejecting an initiative appearing on the same ballot. Proposition 45 was a bid to extend term limits by allowing voters to petition to have their incumbent legislator serve another four years. The initiative was sponsored by a coalition of labor unions, professional organizations, and business groups. They sought to allow legislators a one-time extension if 20 percent of the voters in their district signed a petition asking for the extension. Proposition 45 was solidly opposed in the January 2002 survey (61% no, 31% yes). In the February 2002 survey, a similar 59 percent of likely voters were saying they planned to vote no (see table 2.4). The PPIC survey found that a majority in all political parties opposed extending California's strict rule of three two-year terms in the Assembly and two four-year terms in the Senate, which had been imposed by Proposition 140 in 1990.

Table 2.4: Proposition 45—Extending Term Limits

"Proposition 45 on the March 2002 ballot—the 'Legislative Term Limits, Local Voter Petitions Initiative'—allows votes to submit petition signatures to permit their incumbent legislator to run for reelection and serve a maximum of four years beyond the terms provided for in the constitution if a majority of voters approves. . . . If an election were held today, would you vote yes or no on Proposition 45?"

	Likely Voters	Democrats	Republicans	Independents
Yes	28%	33%	22%	32%
No	59	52	65	62
Don't know	13	15	13	6

"Legislative term limits now allow members of the state Assembly to serve up to three two-year terms and members of the state Senate to serve up to two four-year terms. Do you think the current term limits give state legislators too little, too much, or the right amount of time in office?"

	Likely Voters	Democrats	Republicans	Independents
Too little	24%	31%	19%	20%
Too much	7	4	9	6
Right amount	66	61	70	72
Don't know	3	4	2	2

Source: PPIC Statewide Survey, February 2002.

A follow-up question in February showed why—harking back to the populist aversion to professional politicians, two in three voters said they thought the current eight-year limit gave state legislators "the right amount of time in office," while only one in four said it was "too little." The belief that current term limits allowed state elected officials an adequate amount of time was shared across party lines, and those with this opinion opposed Proposition 45 by a three-to-one majority. A month earlier, just three in ten likely voters in a PPIC survey said their legislators would be more effective if allowed to serve up to four more years, again, with broad agreement across political groups. Only the small minority of voters who thought that longer terms led to more effective legislators supported this initiative.

Proposition 45 fell to defeat in March, with 57.7 percent voting no (see table 2.3). According to the Los Angeles Times Exit Poll (March 5, 2002), Proposition 45 passed among Democrats and liberals, but it was opposed by moderates and independents, and conservatives and Republicans voted solidly against this effort to extend term limits. This relatively mild term-limit reform was defeated by large margins among whites and older, upper-income, and college-educated voters, as well as both men and women.

PARTISAN IMPASSE LEADS TO
A RECORD BUDGET STANDOFF

In the months between the spring primary and the fall election, the California legislature was seized by a partisan standoff over the 2002 to 2003 budget that lasted a record sixty-seven days. The impasse had left state government without a spending plan in place for more than two months during the summer, stalling payments to vendors doing business with the state, cutting some funding for local governments, and preventing the state from paying its rent and utility bills.[4]

The stalemate began in May, when revised budget figures showed the state facing a nearly $24 billion shortfall. To help close the gap, Davis's May budget Revise[5] proposed increasing taxes on vehicles and cigarettes, as well as making substantial cuts to many state programs. Responding in partisan fashion, Republicans rejected a budget bill that included tax hikes, while Democrats balked at the program cuts. The two sides refused to compromise throughout the summer, but finally began to negotiate at the end of August, reaching an agreement that was signed into law on September 5. While the $99 billion spending plan did include reductions in funding for health and social service programs, it appeased partisan interests by allowing Democrats to point out that deeper cuts had been avoided and Republicans to claim they had prevented tax increases. It also created a sizeable deficit for the next fiscal year (*Sacramento Bee*, September 6, 2002).

The record standoff over the budget highlighted the weaknesses of a term-limited legislature that was long on partisanship and short on fiscal experience and political statesmanship. It also called attention to the influence of special interests, such as the state's prison guard union—major contributors to Davis's reelection campaign—which received a substantial pay increase that summer despite the state's budget woes. Davis exacerbated the public's consternation over his campaign finance activities by rushing directly from the budget-signing in Sacramento to a $1,000-a-head fund-raiser in San Francisco (*San Francisco Chronicle*, September 6, 2002).

THE NOVEMBER 2002 ELECTION:
THE GUBERNATORIAL RACE

From the outset, the 2002 gubernatorial election was a contest that many voters found unattractive, either because the candidates did not reflect their political values (i.e., Simon) or because voters were not happy with their performance in office (i.e., Davis). In an August PPIC survey, the majority (54%) of likely voters in the upcoming gubernatorial contest said they were not satisfied with the choice of candidates (see table 2.5). Majorities of Democrats, Republicans, and independents all shared this view. That summer and fall, Californians were exposed to what is widely acknowledged as the ugliest gubernatorial campaign the state had ever experienced (see Baldassare et al. 2004). Both Davis and Simon spent huge sums of money—nearly $80 million—on television advertising so negative that voters found both candidates repulsive in the end.

Throughout the campaign, Davis and Simon continued to wage full-scale attacks on each other. Television advertisements for the Davis side characterized the Republican challenger as an archconservative fanatic, in hopes of turning off liberal and moderate voters. Simon's commercials focused on Davis's voracious fund-raising, portraying his administration as "pay-to-play" politics and beholden to special interests.

It was a contest between "damaged goods versus defective product," Garry South, Davis's chief campaign strategist, told the *Los Angeles Times*.

Table 2.5: Satisfaction with Choice of Candidates

"Would you say you are satisfied or not satisfied with the choices of candidates in the election for governor on November 5?"

	August	*September*	*October*
Satisfied	38%	38%	38%
Not satisfied	54	55	57
Don't know	8	7	5

Sources: PPIC Statewide Surveys, August, September, and October 2002. Likely voters.

South admitted that Davis's campaign advertising "bludgeoned Simon with a blunt object, and it was not a pretty sight" (*Los Angeles Times*, November 11, 2002). Simon's campaign also had its share of political missteps, such as an announcement that he had a photo documenting Davis accepting an illegal donation—which turned out to be bogus—and Simon was dogged by allegations that he had been in a business partnership with a former drug dealer.

Californians were rocked by a nonstop volley of negative advertising launched by both Davis and Simon that spring, summer, and fall, leaving many voters alienated and disgusted. "We don't have to make Gray Davis into the sweetheart of the rodeo," South told the press at the beginning of Davis's campaign (*Los Angeles Times*, March 19, 2002). And they certainly didn't try. By the time the November election rolled around, voters were so disenchanted by the nasty tone of the campaign that nearly six in ten in an October 2002 PPIC survey said they were dissatisfied with all the candidates (see table 2.5). Voter dissatisfaction cut across all political and demographic groups and all regions of the state.

Moreover, Davis's and Simon's almost singular focus on attacking each other intensified the public's concerns that the issues that mattered most to them were being ignored. Two in three voters in surveys that fall said they were dissatisfied with the amount of attention the candidates were giving to the most important issues. The October survey, conducted shortly before the election, found that Democrats (65%), Republicans (66%), and independents (69%) were all highly dissatisfied with the candidates' attention to the issues most important to voters. What did voters want to hear about? Just as they did at the beginning of the year, schools (21%) topped the list, followed by the economy (14%), the state budget (7%), and taxes (7%). What did voters want to learn about the candidates? According to the September survey, 50 percent of likely voters said it was their stands on the issue, with far fewer naming character (18%), experience (11%), intelligence (11%), and party platform (6%). But the campaigns gave voters a heavy dose of character attacks, while skimping on policy, substance, and issues.

As the election neared, voters were increasingly turned off by the contest. A majority of likely voters in the September 2002 PPIC survey said they were less enthusiastic than usual about voting in the upcoming gubernatorial election (see table 2.6). Enthusiasm was low in all demographic groups and regions and especially so among the traditionally high-turnout groups of older, more educated, and more affluent voters. A majority of Democrats (57%), Republicans (52%), and independents (60%) all said they were less enthusiastic about voting in this gubernatorial election than usual.

The 2002 California gubernatorial election was the most expensive in state history to that date. Together, the two candidates spent more than $97

Table 2.6: Voters' Enthusiasm about the Election

"Thinking about the governor's election that will be held this November, are you more enthusiastic about voting than usual, or less enthusiastic?"

	Likely Voters	Democrats	Republicans	Independents
More enthusiastic	27%	24%	30%	26%
Less enthusiastic	55	57	52	60
Same	15	17	16	11
Don't know	3	2	2	3

Source: PPIC Statewide Survey, September 2002.

million on their campaigns, outpacing the previous gubernatorial election by nearly $40 million.[6] Davis, a master fund-raiser, had stored up a huge campaign chest, while Simon financed much of his campaign from his own personal wealth. In the end, however, Davis outspent Simon by a considerable margin—$64.2 million to the Republican's $33.6 million (California Secretary of State, "Campaign Finance," 2002; Baldassare et al. 2004). Much of the funds were spent on television advertising, but to little positive effect: although 75 percent of voters in the September survey and 79 percent in October said they had seen television ads by the candidates in the past month, only about three in ten of them found the ads relevant. The vast majority (71%) of California voters who had seen the candidates' ads said they were of little or no use in helping them decide which man to support. Those who were most likely to say the ads met their information needs were the traditionally low-propensity voting groups: younger voters, those with less education and income, and Latinos.

Meanwhile, residents continued to see California as being in difficult times throughout 2002. In August, the proportion who thought the state was headed in the right direction had reached a new low for PPIC surveys, with only 44 percent thinking things were on the right track while 48 percent said the state was generally going in the wrong direction. And the mood hadn't improved by election time: in the October survey, 56 percent of residents believed their region was in a recession and 51 percent expected bad economic times for the state in the next year.

Voters saw little to encourage their confidence in the leadership of either candidate on the key economic issues facing the state. Throughout the fall, voters remained evenly divided on which one would do a better job handling the economy, with the October survey showing Davis (42%) and Simon (39%) still virtually tied on this issue and one in five not picking either candidate. As for handling the state budget and taxes, voters gave the incumbent a slight edge, with 43 percent in the October survey saying Davis would do the better job in this area, while 39 percent selected Simon. Again, nearly one in five did not express confidence in either man. Voters were divided along party lines in each of these domains—with Democrats favoring Davis and Republicans favoring Simon. Independents did not express strong support for either of the candidates on these issues.

The area in which neither candidate stood out in many voters' perceptions, not surprisingly in light of the campaign commercials, was maintaining high ethical standards in government. Although voters' views of Davis did slip toward the end of the campaign, the October survey still found the governor ahead of his challenger in this area (41% to 29%). Nonetheless, it is significant to note that fully three in ten voters did not think either candidate would lead in this area. In no other issue were voters so reluctant to choose a favorite candidate. Six in ten Democrats chose Davis over Simon, while a similar proportion of Republicans chose Simon over Davis on this issue. Only four in ten independents thought that Davis would be the best at maintaining ethics in office, while one in four named Simon and one in three did not name either candidate.

While the governor's campaign tactics hadn't built voter confidence in his own leadership, they had succeeded in lowering views of his opponent enough that Davis was able to eke out a scant five-point victory over Simon in November (see table 2.7). Although Davis's 47 percent vote fell short of a majority, it earned him a plurality that allowed him to be reelected. But he did so at the cost of the public's confidence.

Voters were so alienated by the 2002 gubernatorial campaign that they stayed away in droves in November. Turnout was a mere 50.6 percent—the lowest turnout for a gubernatorial election in California history (California Secretary of State, "Statement of the Vote," November 2002). Majorities of those who did vote said they had an unfavorable image of both Simon and Davis, according to the Los Angeles Times Exit Poll (November 5, 2002). The top reason Davis voters gave for their choice of candidate was that he was the "best of a bad lot."

The closeness of the election reflected California's partisan divisions, with Democrats and liberals supporting Davis, Republicans and conservatives favoring Simon, and independents and moderates divided. Davis's support

Table 2.7:   November 2002 Election Results

Governor	
Gray Davis	47.3%
Bill Simon	42.4
Other	10.3
Proposition 49: After-School Programs	
Yes	56.7%
No	43.3
Registered voter turnout	50.6%

Source: California Secretary of State, "Statement of the Vote," November 2002.

fell below 50 percent in key groups—whites and older, college-educated, and affluent voters—many of whom had voted for him four years earlier. Less than a year later, the alienation with the campaigns that kept so many voters at home, and dissatisfaction with candidates among the majority of those who did vote in November 2002, would prove to be Davis's undoing when the electorate became energized by the possibility of recalling him from office.

PROPOSITION 49: AFTER-SCHOOL INITIATIVE

Davis's "feel-bad" campaign throughout the 2002 gubernatorial election contrasted sharply with a "feel good" initiative campaign effort being waged at the same time. Arnold Schwarzenegger made his political debut on the California election scene with an upbeat, folksy approach, winning over voters for the after-school program initiative he was promoting for the November 2002 ballot. Pumping handshakes in schools and shopping malls up and down the state, a smiling, tanned, and fit Schwarzenegger was in many ways the antithesis of the cold and dour Davis.

From the start of his campaign for his ballot-box-budgeting initiative, Schwarzenegger hit the populist notes that resonated with the California electorate, portraying it as an issue that voters needed to take into their own hands because state lawmakers had failed to act on it. By April, Schwarzenegger delivered 750,000 signatures—nearly double the number required to qualify the measure for the November 2002 ballot—flanked by schoolchildren helping him carry the bags of petitions to the Sacramento County administrative offices.

The populist theme was echoed in the initiative campaign's inclusive website name, www.joinarnold.com, urging voters to become part of his team effort to improve public schools. It was shown by the crowds who flocked to his campaign appearances calling him by his first name. It was shown in his easy manner and informal language as he described his plan to dedicate up to $550 million from the state's general fund toward after-school programs for elementary and middle school students—without raising taxes. While most voters felt that the candidates for governor were not focusing on the issues most important to them, Schwarzenegger's measure dealt with education—consistently rated by the public as the state's most pressing concern. His confidence and optimism stood in marked contrast to both Davis's and Simon's focus on the negative and provided a tonic to what was seen as partisan warfare. With the public's trust in its elected leaders headed further downhill in light of recent budget deficits and partisan impasse over the solutions, Schwarzenegger's outsider status and direct legislation approach offered a jaded electorate a renewed sense of control over their government.

He was also, of course, a huge celebrity, drawing capacity crowds at nearly every event. He knew how to work a crowd and was a master at setting stages that would showcase him and his causes to maximum effect. One example is a Sunday-morning appearance at one of California's most overpowering structures: Orange County's Crystal Cathedral. Constructed of more than ten thousand glass panels, the megachurch claims to be home to a congregation of more than ten thousand individuals, with Sunday services broadcast to 20 million more television viewers (www. hourofpower. org).

"Crystal Cathedral's famous minister, Robert Schuller, not only embraced Proposition 49 but hailed Schwarzenegger as an old friend and as an agent of the Almighty," *Sacramento Bee* columnist Dan Walters wrote of Schwarzenegger's September 2002 campaign stop at the Crystal Cathedral shortly after a highly successful appearance at the nearby Republican convention. "'Thank you, God, for this man,'" Schuller proclaimed, after hearing Schwarzenegger plug his measure as a means of keeping latchkey kids out of trouble (*Sacramento Bee*, September 30, 2002).

Schwarzenegger clearly enjoyed his new role. "I've had the most spectacular time, pushing for this initiative," the actor told the *San Francisco Chronicle*'s editorial board on a campaign tour through the region a few weeks before the election. "Whether it's the fund-raising, traveling up and down the state to do interviews, answering the questions. . . . I love crowds. I'm not shy. I'm not one of those celebrities who has the bodyguards around to keep the people away. I'm fortunate that I'm a people person" (*San Francisco Chronicle*, October 14, 2002).

Proposition 49 was a classic example of ballot-box budgeting: earmarking funds from the state's general fund for a popular purpose without raising taxes to create extra revenue. Since 1988, when Californians passed the landmark ballot-box budgeting initiative, Proposition 98, the idea of earmarking funds to pay for their favorite state programs has appealed to voters who have lost faith in the way the governor and legislature are spending their money. Proposition 49 was perfectly positioned for voters who were nervous about California's looming deficit, containing provisions that the additional funding requirements for after-school programs would not kick in until the state budget was back in the black.[7] Its campaign messages maintained that the measure would pay for itself, because after-school programs would reduce juvenile crime, thus lowering the need for spending on the criminal justice system.

The public response to this initiative was very favorable. The 2002 surveys showed that two in three likely voters in August and nearly three in four in October agreed that Proposition 49 would help keep children safe from crime (see table 2.8). Moreover, a majority of voters believed that the

Table 2.8: Proposition 49, the After-School Initiative

"Proposition 49, the 'Before and After School Programs Initiative' increases state grant funds available for before and after school programs. . . . If the election were held today, would you vote yes or no on Proposition 49?"

	October	Democrats	Republicans	Independents
Yes	64%	73%	50%	72%
No	27	19	39	20
Don't know	9	8	11	8

"Do you think the additional funding in Proposition 49 for before- and after-school programs will or will not improve children's safety from crime?"

	August	October
Will	67%	73%
Will not	25	21
Don't know	8	6

"Do you think the additional funding in Proposition 49 for before- and after-school programs will or will not raise student test scores?"

	August	October
Will	54%	55%
Will not	33	34
Don't know	13	11

Sources: PPIC Statewide Surveys, August and October 2002. Likely voters.

after-school measure would raise student test scores—a perennial area of focus since the state's education reforms were put into place in the 1990s. In the October survey, six in ten voters said they would vote yes on Proposition 49. There was strong support among Democrats and independents, and substantial proportions of Republicans were also in favor of this state spending initiative. We found majority support among liberals and conservatives, whites and nonwhites, men and women, and even voters without children living in their households.

Although Schwarzenegger was a registered Republican, he made every effort to position his measure as bipartisan, including airing television commercials showing him in his office flanked by the stars and stripes and the California bear flag, with busts of presidents Ronald Reagan and John Kennedy at his side. Enhancing his populist appeal, he drew support from across the spectrum of California politics, including the conservative Howard Jarvis Taxpayers Association, law enforcement officers, the liberal California Teachers Association, and prominent Democrats Willie Brown (then mayor of San Francisco) and Herb Wesson (then speaker of the state Assembly).

The initiative did not attract a highly organized or expensive campaign by its opponents, helping it avoid the label of being supported or opposed by big money from partisans or special interests. Not everyone jumped on the

Schwarzenegger bandwagon, however. A spokeswoman for the California League of Women Voters expressed her group's objections: "We're concerned Proposition 49 will start a pattern, that anyone with fame and money can bypass the legislature and dictate how state funds should be spent from now until kingdom come" (*San Francisco Chronicle*, October 12, 2002). The president of the California Federation of Teachers, a smaller rival to the powerful California Teachers' Association, called it "just bad government. . . . If we get to the point where everybody's sequestering funds for their pet project, we're going to have more funds sequestered than we've got funds" (*Los Angeles Times*, October 4, 2002).

But Arnold Schwarzenegger and his proposition prevailed on November 5, passing with a hearty 57 percent of the vote, while Davis was eking out a scant 47 percent plurality (see table 2.7). The Los Angeles Times Exit Poll (November 5, 2002) found that Proposition 49 was supported by majorities across party groups, whites and Latinos, men and women, liberals and conservatives, and voters in all age, education, and income groups. The direct legislation's broad-based appeal stood in stark contrast to the highly divisive campaign for the governor's office.

Proposition 49 was a political milestone for the budding political career of Arnold Schwarzenegger. Democrats had swept all of the statewide races in the November 2002 election, including the governor's office and six other executive branch positions, leaving Schwarzenegger and his citizens' initiative as the largest vote-getter associated with a GOP politician. Indeed, the Schwarzenegger initiative's 4 million "yes" votes had outpolled Davis himself, who garnered just 3.5 million votes, as well as all of the Democratic winners in the other statewide races. Arnold Schwarzenegger's credentials as a populist candidate with bipartisan appeal were firmly established.

POLITICAL CONSEQUENCES:
A MORE DISTRUSTFUL ELECTORATE

The 2002 California gubernatorial election went down in history as one of the low points in state politics. Despite the record amounts spent on advertising, the campaigns are today best remembered for their nasty tone and lack of discussion of the issues most important to voters. This display of negativity led to the lowest turnout ever in a California gubernatorial election. It also gave rise to widespread voter dissatisfaction.

The events of 2002 exacted a heavy toll on the public's bonds of trust in their elected leaders.[8] Over the course of the year, confidence in state government plummeted—from 44 percent of California voters saying they trusted lawmakers in Sacramento to do what is right "just about always" or "most of the time" in January, to 33 percent giving this response in August (after the March primary and before the start of the fall campaign) to just 30 percent expressing this level of confidence right before the election in November (PPIC Statewide Surveys, January–November 2002) (see table 2.9). Voters' approval for the way the legislature was doing its job had fallen from 56 percent in January of the previous year to 40 percent during the campaign season in September 2002.

Such negative changes in perceptions of state government had been underway for the past thirty years, during which Californians' faith in their leaders weakened and their interest in participating in the electoral process declined (Baldassare 2000). But the trends of voter distrust and disengagement kicked into high gear during the 2002 election.

In the November survey, conducted the week before the election, nearly seven in ten voters said they trusted their state government "only some" or "none of the time" (see table 2.9). During the course of the year, moreover, we noticed a dramatic drop in confidence across the political spectrum, with Democrats (51% to 40%), Republicans (43% to 26%), and independents (41% to 29%) all becoming less likely to trust their state government to act in the public's best interest.

One key factor in the decline in public trust in government may have been the lack of informational content in the gubernatorial candidates' advertising. Although the majority of voters had seen the ads before going to the polls, very few found them helpful in making their voting decision. A Los Angeles Times Exit Poll of voters leaving the voting booth on November 5 found that one in five had just made up their minds that day. For many voters, the lack of information they felt they could use to make an informed choice also appears to have translated into lack of participation in the election (Baldassare et al. 2004).

The candidates' avoidance of topics Californians considered most important reinforced the public's image that their elected leaders were disinterested and out of touch with people like themselves. Two in three voters in the October 2002 survey said they were not satisfied with the amount of atten-

Table 2.9: Trust in State Government, 2002

"How much of the time do you think you can trust the government in Sacramento to do what is right?"

	January	August	November
Always/most of the time	44%	33%	30%
Only some of the time	54	61	64
None of the time (volunteered)	1	5	5
Don't know	1	1	1

Sources: PPIC Statewide Surveys, January–November 2002. Likely voters.

tion the candidates were spending on the issues most important to them. The day-to-day events in Sacramento seemed to reinforce these perceptions. The year was marked by a lack of bipartisan cooperation in dealing with the state budget deficit that culminated in a record budget standoff. The governor and legislature seemed to lack interest in addressing the state's growing fiscal crisis. Meanwhile, Arnold Schwarzenegger and his Proposition 49 initiative campaign offered Californians a way to feel in control of governance again. Similar perceptions by citizens had fueled the populist movement in the early part of the previous century, and it was to motivate voters to take matters into their own hands again soon—in the 2003 recall.

CONCLUSION

The events surrounding the 2002 election cycle raised a number of critical issues for California voters about their current system of representative democracy and the promise of direct democracy. This highlights the role of populism, partisanship, special interests, and voter distrust in shaping public opinion about governing in the state.

Governor Davis was facing increasing criticism at the beginning of his fourth year in office over his handling of the state's economy and budget issues. The apparent failures of the state's electricity deregulation plans and the record budget impasse over the multibillion dollar imbalance between spending and revenues led to even more fundamental questions about the ability of the governor and legislature to make good policy decisions.

Davis's reelection focused voters' attention on partisanship and the role of special interests. His campaign staff chose to use its resources to influence the outcome of the GOP primary and dwell on the negative attributes of his opponent in the general election, rather than address the issues voters considered most important. In a race that was largely devoid of substance, his challenger, Bill Simon, attempted to link the governor's fund-raising with his policy decisions in office. The campaigns had succeeded in making voters dissatisfied with both candidates and managed to so alienate voters that the turnout was a historic low. In the end, a majority of voters viewed both the GOP and Democratic candidates for governor unfavorably. While Davis won a narrow reelection, the year ended on the sour note of growing distrust in state government.

Meanwhile, the 2002 election cycle reaffirmed the value of the initiative process and its populist ideals. Voters soundly rejected an effort by special interests in the March primary—endorsed by some of the majority party's elected officials in the legislature—to relax term limits. Thus, voters took the opportunity to remind party leadership and special interests that they still favored a limited role for elected officials, and that changing initiative-based reforms would be difficult. Arnold Schwarzenegger entered the state's political stage with an after-school funding initiative on the November ballot. This initiative was a classic effort to earmark funds for favorite programs, and thus also took aim at the legislature and governor by limiting their spending power. In its appeal to voters across party lines and avoidance of relying on special interests for campaign funds, the initiative had the trappings of a populist movement. In the end, the biggest winner on the November ballot was Schwarzenegger, through a citizens' initiative.

NOTES

1. For a thorough discussion of the factors contributing to the California energy crisis, see Christopher Weare, *The California Electricity Crisis: Causes and Policy Options* (San Francisco: Public Policy Institute of California research report, 2003), 15–50. See also California State Auditor, *Energy Deregulation: The Benefits of Competition Were Undermined by Structural Flaws in the Market, Unsuccessful Oversight, and Uncontrollable Competitive Forces* (Sacramento, Calif.: 2001) and Cambridge Energy Research Associates, *Beyond California's Power Crisis: Impact, Solutions and Lessons* (Cambridge, Mass.: 2001).

2. For a discussion, see Weare, *California Electricity Crisis*, 51–54.

3. Although this term became widely used to describe negative campaigning, its first reported use was in a Lockyer meeting with *Sacramento Bee* reporters on July 30, 2003, in which he used the term "puke politics" to warn Davis and his campaign consultants that a repeat of the personal attacks on Riordan made during his reelection bid would alienate Democratic voters from supporting him in the recall. See Gary Delsohn, "Davis Is Told: No Trash Talk," *Sacramento Bee*, August 1, 2003, A1.

4. The effect was not more widely felt because the state covered most of its payments with a $7.5 billion loan. In addition, recurrent late budgets in recent years had resulted in court rulings requiring that programs such as welfare, foster care, and adoption and child support services continue to be funded even when the state did not have a spending plan in place.

5. The May Revise is a step in California's budget process in which the governor releases a revised state budget plan for the fiscal year beginning on July 1 incorporating updated figures on state revenues.

6. For a list of spending on recent gubernatorial elections in California, see Mark Baldassare, Bruce E. Cain, D. E. Apollonio, and Jonathan Cohen, *The Season of Our Discontent: Voters' Views on California Elections* (San Francisco: Public Policy Institute of California, 2004), 8.

7. The measure provided that the increased after-school program spending would be triggered when a formula calculating the state budget's peak level of education spending between 2002 and 2005 showed a $1.5 billion rise in state revenues outside of money earmarked for education. This finally took place in the 2006 to 2007 budget year.

8. Further description of the political turmoil of 2002 can be found in Larry N. Gerston and Terry Christensen, *Recall: California's Political Earthquake* (Armonk, N.Y.: M. E. Sharpe, 2004), 45–48; and Shaun Bowler and Bruce E. Cain, *Clicker Politics: Essays on the California Recall* (Upper Saddle River, N.J.: Pearson-Prentice Hall, 2006), 2–3.

3

Voters' Revolt: The Gubernatorial Recall and 2003 Special Election

The chapter details the historic 2003 recall from its inception in the signature gathering by citizens' groups that began in February, through the qualifying stages and announcement of replacement candidates in the summer, to the October special election. The success of the recall movement is shown to be highly dependent on the enabling factors of populist attitudes and voter distrust, with evidence that concerns about the influence of partisan groups and special interests also contributed to the recall effort along the way.

Davis's downfall was tied to perceptions of his being a career member of the political establishment and his voracious appetite for fund-raising, linking him to special interests in the public's view. Schwarzenegger's victory is credited to his embracing the themes of populism and the tools of direct democracy while avoiding the pitfalls of partisan identification and debts to special interests. His campaign as an outsider to Sacramento politics also succeeded by offering hope to California voters, who were cynical about state government and its entrenched politicians. The high turnout for the special election, running counter to the overall trend of declining voter participation, indicates that Californians were attentive to the recall election and enthusiastic about using this unique tool of direct democracy to remove the incumbent governor and replace him with a political newcomer.

Public opinion throughout the campaign was a major catalyst for change, including broad public support for the recall provision, a high, bipartisan level of pessimism about the state of the state, and significant dissatisfaction with representative government and its practitioners. The events of 2003, involving the deficit-ridden state budget and other legislative decisions, further fueled voters' feelings of alienation and desire for change. Nonetheless, the outcome of the special election illustrates Californians' selective approach to direct democracy: while the recall succeeded, two state propositions on the same ballot (racial classification and infrastructure spending) failed by wide margins. The events of 2003 overturned the political status quo and emphasized to voters the importance of their direct involvement in setting public policy.

THE RECALL MOVEMENT BEGINS

On January 6, 2003, Gray Davis took the oath of office, beginning his second term as governor of California. "I am humbled and inspired to be standing in the footsteps of giants like Hiram Johnson, Earl Warren, Ronald Reagan and Pat Brown," the sixty-year-old Davis, who had spent most of his career in public office, told the audience at Sacramento Memorial Auditorium (Davis, "Governor's Inaugural Address," 2003). Little did he know that, less than a year later, the legacy of one of those giants—governor Hiram Johnson—would contribute to having his time in office drastically shortened. Davis would make history as the first California governor to be recalled from office by the voters.

The California recall was officially born on February 5, 2003, when Ted Costa, head of the taxpayer-rights group, People's Advocate, announced the beginning of an effort to gather signatures to recall the governor. Costa's organization, founded by Proposition 13 coauthor Paul Gann, had been a major sponsor of legislation by citizens' initiative over the years, with efforts including passage of the "Gann Limit" (restricting increases in state spending), legislative and congressional term limits,[1] and an unsuccessful bid to place caps on legislators' salaries. The Costa recall petition claimed that Davis had committed "gross mismanagement of California finances by overspending taxpayers' money, threatening public safety by cutting funds to local governments, failing to account for the exorbitant cost of the energy fiasco, and failing in general to deal with the state's major problems until they get to the crisis stage" (California Secretary of State, "Official Voter Information Guide," 2003).

A second recall effort, sponsored by former Republican assemblyman Howard Kaloogian, was announced the same day, charging the governor with "malfeasance in office and lies to Californians" (RecallGrayDavis.com 2003). But the underlying force behind both organized efforts was anger over Davis's meddling in the GOP primary ten months earlier, a move that helped bring him victory in November, but enraged Republicans and ultimately cost him the goodwill of the voters.

In reality, discussions of the organized recall effort began shortly after Governor Davis's reelection in November 2002. Two weeks after Davis's five-point victory over Bill Simon, according to Costa associate Mark Abernathy, he and Costa discussed the idea of recalling Davis in a telephone conversation on November 17, 2002.

"We were talking about what to do about this, in our view, terrible election that happened in November; when there was a very small turnout, and people didn't feel like they had a legitimate choice," Abernathy recalled. "So Ted said, 'You know, maybe we ought to recall him.' And we said, 'Well yeah. What does that take?' So we went to the Constitution and started reading."[2]

Costa and Abernathy quickly realized that to mount a recall against Governor Davis, they would need signatures from just 12 percent of the voters who cast ballots in the previous gubernatorial election. Because of the record low turnout—only a little more than 7.7 million voters participated in the November 5, 2002, election and fewer than 7.5 million cast valid votes in the gubernatorial contest (California Secretary of State, "Statement of the Vote," November 5, 2002)—that translated to less than 900,000 voter signatures needed to qualify a recall for the ballot. While this may represent a large number for a statewide petition campaign, many more voter signatures would have been needed to qualify a gubernatorial recall after the 1994 or 1998 elections, which had much higher turnouts. "This is a thing of beauty," Abernathy recalled saying to Costa when they realized the governor's recall was achievable, "'A thing of beauty,' which I continued to repeat throughout the process as it continued to unfold."[3]

POLITICAL AND FISCAL CONTEXT

The recall effort got underway as Californians' confidence in their elected leaders was crashing. Although Davis had eked out a five-point victory the previous year in which he intervened in the Republican primary to face a weak opponent in November, his tactics had alienated voters. The public was further turned off by a ballooning state budget deficit and a state government that seemed unable to take action to resolve it. In a PPIC survey conducted in February 2003, Davis's approval ratings had fallen to 33 percent, while six in ten said they disapproved of the job he was doing as governor (see table 3.1). This was a nineteen-point drop from Davis's ratings just before his reelection in an October 2002 survey (52%). Davis fared even worse among likely

Table 3.1: Davis's Job Approval Ratings

"Do you approve or disapprove of the way that Gray Davis is handling his job as governor of California?"

	Adults	Democrats	Republicans	Independents
Approve	33%	41%	14%	27%
Disapprove	60	54	83	68
Don't know	7	5	3	5

Source: PPIC Statewide Survey, February 2003.

voters, of whom only 24 percent approved, while 72 percent in the February 2003 survey disapproved of his performance as governor. His approval was below 50 percent in all political parties, including Democrats (41%), independents (27%), and Republicans (14%) and in all regions of the state. As if that wasn't enough bad news for the governor, his approval ratings worsened among citizens who traditionally are most likely to participate in the political process—older, more educated, and higher-income residents.

It is important to note that disapproval with the state's elected representatives was not confined to the governor. In the same survey, only 36 percent of all adults and 29 percent of likely voters said they approved of the way the California legislature was handling its job. Four in ten Democrats, half of independents, and six in ten Republicans had a negative assessment of the legislature, and disapproval increased with age, education, and income. Five months earlier, in September 2002, 45 percent of California adults had approved of the legislature's job performance. Given the public's dissatisfaction, legislators could take solace in the fact that there was no provision for recalling the entire state Senate and Assembly.

The public was generally in an ugly mood in February, 2003. Fully six in ten adults thought things in the state were headed in the wrong direction, and only 28 percent had an optimistic view (see table 3.2). This was a twenty-eight-point drop since the beginning of the previous year, when 56 percent thought things were going well in California. It was the most negative outlook we had seen since we began asking this question in April 1998, when 55 percent had a positive evaluation. Whites, older residents, and those with more education and income were especially negative about the direction the state was taking. Just three in ten Democrats thought the state was headed in the right direction, and even fewer Republicans and independents held this positive view.

The events of the previous year had severely damaged Californians' confidence in their state government and there were no signs of improvement. In the February 2003 survey, just 36 percent said they felt they could trust the government in Sacramento to do what is right "just about always" or "most of the time," while six in ten said they trusted their leaders "only some of the

Table 3.2: Overall Mood

"Do you think things in California are generally going in the right direction or the wrong direction?"

	2000	2001	2002	2003
Right direction	65%	62%	56%	28%
Wrong direction	27	29	36	60
Don't know	8	9	8	12

Sources: PPIC Statewide Survey, February 2000, January 2001, February 2002, and February 2003. All adults.

time" (58%) or "none of the time" (4%). The low percentage of residents expressing confidence in state government that February was identical to what it had been just before the November 2002 election (37%)—and well below the trust measured one year earlier (47%) in a January 2002 survey.

Moreover, confidence was shaken in every political group, with only a minority of Democrats (36%), Republicans (25%), and independents (29%) feeling they could generally trust their state government. Likely voters were especially skeptical, with only 28 percent saying they trusted their leaders in Sacramento to do what is right all or most of the time. The only group expressing a higher amount of confidence was Latinos, of whom 49 percent felt they could generally trust the state government, a faith shared by only 29 percent of whites. And once again, the Californians with higher incomes, education, and age were especially negative in their political evaluations.

The days of California's dazzling economy were a distant memory in early 2003, and the governor and legislature were grappling with huge budget shortfalls. The revenue windfalls of the previous years had been funneled into tax cuts and funding for state programs. With the economy now hovering near recession, state revenues that were highly dependent on personal income from capital gains had plunged along with the stock market, while spending commitments remained the same. Davis warned Californians that the state now faced a nearly $35 billion shortfall.[4] "We have to find a way to wean state government off the feast-and-famine budgeting it's experienced for more than 25 years," Davis had said in his January inaugural speech. "Our task is far greater than balancing the books. We must rewrite the book on California budgets" (Davis, "Governor's Inaugural Address," 2003).

The austere budget proposal he had presented in January included cuts in virtually all state programs, including $1.7 billion less for K–12 public schools. The impact of the state budget cuts would be especially strong at the local level, with $5.1 billion in resources shifted away from local governments. The plan also included income tax increases for the wealthiest Californians, as well as a one-cent hike in the sales tax and a doubling of the state's cigarette tax, (Legislative Analyst's Office, "Overview of the 2003–04 Governor's Budget," 2003).

Partisan and special interest battle lines formed almost immediately after the release of Davis's budget proposal. City officials decried the loss of local programs, the powerful California Teachers Association vowed to fight the cuts to school funding, and lobbyists for a myriad of causes queued up at the capitol to plead for their group. Republican legislators, meanwhile, refused to sanction any tax increases and insisted the deficit be made up entirely through belt-tightening. Privately, however, some GOP leaders were suggesting an increase in the state's vehicle registration fee, which had been reduced when the state was flush with cash three years earlier. Raising the license fee would net the state an additional $4 billion, and offered an attractive solution for Republicans because, unlike the two-thirds vote requirement for raising taxes, this fee could be increased with a simple majority vote in the legislature. Thus, Republicans could support the fee hike without having to actually vote for it (*Los Angeles Times*, January 15, 2003).

As legislators argued over the state budget in early 2003, the deficit weighed heavily on Californians' minds. Three in four (74%) called it a "big" problem in the February 2003 survey, and 63 percent were "very concerned" that it would lead to severe cuts in state programs, such as education, health care, and the environment. Concern about cuts to state programs was especially high among whites, women, and Democrats. Moreover, two in three Californians were very closely or fairly closely following the news about the state's deficit—even as Iraq and terrorism competed for their attention.

Californians felt they were looking at a bleak future in February 2003. Fully 71 percent expected the state to undergo bad financial times in the year ahead, while only 20 percent anticipated good times. This was a twenty-six-point drop from the percentage giving a positive forecast just one year earlier (46% in February 2002) and was the lowest this measure had been since we began asking the question in February 2000 (78%).

The public held both Davis and the legislature responsible for much of the state's fiscal troubles. More than six in ten Californians (63%) in the February 2003 survey disapproved of the way the governor was handling the state budget and taxes—placing the governor slightly ahead of the legislature (57% disapprove) in the blame game (see table 3.3). Nonetheless, only about one in four residents approved of the way either entity was handling state budget and tax issues. Strong majorities of voters in all party groups disapproved of the job both the governor and the legislature were doing in the fiscal arena.

Davis came out on top in the public's assignment of primary responsibility for the budget deficit, with 23 percent in the February survey naming the governor as the main reason for the problem, while 17 percent named

Table 3.3: Fiscal Approval Ratings

"Do you approve or disapprove of the way . . . is handling the state budget and taxes?"

	Adults	Democrats	Republicans	Independents
Governor Davis				
Approve	26%	32%	11%	24%
Disapprove	63	57	84	68
Don't know	11	11	5	8
California Legislature				
Approve	26%	27%	18%	23%
Disapprove	57	57	69	63
Don't know	17	16	13	14

Source: PPIC Statewide Survey, February 2003.

population growth and immigration, 16 percent blamed the state's economic downturn, 13 percent mentioned the energy crisis, and 10 percent named the legislature. Not surprisingly, Republicans were highly inclined to place the main blame on Davis (40%). However, about one in five Democrats (18%) and independents (21%) also saw the state's budget deficit as primarily the governor's fault.

When asked in the February survey about the overall role of state government in the budget deficit, 43 percent of adults said that Governor Davis and the legislature deserved "a lot" of the blame for the problem. Only 14 percent of Californians thought their state leaders deserved "very little" or no blame. Two in three Republicans, nearly half of independents (46%), and 36 percent of Democrats blamed state government for the deficit in great measure.

It was in this grim climate of finger-pointing and economic fear that the recall took hold. Voters were being asked to sign petitions to remove the top state official at a time when many were eager to find a way to express their displeasure to their elected representatives in Sacramento. The recall amounted to a protest movement against the status quo, combining elements of populism with voter distrust.

POPULISM IN THE AGE OF NEW TECHNOLOGY

Initially, the recall effort was written off by the political establishment as "partisan mischief" (*Sacramento Bee*, February 14, 2003) and snickered at by the mainstream media.[5] It was seen by many political observers as no different from recall attempts faced by every California governor for the previous thirty years. Beginning with Pat Brown in 1960, some type of recall effort had been launched against California governors representing the political spectrum from Ronald Reagan to Jerry Brown. But none to date had reached a ballot, because they lacked the combination of money, organization, and voter support required to gather enough signatures to qualify.

However, this time, against the backdrop of voter distrust and political activism, the recall petition signature drive was proceeding apace. Volunteer signature-gatherers were standing outside Wal-Marts and Home Depots up and down the state and angry voters were adding their names to the petitions. With little money in the bank, recall backers did not have the funds to buy campaign ads or pay for professional signature-gatherers. Instead, their approach capitalized on the tools of populism in the age of new technology—utilizing the Internet and talk radio programs to spread their message.

As soon as the recall effort was announced, both campaigns launched websites and began making the rounds of radio call-in shows. Within the first few weeks of its launch, members of the Kaloogian-backed recall effort claimed that their Internet site had received 2.5 million hits, gotten 50,000 e-mails, and collected $100,000 (*Sacramento Bee*, March 9, 2003). According to Sal Russo, campaign manager for the Kaloogian-sponsored effort, their website, www.RecallGrayDavis.com, was the number one–ranked website in politics until Schwarzenegger entered the race. Visitors to the site were encouraged to download recall petitions and circulate them among their friends and colleagues. Russo speculated that "there's probably a couple million petitions that were printed and out into the world as a consequence" of being posted on the website.[6]

Meanwhile, conservative talk radio programs were broadcasting the Davis recall message to wide audiences throughout the state. The deliberately incendiary programs, where listeners called in to air their views on issues fielded by "talk jocks" with a primarily conservative or antiestablishment bent, served as the perfect medium to spread the recall's theme of righteous indignation. The recall campaigns made a concerted effort to blitz talk radio stations—Russo claimed that forty-five talk show hosts up and down the state were taking recall campaign materials and using them in their broadcasts every day.[7]

Both these new technologies provided inexpensive and relatively easy ways to reach large numbers of people in a very short time. By nature, both the Internet and talk radio appealed to voters' penchant for a populist approach, lacking the "slick" appearance of professional campaign advertising and literature. Both were accessible virtually around the clock (many talk radio stations broadcast twenty-four hours a day). Both also had a "multiplier effect"—for instance, directing listeners to a website or providing a link to a radio program—thus further extending their reach. The "new populist" technologies played a significant role in propelling the Davis recall effort farther than any previous attempts to recall a California governor had gone. On March 25, 2003, with the two efforts joining forces in using a version of the Costa petition to gather signatures, the recall was certified for circulation by then California Secretary of State Kevin Shelley.

PROPOSITION 13 REBORN

The recall movement quickly succeeded in gaining a following. "When we got the first petition on March 25, finally, Ted (Costa) took the petition out to a Wal-Mart," Abernathy recalled. "After about an hour, he called me on his cell phone and said, 'Mark, they're lined up 30-deep to sign this thing. You know, they're running across the parking lot to sign it. This is going to be a prairie fire." "I've never felt anything like this since Prop. 13," Abernathy quoted Costa as telling him over the phone that day. "This feels like Prop. 13."[8]

In many ways, the populist movement seen in these early stages of the recall was like Proposition 13. Ironically, 2003 was the twenty-fifth anniversary of the passage of the historic citizens' initiative. The tax-limiting measure was as popular at twenty-five as it had been shortly after its passage in June 1978. In the February 2003 survey, 57 percent of Californians felt that Proposition 13 had turned out to be "mostly a good thing," identical to the 58 percent who felt that way in the 1979 survey for the California Tax Revolt Study (see Sears and Citrin 1982). Likely voters in the February 2003 survey were even more approving, with 65 percent saying the outcome of Proposition 13 had been primarily positive for California. As further evidence that its populist and nonpartisan appeal persisted, solid majorities across regions and political and demographic groups agreed that Proposition 13 was a good thing for California.

Proposition 13 stands out as one of the most significant events in California's history (see Baldassare 2002; Citrin 1979; Lo 1990; Schrag 1998, 2006; Sears and Citrin 1982). Placed on the ballot by Howard Jarvis, an antitax activist from Los Angeles, the measure was a major catalyst for the explosion in initiative use in the twentieth century (see chapter 1). The initiative rolled back property rates and sharply limited increases while the property remained with the same owners. It also severely restricted state and local governments' ability to pass new taxes, requiring a two-thirds vote from the California legislature for passage of any new state taxes and a two-thirds vote from local voters for passage of any local special taxes.

The effect was immediate and far-reaching: state revenues plunged and the measure's centralized allocation formulas caused local governments to become dependent on state government to provide funding for local services. Voters gained an unprecedented amount of control over the workings of their government, as well as a big stick to wave at any elected officials who dared to speak of raising taxes. The passage of Proposition 13 also opened the gates for a flood of citizens' initiatives to follow in California and other states with direct democracy provisions, with far-reaching effects such as term limits, earmarking state spending, and campaign finance reform.

Despite some of Proposition 13's consequences, such as reducing the amount of money going to local services and severely cutting funding for public schools (see, for example, Baldassare 1998; Baldassare et al. 2000; Raymond 1988; Schrag 1998, 2006; Shires, Ellwood, and Sprague 1998; Shires 1999; Silva and Barbour 1999), the measure remained immensely popular at its silver anniversary. The popularity of Proposition 13 increases among high-propensity voters and declines sharply among those who aren't registered to vote in elections (Baldassare 2006). Given the makeup of the electorate—mostly homeowners, long-term residents, and affluent households—efforts to change any features of Proposition 13 would face formidable opposition.

As for the measure's effect on local services, Californians were somewhat less positive during the belt-tightening year of 2003. Only a quarter of adults in the February 2003 survey (27%) said Proposition 13's outcome in this area had been mostly positive, compared to 38 percent giving a thumbs-up in a September 1998 survey conducted on the measure's twentieth anniversary. Still, fewer than one in four residents in 2003 said there had been bad effects on local government services from the property tax limitations.

Moreover, residents staunchly opposed changing the supermajority vote provision of Proposition 13, which made it difficult for cities and counties to compensate for property tax cuts by raising other local taxes. By nearly a two-to-one margin (60% to 32%), residents opposed allowing local special taxes to pass with a simple majority vote. For likely voters, opposition to this change rose to 63 percent, and among homeowners, 66 percent were opposed. Five years earlier, in a September 1998 survey, a similar six in ten residents were opposed to changing the supermajority vote. In both good and bad economic times, Californians voiced strong support for Proposition 13 and its features.

SPECIAL INTEREST MONEY

Costa and Abernathy were right that the recall had tapped into a vein of populist sentiment just like Proposition 13 had done. But times had changed considerably since 1978, and direct democracy efforts that relied primarily on grassroots campaigns were largely a thing of the past. While the signature gathering to qualify Proposition 13 for the ballot had been conducted mainly by volunteers,[9] recent efforts almost invariably employed professionals paid $1–$2 a signature to perform this task.

The total amount raised by the "Yes on 13" campaign was $2.1 million, with most of the money coming from small contributors in amounts of less than $100. By contrast, in 1998, proponents of Proposition 5 spent nearly $67 million on the initiative legalizing gambling on Indian reservations in California (California Secretary of State 1999). The previous fall, backers of Arnold Schwarzenegger's more modest Proposition 49 had nonetheless spent $10 million on the campaign. In addition, the signature requirement to qualify the recall—12 percent of votes cast in the last gubernatorial election—posed a considerably higher bar than the signature requirements for state consti-tutional (8%) or statute (5%) initiatives. The task of collecting the needed signatures in a short time—thus forcing a special statewide election in 2003 rather than having a recall on the ballot in a regularly scheduled statewide election in 2004—was not a certainty without paid help from professional signature-gatherers.

By the end of April 2003, only about 100,000 unverified signatures had been gathered—well short of the approximately 1.2 million signatures that would guarantee the recall bid's qualification for election.[10] With little money on hand, the campaign lacked the $1 million or more needed to hire professional petition circulators. Instead, the signature-gathering effort was relying primarily on the Internet and campaign insiders admitted that it was not proceeding as quickly as they would like.

Suddenly, the recall campaign was rescued from the doldrums by an infusion of cash. Congressman Darrell Issa, a Vista (San Diego County) Republican who made millions in the car alarm business, announced in early May that he was donating $100,000 to the recall effort. Issa also indicated that he was considering a run for governor if the recall succeeded. The May 8 donation allowed the recall campaign to begin hiring professional signature-gatherers. It also opened the gates for others to join in. A week later, the conservative Lincoln Club of Orange County gave another $100,000 to the Davis recall, followed by another $345,000 cash infusion from a company owned by Issa. Donations began to filter in from GOP lawmakers and political action groups. The fund-raising quickly snowballed from there, feeding a populist campaign with funds from special interests and partisan donations.

Without Issa's donations (ultimately totaling nearly $2 million) allowing the campaign to hire professional signature-gatherers and greatly speed up this effort, it is unlikely the recall would have qualified in time for a 2003 election.[11] It was ironic that this populist effort, in large part a backlash against the perceived influence of special interests in state government, was enabled by the cash contributions of a wealthy businessman. Moreover, as a declared replacement candidate, Issa stood to benefit from the effort he was bankrolling. But for proponents of the recall, this irony seemed to have little impact.

PARTISAN GRIDLOCK ON THE BUDGET DEFICIT

As the recall movement picked up steam that spring, the budget deficit continued to plague Californians. Just as in 2002, the governor and state legislators seemed impotent to act on this crisis, and were locked in a partisan battle over the prospects of raising taxes, cutting spending, or covering the deficit with massive borrowing. More than nine in ten residents called the deficit a problem in a June 2003 survey, including 73 percent calling it a "big problem," with the public seeing no progress since February (see table 3.4). A majority in all demographic groups and regions of the state called the budget deficit a "big problem" in June. While Republicans were especially likely to see the budget deficit as a major problem (85%), three in four Democrats

Table 3.4: Budget Deficit at Midyear

"Do you think the size of the California state budget deficit is a big problem, somewhat of a problem, or not much of a problem for the people of California?"

	February	June
Big problem	74%	73%
Somewhat of a problem	21	21
Not a problem	3	4
Don't know	2	2

Sources: PPIC Statewide Survey, February and June 2003. Adults.

(77%) and independents (75%) agreed. The issue continued to command the public's attention, with six in ten closely following news about the state budget in June, similar to February.

The June survey also illustrated that the public was as divided along partisan lines on the issue of government spending for state services as their elected representatives were at the time. Overall, Californians were evenly split on the fundamental question of the size of government, taxes, and public services. Half (49%) said they would rather pay higher taxes to support a larger government with more public services, while 45 percent opted for lower taxes and fewer services (see table 3.5).

However, Democrats favored a larger government with more services over lower taxes and a leaner institution by nearly a two-to-one margin (61% to 31%). Republicans, meanwhile, were even more adamant in expressing the opposite preference: more than four times as many wanted lower taxes and smaller government as favored a larger one with more public services (76% to 18%). The partisan nature of this issue was further reflected in the views of independents, who had chosen not to align with either of the major parties. Voters in this group were cut right down the middle—with half (45%) favoring larger government and more services, while the other half (47%) wanted lower taxes and fewer services. And the issue illustrated the opinions of the state's electorate appearing to be at odds with those who do not participate in the political system—among likely voters, 54 percent preferred having a

Table 3.5: Partisan Divide on Public Spending

"Which statement do you agree with more: I'd rather pay higher taxes to support a larger government that provides more services, or lower taxes and have a smaller government that provides fewer services?"

	Adults	Democrats	Republicans	Independents
Higher taxes, more services	49%	61%	18%	45%
Lower taxes, fewer services	45	31	76	47
Don't know	6	8	6	8

Source: PPIC Statewide Survey, June 2003.

smaller government and lower taxes. By contrast, the majority of Californians who were not registered to vote wanted a larger government rather than a smaller one.[12]

While voters had philosophical differences over government and taxes, the June survey found agreement across party lines that they did not want their elected representatives to respond with budget reductions in the major categories of state spending. Majorities of Democrats, Republicans, and independents alike were opposed to cutting spending on K–12 public schools, public colleges and universities, and health and human services—spending categories that account for most of the state budget. Majorities in all parties were opposed to reinstating the vehicle license fee as a way to deal with the budget deficit, while voters were split along party lines on the prospects of raising the income tax on the wealthiest Californians or increasing the state sales tax. The option of selling bonds to reduce the current deficit also divided voters and fell short of majority appeal. This left the governor and legislature with few options that would please their partisan constituencies.

These opinions were expressed in the wake of Governor Davis's May Revise of the state budget. The May figures revealed that the size of the budget deficit had climbed to $38 billion. Over the course of the spring, lawmakers had already approved about $15 billion in cuts, including reduced funding for public schools. There was serious talk of increasing the state vehicle license fee, to bring in an extra $4 billion. Davis proposed making up the rest of the shortfall by borrowing $10.7 billion and paying it back over the next several years with a half-cent hike in the sales tax. But negotiations soon faltered. Republicans balked at the tax increase, while Democrats refused to approve any more budget cuts. The capitol was filled with acrimony as the summer wore on, with one legislator reported to have stormed out of session, swearing. However, finally, a month after it was due, a budget was approved. It included a five-year rollover of the state debt and no new taxes (*San Francisco Chronicle*, August 3, 2003). By then, the recall was headed for the ballot.

THE RECALL BECOMES A REALITY

Although the recall was now receiving partisan donations and the professional support needed to make it a viable effort, it retained its populist appeal. Asked in the June 2003 survey how they would vote in a special election to recall Davis from office, more Californians said they would vote "yes" (48%) than "no" (41%). Among likely voters, a majority wanted to remove the governor (51%) (see table 3.6). Voters' response to the recall did reveal a partisan split: Republicans were overwhelmingly in favor of the effort (75% yes to 20% no), while most Democrats were opposed (57% no to 35% yes).

Independent voters, however, were torn, with 47 percent opting for the governor's recall and 41 percent wanting to keep Davis in office. Still, the fact that some Democrats and many independents did support the recall showed that its appeal went beyond partisan politics. Demographic groups that would be most likely to turn out in the special election displayed modest support, including college graduates (44%), upper-income residents (50%), and those aged fifty-five and older (45%). It is important to note, however, that support for the recall at this point was measured in a political vacuum—the poll did not include mention of candidates as replacements for the unpopular governor, as none were certified at the time.

Perhaps one reason for some Californians' initial ambivalence about recalling Davis was their belief that doing so would have little effect on the state's budget woes. Only one in four residents (24%) or likely voters (26%) said they thought removing Davis would make the deficit easier to solve, while 52 percent in both groups said it would make no difference. A majority of Democrats (57%) and independents (55%) believed a recall would neither help nor hurt the state's fiscal troubles. Even Republicans were more likely to think that removing Davis would have no effect on the budget crisis than that it would make the deficit easier to resolve (47% to 40%).

Nonetheless, few Californians were happy about Davis's performance. Only 28 percent in the June survey approved of the way he was handling his job as governor, while two in three (64%) disapproved—making him even more unpopular than the state legislature (44% disapproved). Davis's approval ratings had dropped five points since the February survey (33%) and were twenty-four points lower than in October 2002, shortly before his reelection (52%). Likely voters were even more critical in June, with only 21 percent approving of his job performance. Majorities in all parties were unhappy with Davis. Since the previous October, the percentage of voters who disapproved of his performance as governor had risen twenty-one points among Republicans (67% to 88%), twenty-nine points among independents (42% to 71%), and twenty-seven points among Democrats (29% to 56%).

Table 3.6: Early Support for the Recall

"There is an effort under way to remove governor Gray Davis from office in a recall election. If a special election to recall governor Davis were held today, would you vote yes to remove Davis as governor or no to keep Davis as governor?"

	Likely Voters	Democrats	Republicans	Independents
Yes, remove Davis	51%	35%	75%	47%
No, keep Davis	43	57	20	41
Don't know	6	8	5	12

Source: PPIC Statewide Survey, June 2003.

Californians' trust in their state government, meanwhile, continued to languish. Only 34 percent of residents in the June 2003 survey said they trusted the government in Sacramento to do what is right "just about always" or "most of the time," while six in ten said they did so "only some of the time." Among likely voters, trust was even lower (31%). Confidence in their state leaders was low among Democrats (39% trust always/some of the time), Republicans (26% trust always/some of the time), and independents (30% trust always/some of the time) alike—providing a receptive public when Issa-funded professional signature-gatherers came knocking.

"What Darrell Issa's money did was it gave those angry people opportunity," said Carroll Wills.[13] Wills served as a spokesman for Taxpayers against the Governor's Recall, a group formed by Davis supporters in late May to fight the recall once they realized it was a serious possibility. "What the petition signature-gatherers, the actual people on the ground, did was give those people who maybe heard about it [the recall] on talk radio a place to go and an easy way to sign those petitions," Wills explained.

The Davis effort began circulating its own petition opposing the recall. Advisors included some of the strategists responsible for Davis's campaigns the previous year. Soon, newspapers began running stories about Issa's arrests on illegal weapons charges in the 1970s and other brushes with the law. Issa admitted the incidents, but dismissed them as old news and efforts by Davis to smear his reputation. However, the intense media scrutiny appeared to fluster Issa, and he began giving confusing and contradictory responses on his political record, eventually dropping out of the race.[14]

Another tack taken by the Davis team was to portray the recall as a partisan effort, a power-grab by right-wing Republicans seeking to overturn the November 2002 election. The result was to draw Republican Party leaders, who previously had steered clear of the recall, into the effort. On July 9, the chairman of the California Republican Party announced that his party was endorsing the recall, maintaining, "People are fed up with what's going on in California. . . . It's unlike anything I've seen in California since Proposition 13" (*San Francisco Chronicle*, July 10, 2003). However, PPIC surveys found little evidence that the involvement of the Democratic and Republican parties rallied Democrats to Davis's defense or deterred independents from supporting a partisan cause.

Two weeks later, on July 23, 2003, California secretary of state Kevin Shelley certified the recall petition. In his announcement that day, Shelley said that nearly 1.4 million valid signatures had been submitted—yielding many more signatures than the amount required (*Los Angeles Times*, July 24, 2003). The next day, lieutenant governor Cruz Bustamante called a special election for the recall as stated by constitutional law and set the date for October 7, 2003—seventy-five days after the certification of the petition. The recall ballot was in two parts—a yes or no vote on the recall of Davis and a vote for his replacement if the recall succeeded—and included two state propositions that had qualified to be placed on the next state election (racial classification and infrastructure spending).

What followed was a free-for-all, as nearly five hundred candidates took out papers to file as candidates for governor. Two weeks later, the August 9 closing date for candidates to file, 135 Californians had met the requirements to run—paying $3,500 and submitting valid signatures from sixty-five registered voters.

Among the candidates were Mary "Mary Carey" Cook, an actress in pornographic films, whose platform called for boosting state revenues with a tax on plastic surgery; Larry Flynt, the publisher of *Hustler* and other "adult" magazines; actor Gary Coleman, who starred in the 1970s sitcom "Diff'rent Strokes"; watermelon-smashing comedian Leo Gallagher; Los Angeles billboard model Angelyne, whose motto was "We've had Gray. We've had Brown. Now it's time for some blonde and pink"; as well as a lilac farmer, a bounty hunter, a sumo wrestler, and a host of others.

The individuals considered to be "serious" candidates were Democratic lieutenant governor Cruz Bustamante, conservative state senator Tom Mc-Clintock (R-Thousand Oaks), Green party activist Peter Camejo, Republican-turned-liberal-independent Arianna Huffington, GOP businessman Peter Ueberroth, defeated GOP gubernatorial candidate Bill Simon, and movie star and registered Republican Arnold Schwarzenegger. The list of replacement candidates helped solidify the public's perception of the recall as populist and nonpartisan, since voters could choose without the interference of party primaries as well as select from independents and those with no political experience.

Schwarzenegger's surprise announcement of his candidacy before a national audience on the "Tonight Show" on August 6 caught even his handlers off guard.[15] The actor had been testing the political waters since the previous year with his successful campaign for Proposition 49, the after-school initiative. But it had generally been expected that Schwarzenegger would sit out the recall, leaving the field clear for his friend, Richard Riordan, who had lost in the GOP gubernatorial primary the year earlier. Even that morning, Schwarzenegger's would-be campaign manager issued a statement saying that the actor was leaning toward staying out of the race (*Los Angeles Times*, August 7, 2003).

The decision by Democratic U.S. senator Dianne Feinstein to not be a replacement candidate because of her general opposition to the recall meant there was no candidate who stood out in experience, name recognition, and popularity. This decision created a ripe opportunity for Schwarzenegger in a field of Sacramento insiders and inexperienced or unknown candidates.

Joking with the program's host, Jay Leno, on national television that evening, Schwarzenegger said that the decision to run for governor was the toughest call he had made since deciding to get a bikini wax. Turning serious, he announced, "The man that is failing the people more than anyone is Gray Davis. He is failing them terribly, and this is why he needs to be recalled, and this is why I am going to run for governor" (*New York Times*, August 7, 2003).

Schwarzenegger's entry into the recall election made for a populist dream come true.[16] From the beginning stages of his campaign, his down-to-earth approach hit all the right notes: portraying himself as folksy, independent and upbeat, and not beholden to special interests. He shared and encouraged voters' distrust, especially when it came to special interests.

"What they have is self-interest and special interest first. We have to change all of that around," Schwarzenegger said of the state government during rounds of interviews after his announcement. "I am rich enough that I don't have to take anyone's money. I can go to Sacramento and I make decisions that are the wisest decisions for the people and not what is best for the special interests" (*San Jose Mercury News*, August 10, 2003).

OPINIONS ON THE RECALL ELECTION

In contrast to their lack of interest in the gubernatorial contest the previous year, Californians were energized and engaged by the recall election. The August 2003 survey found that nine in ten (89%) likely voters were closely following news about the recall election, including 45 percent saying they were following it "very closely." The level of interest in the recall far surpassed that expressed during polling on the gubernatorial election in October 2002 (75% following news very or fairly closely). High numbers in all political parties, demographic groups, and regions of the state were paying close attention to the recall in August.

Moreover, about half of likely voters (49%) said they were satisfied with the candidate choices in the recall election, while 40 percent were not satisfied. Voters were more satisfied with their choices in the recall than they were in the 2002 gubernatorial election, when only four in ten were satisfied with the candidate options. Satisfaction varied by party and support for the Davis recall, however: two in three of those who wanted to keep Davis in office and half of the Democrats were not satisfied with the recall choices.

Support for removing Davis from office had risen to 58 percent among likely voters in the August 2003 survey taken after the list of replacement candidates was announced—a twenty-two-point lead over the percentage wanting to keep him as governor (36%). Solid majorities of Republicans (84%) and independents (60%) favored recalling the governor, while most Democrats (56%) wanted him to finish out his term.

In the race among the replacement candidates, Schwarzenegger had jumped out to an early, though small, lead over Bustamante (23% to 18%) in August. No other candidate received more than 10 percent of the vote, and one in three voters had not made up their minds at the time. Most Democrats favored Bustamante, and most Republicans backed Schwarzenegger, but many partisans were not sure whom they would support in the recall. Among independents, four in ten were undecided, while Schwarzenegger had a slight edge over Bustamante.

Compared to the personable Schwarzenegger, Davis appeared stiff-necked and aloof, and voters continued to be turned off by his style and substance. Nearly half (48%) in the August survey said they disliked both the man and his policies. A majority of Republicans (70%) and independents (55%) had this view of Davis, and even three in ten Democrats agreed. Davis's job approval ratings remained low among all Californians (67% disapprove) and likely voters (72% disapprove), with a majority of Democrats (56%), Republicans (89%), and independent voters (73%) all disapproving of the way he was handling his job as governor.

Once again, voters were more negative toward Davis than the legislature, although ratings of the state lawmaking body were also low (68% disapprove). Nearly half said they thought California would get better if Davis were removed from office (47%), while 28 percent said it would make no difference. Only 17 percent of likely voters in the August survey thought things would go downhill if the governor were recalled.

Although the legislature had managed to pass a state budget in early August, the issue remained a source of highly partisan conflict. Most voters (61%) were dissatisfied with the budget package and opposed (64%) the government's plan to borrow money to cover part of the $38 billion deficit. While majorities in all parties held these views, there was little agreement on what else could be done to make up the shortfall. Half the voters (46%) thought tax increases should have been included in the budget plan, while an equal proportion (48%) said no. Most Democrats (53%) favored raising taxes to offset the deficit, while most Republicans (59%) were opposed. On this issue, independents showed their fiscally conservative side, with a majority (53%) saying no to tax increases. Thus, partisan conflict and voter unhappiness over the handling of the state budget continued to help propel the recall movement forward.

The recall had riveted public attention on California's tools of direct democracy. Likely voters in the August 2003 survey overwhelmingly (80%) believed that the recall provision was a "good thing" and just one in six (17%)

Table 3.7:   Perceptions of the Recall Process

"Do you think that the current effort to recall the governor is an appropriate use of the recall process?"

	Likely Voters	*Democrats*	*Republicans*	*Independents*
Yes	52%	33%	78%	54%
No	43	62	18	41
Don't know	5	5	4	5

Source: PPIC Statewide Survey, August 2003.

described it as a "bad thing." At least seven in ten voters in all parties, demographic groups, and regions of the state thought it was good that California's Constitution gave residents the ability to recall elected officials such as the governor.

The majority of voters (52%) in the August survey also saw the 2003 recall effort as an appropriate use of the process, while 43 percent disagreed (see table 3.7). However, while a majority of Republicans (78%) and independents (54%) thought the current recall was justified, most Democrats (62%) did not think it was a warranted use of the provision. Still, substantial proportions of Californians in all parties, as well as in all regions and demographic groups, supported this particular use of the recall provision.

One aspect of the recall that did concern a majority of voters was the expense of mounting a special election. When told that the election would cost an estimated $50 million to $70 million in state funds, 53 percent said it was a "waste of money," while 44 percent called it "worth the cost." Opinions broke down sharply along partisan lines—seven in ten Republicans thought the expense was justified and 74 percent of Democrats said it was a waste of public funds. Independents were evenly divided, with 48 percent saying the special election was worth the cost and 47 percent calling it a waste of money. Of course, these opinions were closely related to support for the recall of Davis.

THE RECALL AND
REPLACEMENT CANDIDATE CAMPAIGNS

Californians were treated to a spectacle that August and September and the world watched it over their shoulders. It was not the first time a movie star had run for political office in the Golden State—actor Ronald Reagan had served two terms as governor before going on to the White House and Clint Eastwood was mayor of the city of Carmel, among other entertainment celebrities in government. But Schwarzenegger campaigned with a flair never before seen in state politics. Drawing on his action films for inspiration, his antics included cruising the state in a caravan of buses, named "Running

Man," "Total Recall," and "Predator 1" through "Predator 4." His stump speeches were peppered with lines from his popular *Terminator* movies, such as telling voters to say "Hasta la vista, baby" to Davis, speaking of the need to "terminate" the car tax, and calling Davis and Bustamante the "Twin Terminators of Sacramento" (*Los Angeles Times*, September 26, 2003). His star appeal drew crowds wherever he went.

But Schwarzenegger's pull went beyond his marquis appearances. Using the same folksy approach as in his Proposition 49 campaign, Schwarzenegger tapped into Californians' populist spirit and made people feel as if they were all part of a grassroots effort to take back control of their state. Campaigning as an outsider, the candidate appealed to voters who were distrustful of "career politicians." Using incendiary rhetoric, he drummed up the public's long-standing fears about special interests controlling state government, such as in a September 2003 television ad declaring, "Special interests have a stranglehold on Sacramento. Here's how it works. Money comes in, favors go out. The people lose."[17] Then he allayed those fears by trumpeting his personal wealth and vowing that he would not take money from such groups. And despite being a Republican, Schwarzenegger avoided falling into the usual pattern of partisan bickering by positioning himself as a political moderate—leaning liberal on social issues and conservative on fiscal issues—earning him a broad, bipartisan base of support.

His main challengers, by contrast, wore unmistakable partisan labels. Bustamante, a Democrat, was his party's best hope at retaining control in Sacramento if the Davis recall succeeded. The second-in-command in state leadership, he risked being linked with Davis even though he had been elected independently. Tom McClintock, a state senator from Southern California, was a conservative Republican with a long history in state politics. Peter Camejo, who had run for governor on the Green Party ticket in 2002, was a hard-core liberal whose solutions to many of the state's problems involved making wealthy Californians pay higher taxes. Other contenders initially considered to be among the "serious" candidates—Bill Simon, the Republican businessman defeated by Davis in 2002; Arianna Huffington, ex-wife of conservative former congressman Michael Huffington, now reborn as a liberal; and Peter Ueberroth, former baseball commissioner and booster for state businesses—dropped out during the course of the campaign.

Voters continued to back the recall as the campaign proceeded, with 53 percent in a September survey saying they planned to vote to remove the governor while 42 percent would vote to keep him in office. This was a slight improvement for Davis from the August survey, when 36 percent said they would vote against the recall, but it wasn't enough of a shift to make a difference in the race. Republicans overwhelmingly supported the recall (86%), while two in three Democrats were opposed (65%). The key bloc of independent voters remained on the fence (48% yes on recall, 48% no).

Bustamante, meanwhile, had pulled even with Schwarzenegger in September, with 28 percent of likely voters supporting the lieutenant governor, 26 percent backing Schwarzenegger, and 14 percent going for McClintock. None of the other candidates drew more than 3 percent of voters. Part of the reason for Bustamante's surge was his gains among Latinos, who went from 27 percent supporting him in August to 49 percent in September. Bustamante had also made sizeable gains among Democrats (34% to 49%) and independents (14% to 24%) as voters in these groups made up their minds. While Schwarzenegger drew the biggest share of Republican votes (47%), a sizeable 24 percent in the party was supporting McClintock in September.

The recall effort and replacement candidates benefited from the public's persistent dark mood. Two in three adults (67%) and 75 percent of likely voters in the September survey believed that California was headed in the wrong direction, continuing the six-year high in pessimism about the state we had seen in August. Older and more affluent voters were especially negative. A majority of residents (58%) continued to think their region was in a recession, and 50 percent expected bad economic times over the next twelve months.

For his part, Davis attempted to counter voter negativity by softening his stiff image and meeting the public in a series of "Town Hall" type meetings around the state. In an August 19 speech at UCLA, he admitted that he had been too slow to respond to the energy crisis and not tough enough with reining in state spending. "We made our share of mistakes, and like you, I wish I had known then all I know now," Davis told a live television audience that day, calling the recall "part of an ongoing national effort to steal elections that Republicans cannot win" (*Los Angeles Times*, August 20, 2003).

Nonetheless, Governor Davis's popularity remained low, creating a large base of support for the recall. Two in three adults (65%) and seven in ten likely voters (71%) in the September survey disapproved of the way he was handling his job as governor, similar to the ratings in August. A majority of residents (65%) and likely voters (69%) disapproved of the way Davis was handling the state's economic issues. And most adults (70%) and voters (74%) also disliked the way he was handling the budget. While the governor's ratings were especially negative among Republicans and independent voters, even a majority of Democrats disapproved of his performance in all these areas.

As the replacement candidates hammered away at Davis and focused attention on the state's problems that fall, public confidence in the state government reached a new low. Only 27 percent of Californians in the September survey felt they could trust leaders in Sacramento to do what is right "just about always" or "most of the time"—a seven-point drop from three months

Table 3.8: Trust in State Government

"How much of the time do you think you can trust the government in Sacramento to do what is right?"

	November 2002	February 2003	June 2003	September 2003
Just about always/most of the time	36%	36%	34%	27%
Only some of the time	59	58	60	61
None of the time (volunteered)	4	4	4	9
Don't know	1	2	2	3

Sources: PPIC Statewide Survey, November 2002, February 2003, June 2003, September 2003. Adults.

earlier (see table 3.8). Among likely voters, an even lower 21 percent said they generally trusted their state government. A significant 9 percent of adults and 12 percent of voters in the September survey volunteered the response that they could not trust their state leaders any of the time.

VOTER ENGAGEMENT

A deluge of reporters from all over the world descended on California to cover the quirky election, lending a circus-like atmosphere to the event. Newspapers and broadcasts devoted what seemed like an unprecedented amount of space to covering the campaigns. In addition, the airwaves were filled with paid messages both for and against the recall, as well as advertisements by the replacement candidates.

Californians were paying rapt attention. More than nine in ten likely voters (92%) in the September survey said they were closely following the news about the recall election, including 49 percent following it "very closely." This was a four-point increase from the number paying such close attention in August (45%). Interest continued to be high in all political groups, but had risen among Republicans (from 48% to 57% paying very close attention) and independents (from 44% to 48% paying very close attention) since August, while Democrats remained the same (43% paying very close attention).

Similar to the 2002 gubernatorial election, eight in ten voters (83%) had seen television advertisements about the recall in the past month. Also similar to that previous campaign, few (24% in September 2003; 29% in October 2002) found the ads helpful in deciding how to vote. Those voters most likely to find the recall ads helpful in September were Latinos (39%), voters who did not attend college (39%), and those with incomes below $40,000 (37%). Although those were traditionally low-turnout voter groups, they stood to play a crucial role in the special election if it managed to attract large numbers of new or infrequent voters. And given the unprecedented attention to the recall, a large turnout was an increasingly likely scenario.

Voters in September were looking forward to the upcoming candidates' debate, sponsored by the California Broadcasters Association. Although some of the candidates had previously squared off in public discussions around the state, Schwarzenegger had so far been absent. He agreed to participate in only one debate, to be held two weeks before the election, in which he and the other candidates would receive the questions in advance.

In the September survey, conducted shortly before the September 24 debate, two in three voters said the candidates' performances during the event would be "very important" (27%) or "somewhat important" (40%) in their decision on how to vote in the recall election. Democrats (29%), Republicans (27%), and independents (24%) were equally likely to consider the debate very important. The candidates' performances were considered especially important by younger, less affluent, and less educated voters—the less frequent voters who were being drawn into the recall election by the drama surrounding the event.

What did voters consider most important about the debate? "Learning about the candidates' stands on the issues," 50 percent of the voters in the survey responded. Much less importance was placed on the candidates' experience (17%), character (15%), or intelligence (11%). Voters in all parties agreed that the candidates' stands on the issues were the most important consideration. But Republicans (23%) were more likely than Democrats (8%) or independents (13%) to say that a candidate's character also mattered to them.

The debate, held at Sacramento State University, proved to be good theater for the worldwide audience following it. More than five hundred members of the press had requested credentials to cover the event, which was broadcast as far as England and Japan (*New York Times*, September 25, 2003). Candidates Bustamante, Schwarzenegger, McClintock, Camejo, and Huffington traded insults and frequently interrupted each other during the ninety-minute debate. Schwarzenegger managed to get off a number of zingy one-liners, including accusing Bustamante and legislative Democrats of "having an addiction problem . . . because you cannot stop spending" and telling Huffington that he had a part for her in his *Terminator 4* movie, (*Los Angeles Times,* September 25, 2003). The proceedings were so chaotic that at one point the moderator was prompted to remind the candidates that "This is not *Comedy Central*" (*San Jose Mercury News*, September 25, 2003).

For the most part, the five candidates stuck to the positions they had already carved out for themselves in their predebate campaigning. Bustamante, who was in the tough spot of opposing the recall while promoting himself as the best replacement choice, advocated solving the state's budget problems with higher taxes on the wealthy, alcohol, and tobacco. McClintock vowed that he would never raise taxes, maintaining that the deficit could be eliminated by cutting state programs and contracting out state services to the lowest bidder. Huffington said she would fix the state's budget woes by closing the loopholes in corporate taxes. Camejo advocated for making the state's wealthiest residents pay their fair share of taxes. Schwarzenegger promoted a business-friendly platform of improving the state's economy by loosening regulations on companies.

One of the most contentious issues in the debate and the political discourse that fall was a new law allowing illegal immigrants in California to get state driver's licenses. The bill, promoted by Democrats, had been vetoed by Davis twice before. But on September 5, 2003, in what was seen as a desperate bid to court the Latino vote, Davis had signed the measure into law. The move tapped into the touchy public attitudes about the state's burgeoning immigrant population that had been swirling since the passage of Proposition 187 in 1994. That measure, which prohibited illegal immigrants from receiving state services, was subsequently invalidated by the courts. But the driver's license bill reignited deep feelings of resentment among many of the state's white voters, and Schwarzenegger advanced his cause by publicly ridiculing the new drivers' license law. "I am against the driver's licenses [for undocumented immigrants] because that is without any background check and without any fingerprints or anything. Therefore, it is dangerous for the security of California," Schwarzenegger maintained during the debate, pointing out that Davis had opposed the bill earlier for that reason. "Notice now because it is an election coming up on October 7, now all of a sudden, it is a great idea," Schwarzenegger said, accusing Davis of pandering to Latino voters. "The governor is supposed to represent the people of California, not special interests. That is the problem."[18]

Pundits analyzing the candidates' performances in the debate generally agreed that there was no clear winner. But Schwarzenegger had shown the world that he could hold his own in a public forum, and communicated his themes of populism, independence from partisan politics, and fighting against special interests while giving voice to the distrust of average voters. It was an important turning point for his campaign.

The PPIC survey taken the week before the special election found the recall favored by an eight-point margin. Schwarzenegger had a significant lead over Bustamante in the race among the replacement candidates. Only one in six voters feared that things in California would get worse if the recall against Davis succeeded. Most voters were familiar with the debate and said it had helped them decide which candidate to support in the upcoming election. Nearly half of likely voters said they were more enthusiastic than usual about voting in the October 7 election. Eight in ten continued to think the recall was a good thing and a similar proportion claimed to know a substantial amount about how the state's recall process worked. Clearly, the idea of the recall provision, its specific use against Governor Davis, and the candidacy of Arnold Schwarzenegger had all struck chords with voters seeking a historic opportunity to make significant changes at the ballot box.

THE OCTOBER SPECIAL ELECTION

The final days of the recall campaign were tumultuous. One week before the election, the *Los Angeles Times* published the results of an investigation its reporters had conducted into Schwarzenegger's behavior toward women. One article included claims by six women that Schwarzenegger had groped them against their wishes (*Los Angeles Times*, October 2, 2003). More women came forward in subsequent articles, totaling sixteen in all. Schwarzenegger publicly apologized for his earlier actions. Davis attempted to use the allegations to call Schwarzenegger's character into question, but to little avail.

The recall easily passed with 55.4 percent of the vote on October 7 (see table 3.9). In the follow-up question on who should replace the recalled governor, Arnold Schwarzenegger was the choice of 48.6 percent of California voters, easily beating Cruz Bustamante (31.5%), Tom McClintock (13.5%), Peter Camejo (2.8%), and a field of more than a hundred other candidates. Just under 5 million Californians voted in favor of the recall in the special election, and just over 4 million voted against it, while about 5 percent of voters (429,431) in the special election did not cast a ballot on the recall question.

More than six in ten registered voters turned out for the recall election, adding

Table 3.9: October 2003 Vote

Recall Gray Davis	
Yes	55.4%
No	44.6
Governor	
Arnold Schwarzenegger	48.6%
Cruz Bustamante	31.5
Tom McClintock	13.5
Peter Camejo	2.8
Other candidates	3.6
Proposition 53: Funds Dedicated for State and Local Infrastructure	
Yes	36.2%
No	63.8
Proposition 54: Classification by Race, Ethnicity, Color, or National Origin	
Yes	36.1%
No	63.9
Registered voter turnout	61.2%

Source: California Secretary of State, "Statement of the Vote," October 2003.

to the legitimacy of this first-ever use of this direct democracy tool to remove a governor in California. The 9.4 million votes cast in the 2003 special election exceeded the number who had participated in the 2002 gubernatorial election by 1.6 million votes (California Secretary of State, "Statement of the Vote: 2003 Statewide Special Election," 2003). In fact, the 4.2 million votes cast for Schwarzenegger surpassed the 3.4 million votes for Davis in 2002, as well as the 4 million votes against the recall in 2003. Such a high turnout appeared to invalidate claims by some critics that a recall would be unfair because it would only reflect the will of an activist minority, rather than the general public.

A Los Angeles Times Exit Poll found that three in four voters who participated in the special election thought the state was headed in the wrong direction and the economy was doing badly. In all, according to the exit poll, 88 percent of Republicans, 52 percent of independents, and 24 percent of Democrats had voted to recall Davis as governor. On the replacement question, 77 percent of Republicans, 46 percent of independents, and 21 percent of Democrats chose Schwarzenegger. Despite the groping allegations, the exit poll found that more women voted for Schwarzenegger (45%) than any other candidate. The Austrian born muscleman was the choice of 54 percent of white voters, 53 percent of men, and 54 percent of voters earning $75,000 a year or more. Fifty percent of voters who were casting ballots for the first time in the October 7 special election voted for Schwarzenegger. Interestingly, 45 percent of Latinos voted for the recall of Davis and 33 percent chose Schwarzenegger over Bustamante despite their Democratic leanings. One in five voters who supported Davis in the 2002 gubernatorial election turned on him and voted for both the recall and Schwarzenegger in 2003 (Los Angeles Times Exit Poll, October 7, 2003).

However, voters' enthusiasm for the recall did not extend to two other items that had piggybacked onto the special election ballot. Proposition 53, a legislative constitutional amendment that would have dedicated up to 3 percent of the state budget to improve roads, bridges, and public buildings, got little attention in the noise surrounding the recall election. The measure failed badly, with nearly 64 percent voting no (see table 3.9).

Proposition 54, a citizens' initiative put up by businessman and University of California Regent Ward Connerly, who had previously won an effort to do away with race-based affirmative action in state agencies (Proposition 209 in November 1996), would have prohibited public agencies from collecting information on their clients' race or ethnicity. Although Proposition 54 attracted considerably more media attention than Proposition 53, it too was drowned out by the recall, and failed with 63.9 percent voting against it (see table 3.9).

The Los Angeles Times Exit Poll found that majorities in all political parties opposed Proposition 53 (infrastructure spending), as did majorities across age, education, income, and racial/ethnic categories. As for Proposition 54 (racial/

ethnic classification), majorities of Democrats and independents were opposed, while majorities of Republicans were in favor. There was solid opposition to this initiative in all age, education, income, and racial/ethnic categories.

As further indication of the lack of voter interest in these two ballot items, nearly 1.1 million special election participants did not cast a vote for Proposition 53, and 728,022 skipped the question on Proposition 54. Each measure received only about 3 million "yes" votes in the special election. The difference between the rates of participation for the recall and the propositions shows voters again demonstrating their interests and ability to pick and choose among the tools provided by direct democracy.

CONCLUSION

California's historic use of the recall in 2003 as an extension of the direct democracy system had reinvigorated a disenchanted electorate's interest in elections and politics. From a low of 7.7 million registered voters turning out to cast ballots in the November 2002 gubernatorial election, more than 9.4 million had showed up on election day for the recall less than one year later (California Secretary of State, "Statement of the Vote: 2002 General Election," 2002; "Statement of the Vote: 2003 Statewide Special Election," 2003). The political events of that year, measured in the ebb and flow of public opinion, were stunning examples of the powerful forces at work—populism, partisanship, special interests, and voter distrust—that are increasing the role of direct democracy and shaking up elected representatives today. The likelihood that the recall in California would have political consequences in other places was heightened by the unprecedented attention it received from the national and international media.

The populist recall had stirred up Californians' long-standing independent streak and set the stage for a diminished role for the major political parties. While the total number of registered voters remained fairly constant in California (15,303,469 in November 2002; 15,383,526 in October 2003), a shift in party affiliation indicated voters' growing disaffection for partisan politics. Despite electing a GOP governor in October 2003, Republican registration rose only by about 40,000 voters between Davis's election and his recall. The number of registered Democrats, meanwhile, fell by more than 100,000 during that time. The most significant gains in new voters called to action by the recall were those who declined to affiliate with either major party—a number that climbed by more than 146,000 Californians.

The recall also spurred voters to learn about the workings of direct democracy in their state. Eight in ten voters in the October survey said they knew "a lot" (32%) or "something" (49%) about the way the recall process operated in California. But with knowledge and experience came concerns over the issue. Nearly six in ten voters in October thought the system was in need of changes, including 32 percent saying it needed "major changes." Only one in three said the recall process was "okay the way it is." Most Democrats and independents and a sizeable proportion of Republicans in the October survey said California's recall provision was in need of changes.

Majorities of voters preferred changes, including raising the signature requirements for qualifying the recall (56%) and replacement candidates (68%). On the other hand, the majority of voters wanted the recall to be on a special election ballot rather than the next scheduled election (67%) and wanted the recall and choice of replacement on one ballot rather than in two separate elections (59%). While voters could see areas for improvements in the recall process and its uses, 76 percent said it was a good thing to have the recall process as one of the tools for direct democracy. The majority of voters (52%) also said the recall election had made them more interested in California politics.

The historic year of 2003 had started with another governor in California facing the threat of a recall. This time, however, a populist movement fueled by high levels of voter distrust (with timely help from GOP partisans and self-interested political climbers) succeeded in mounting an effective petition drive, followed by a campaign that unseated the incumbent Democratic governor in a blue state.

The factors that enabled the recall's success in 2003 included the public's widespread displeasure with the governor and legislature, especially in their inept handling of the state budget, and the entrenched partisanship at the state capitol. Davis's appearance of being overly tied to special interest money also turned the public against him. Voters had positive feelings about the tools of direct democracy and with high hopes for Schwarzenegger, they responded eagerly to his populist approach, his seeming avoidance of partisanship, and his promise not to take money from special interests.

The overriding theme in 2003—hurting Davis and helping Schwarzenegger—was voters' widespread distrust in the state's elected leaders. Immediately after the recall, the November PPIC survey found that likely voters approved of their new governor's plans and policies by a two-to-one margin, with strong support in all political parties. Now, it was Schwarzenegger's turn to see if he could rebuild public trust through a combination of direct and representative democracy.

NOTES

1. Both Proposition 140, limiting the terms of state legislators, and Proposition 164, extending term limits to California members of Congress, passed. However con-

gressional term limits were ruled unconstitutional by the U.S. Supreme Court, acting on a similar law in Arkansas. That decision invalidated Proposition 164 and congressional term limits were never imposed in California.

2. Conversation recalled in Gerald C. Lubenow, ed., *California Votes: The 2002 Governor's Race and the Recall That Made History* (Berkeley, Calif.: Berkeley Public Policy Press [University of California], 2003), 176–77.

3. Lubenow, *California Votes*, 177.

4. The size of the deficit was in dispute in early 2003. While Davis pegged it at $34.6 billion in his January budget proposal (California Department of Finance, "Governor's Budget Summary 2003–04," Sacramento, Calif.: January, 2003), the Legislative Analyst's Office maintained that that figure was inflated and put it closer to $26 billion (Legislative Analyst's Office, "Overview of the 2003–04 Governor's Budget," Sacramento, Calif.: January, 2003). When the revised budget was released in May, the deficit was adjusted upward to $38 billion—with both the legislative analyst and the governor agreeing on this figure.

5. See, for example, Patt Morrison, "Total Recall," *Los Angeles Times*, February 10, 2003, B3; and Phil Yost, "Davis Wants to Close the Budget Gap: His Foes Just Want His Head," *San Jose Mercury News*, February 9, 2003, OP1.

6. Lubenow, *California Votes*, 189.

7. Lubenow, *California Votes*, 172.

8. Lubenow, *California Votes*, 194.

9. The signature-gathering effort for Proposition 13 is described in David D. Schmidt, *Citizen Lawmakers: The Ballot Initiative Revolution* (Philadelphia: Temple University Press, 1989), 130.

10. Although the actual requirement was 897,158 verified signatures, recall backers estimated that this higher figure was needed to provide a safety margin against unverifiable and duplicate signatures. See Lubenow, *California Votes*, 177. Similar strategies are often employed for signature-gathering by citizens' initiative campaigns.

11. For a detailed account of Issa's contributions to the recall effort and campaign as a replacement candidate, see Larry N. Gerston and Terry Christensen, *Recall: California's Political Earthquake* (Armonk, N.Y.: M. E. Sharpe, 2004), 57–59; Lubenow, *California Votes*, 171–74 and 181–94.

12. A more detailed analysis of the differences in public policy preferences between voters and nonvoters can be found in Mark Baldassare, *California's Exclusive Electorate* (San Francisco: Public Policy Institute of California, 2006).

13. Lubenow, *California Votes*, 187.

14. See description in Gerston and Christensen, *Recall*, 59.

15. For an account of the events surrounding Schwarzenegger's announcement, see Gerston and Christensen, *Recall*, 71–74.

16. For works that discuss the public appeal and life and personality of Arnold Schwarzenegger leading up to his candidacy in the 2003 recall, see Michael Blitz and Louise Krasniewicz, *Why Arnold Matters: The Rise of a Cultural Icon* (New York: Basic Books, 2004); Gerston and Christensen, *Recall*; Laurence Leamer, *Fantastic: The Life of Arnold Schwarzenegger* (New York: St. Martin's Press, 2005); Joe

Mathews, *The People's Machine: Arnold Schwarzenegger and the Rise of Block-buster Democracy* (New York: Public Affairs, 2006).

17. See discussion of this ad in an article by Dion Nissenbaum, "Reality Check: An Analysis of Campaign Commercials," *San Jose Mercury News*, September 4, 2003, A17. Ironically, this sound clip was to be used against him in 2006, when proponents of Proposition 89, a campaign finance reform initiative, aired it in ads attempting to show Schwarzenegger as a hypocrite about accepting funds from special interests. See Jim Sanders, "Prop. 89 Spot Draws on Governor's Quotes," *Sacramento Bee*, October 15, 2006, A3.

18. From a list of debate quotes compiled by Jia-Rui Chong and Eric Malnic, "In the Recall Candidates' Words," *Los Angeles Times*, September 25, 2003, A23.

4

The Year of Recovery: Bipartisan Cooperation and Populism in 2004

Schwarzenegger's term started off on a bright note, with the promise of a new era of legislative cooperation and partisan compromise in his State of the State address. Public expectations were raised about the abilities of the new governor to represent the people in the policy process and he received sky-high approval ratings as he took charge of the state government. However, voters continued to express considerable distrust in the state government and negative perceptions of the legislative process, indicating that the political environment in California had undergone a lasting transformation. In some ways, Schwarzenegger actually fueled this distrust by calling for a "California Performance Review" to uncover waste, fraud, and abuse in state government. He also repealed a law passed by the previous governor and legislature—issuing driver's licenses to illegal immigrants—that was unpopular with the state's white voters. In doing so, however, he alienated the Latino voters who had supported him in the recall election.

Schwarzenegger inherited a number of controversial policy issues, including a persistent multibillion dollar budget deficit and the long-overdue reform of the state's workers' compensation system. He gained Californians' cooperation in resolving these problems by asking them to be part of the policy process and take charge of their state government. In the March 2004 primary, the success of Schwarzenegger's populist approach was demonstrated by voters overwhelmingly passing a package of state bond measures and legislative spending limits he had convinced the legislature to place on the ballot. Meanwhile, using the threat of putting up an initiative if they did not comply, the governor got legislators to enact a package of reforms to the state's costly workers' compensation program. In these early acts, voters and lawmakers joined force in bipartisan cooperation to enact policy reforms that were unheard of in prior times. But the goodwill soon faded, and by summer, the governor and legislature were fighting over the details of the budget for the next year. In the end, he could not resist the temptation of bullying those who stood in his way with insults, name calling, and public ridicule.

The partisanship Schwarzenegger showed by trying to get Republican candidates elected in the spring was further demonstrated in the fall when he delivered a keynote speech at the GOP convention and later flew to Ohio to campaign for President Bush. Still, the governor remained a populist figure at home by taking sides for and against state propositions and citizens' initiatives that spanned the political spectrum—stem cell research, three strikes reforms, taxes on mental health funding, employer mandates for employee health coverage—following the lead of Republican interests in some instances, endorsing Democratic causes on others, and sometimes taking bipartisan positions. Most of his ballot choices were approved by the electorate, providing further evidence of his uncanny sway with the voters. Yet his efforts to reshape the legislature failed, and there was no change in the partisan makeup of the Senate or Assembly. Moreover, California remained a solidly "blue" state, which GOP President Bush lost by a large margin, while Democratic senator Barbara Boxer won by a landslide and the California Congressional delegation remained firmly in Democratic hands. In the aftermath of the November 2004 election, both Schwarzenegger and the Democrat-controlled legislature concluded they were politically invincible and assumed the voters were on their side. The parties became increasingly polarized throughout the fall and partisan trenches were being dug.

THE NEW BIPARTISAN SPIRIT

"Okay, I changed my mind. I want to go back to acting," governor Arnold Schwarzenegger told California lawmakers assembled at the state Capitol to hear his first State of the State Address on January 6, 2004. "No, no, just joking. Ladies and gentleman, that is not true at all," Schwarzenegger quickly continued in the speech, carried live on more than a hundred television and radio stations. "I love working for the people of California," he added later in the address. "It is better than being a movie star. It gives me great joy and satisfaction. I am honored to do this work for the people" (Schwarzenegger, "Governor Schwarzenegger's 2004 State of the State Address," 2004).

This jocular beginning to his first major public address since his swearing-in six weeks earlier was in many ways illustrative of Schwarzenegger's approach to governing California as his term got underway. The self-deprecating humor served to humanize this larger-than-life figure and make him seem more like a "regular guy." The portrayal of himself as the servant and the people of California as his masters reinforced his efforts to create the image of a populist governor. The Schwarzenegger administration, he implied, would be run by and for the public—free from the influence of special interests, partisan warfare, and out-of-touch career politicians Californians associated with their state government.

The approach was an immediate hit. A January 2004 survey showed Schwarzenegger with sky-high ratings—six in ten adults (59%) and nearly two in three voters (64%) said they approved of the way he was handling his job as governor (see table 4.1). Schwarzenegger's job approval was nearly twice as high as the 31 percent Davis had received the month before he was recalled from office. The new governor's 59 percent rating appeared to be higher than Davis's was early in his first term, when 51 percent of Californians in September 1999 said he was doing an "excellent" or "good" job. What's more, Schwarzenegger's popularity crossed partisan boundaries, with voters in all parties more likely to approve than disapprove of the way he was doing his job. Although he was viewed most positively by Republicans (87%) and independents (62%), even 46 percent of Democrats gave him a favorable rating in January.

Schwarzenegger wasn't succeeding equally on all fronts, however. One of his first acts in office had been to repeal the 2003 law granting driver's licenses to illegal immigrants, and the move appeared to have opened up a racial/ethnic gap in his ratings. Fewer than half of Latinos (43%) liked the way he was doing his job in January, significantly lower than the two in three whites (68%) giving him a thumbs-up. Schwarzenegger was also viewed somewhat less favorably by women than men (53% to 65%), although a majority in both groups had a positive image of him.

The public's mood had also undergone a remarkable turnaround since Schwarzenegger took office. In January, residents were more inclined to say the state was going in the "right direction" (43%) than the "wrong direction" (40%). Just before the recall in September 2003, two in three Californians (67%) had said the state was headed in the wrong direction and only 24 percent thought things were going well. Nonetheless, the public's optimism remained lower in January 2004 than it had been before Davis's reelection and subsequent recall, when six in ten Californians (59%) in the January 2002

Table 4.1: Governor's Ratings in January

"Do you approve or disapprove of the way that Arnold Schwarzenegger is handling his job as governor of California?"

	Adults	Democrats	Republicans	Independents
Approve	59%	46%	87%	62%
Disapprove	22	27	3	18
Don't know	19	27	10	20

Source: PPIC Statewide Survey, January 2004.

survey said things were going in the right direction. On this issue, Republicans (59%) had a brighter outlook than independents (39%) or Democrats (34%), although pessimism had declined in all groups since the new governor took office. Those with more education also tended to be more negative about the state's direction, while Latinos (41%) and whites (45%) had similar levels of optimism about the state.

OPTIMISM WITHOUT TRUST

One of Schwarzenegger's first orders of business was to restore public confidence in the government, at least according to his inaugural address in November. But after the bashing state government had received during the 2003 recall, including by Schwarzenegger's own campaign against the Sacramento political establishment, he had a tough task ahead of him. Despite the new governor's high job approval ratings and the recent turnaround in the public mood, Californians remained mistrustful of their leaders.

Only one in four (27%) residents in the January survey said they could trust the state government to do what is right "just about always" or "most of the time"—the same low confidence numbers we had seen during the heat of the recall drive the previous September (see table 4.2). Two in three Californians (64%) felt they could trust their leaders "only some of the time" and 6 percent volunteered the response that they never trusted state government. Trust levels among likely voters (26% always/most of the time) were similar to those of all adults, and were low in all political groups.

One of the reasons for the lack of trust in state government was the public's lingering perception in the wake of the recall campaign and state budget deficit that government officials were wasting their tax dollars. A majority of adults (56%) and likely voters (58%) in the January 2004 survey said state government wasted "a lot" of the money Californians paid in taxes and another 35 percent in both groups said it wasted "some." While Republicans were especially likely to think a significant amount of

Table 4.2: Trust in State Government

"How much of the time do you think you can trust the government in Sacramento to do what is right?"

	Adults	Democrats	Republicans	Independents
Just about always/most of the time	27%	28%	23%	22%
Only some of the time	64	66	66	71
None of the time (volunteered)	6	5	9	6
Don't know	3	1	2	1

Source: PPIC Statewide Survey, January 2004.

tax revenue was wasted (70%), 56 percent of independents and even 50 percent of Democrats agreed.

The vision of special interests influencing Sacramento politics also continued to haunt Californians, who had heard this allegation made repeatedly by Schwarzenegger and others during the recall. Two in three (65%) adults in the January survey saw the state government as being "pretty much run by a few big interests looking out for themselves," well outnumbering the 25 percent who believed it was "run for the benefit of all of the people." While Schwarzenegger may have been elected at least in part on his claims that he would be immune to special interests, the accusations made against Davis during the recall had a lasting impression on the public. The percentage of Californians who thought state government was largely run by special interests was significantly higher in January 2004 than in the January 2002 (54%) or January 2001 (60%) surveys. And at least two in three voters in all political groups shared this postrecall view that their legislature put the needs of big interests ahead of average residents in deciding state policy.

BLOWING UP BOXES

Probably the most memorable line in Schwarzenegger's 2004 State of the State address was his promise to free state government from the constraints imposed by bureaucracy and disconnection from the public, a move he likened to blowing up boxes. "Every governor proposes moving boxes around to reorganize government. I don't want to move boxes around; I want to blow them up," Schwarzenegger told legislators. "The executive branch of this government is a mastodon frozen in time and about as responsive" (Schwarzenegger, "Governor Schwarzenegger's 2004 State of the State Address," 2004).

Schwarzenegger went on to outline a number of specific plans for getting California on the road to recovery. One of the most controversial to government insiders was ordering a total review of the government's performance, in an effort to root out the waste and inefficiency he believed lay within. Schwarzenegger told state lawmakers he would find and abolish overlapping governmental departments and boards that served no purpose. In doing so, he was reaffirming his credentials as a Sacramento outsider and reinforcing the public's view of their state government as a large and wasteful bureaucracy. This populist position endeared him to voters who had elected him because they distrusted the state's political establishment.

He also proposed giving public schools more autonomy over their spending, overhauling the state's expensive workers' compensation insurance system, and building a "hydrogen highway" by promoting research on alternative automobile fuels. These were remarkably ambitious plans, reaching

Table 4.3: Reactions to "State of the State" Speech

"Overall, do you have a favorable or an unfavorable impression of the plans and policies for California that Governor Schwarzenegger presented in his 'State of the State' speech?"

	Adults	Democrats	Republicans	Independents
Favorable	44%	35%	71%	51%
Unfavorable	18	27	4	18
Didn't hear the speech (volunteered)	30	28	20	27
Don't know	8	10	5	4

Source: PPIC Statewide Survey, January 2004.

out to an array of constituencies including education, business, and environmentalists. While he espoused the Republican themes of cutting spending, helping industry to overcome regulations, and promising no tax increases, he also took care not to ruffle Democrats' feathers.

As for the public response to the specific plans and policies laid out in the State of the State address, the reaction was generally positive: 44 percent overall, and 53 percent of voters, had a favorable impression (see table 4.3). Only one in six in either group (18%) was unfavorable. However, a sizeable 30 percent of adults and 23 percent of voters said they had not heard the speech, so had no opinions on the plans that were outlined. A solid majority of Republicans (71%) and about half of independents (51%) had a favorable impression of Schwarzenegger's agenda, while Democrats were more divided between favorable (35%) and unfavorable (27%) reactions.

DEALING WITH THE DEFICIT

Three days after his State of the State address, Schwarzenegger released his budget proposal for the 2004 to 2005 fiscal year. True to his promise, the governor's $99 billion spending plan attempted to close the state's persistent budget shortfall—estimated at $14 billion for the coming year—without raising taxes. Instead, it cut deeply from social services and higher education: raising tuition at the state's colleges and universities, limiting low-income residents' enrollment in public health programs, and deferring $2 billion in Proposition 98–mandated funding guarantees for public schools. The budget also cut $1 billion from transportation projects funded by the state's gasoline tax and diverted $1.3 billion in local property tax funds from cities and counties to the state (California Department of Finance, "Governor's Budget, 2004–05," 2004). As expected, the proposed spending cuts were met with considerable opposition.

In many ways, though, Schwarzenegger's proposed spending plan trod the middle ground between parties. In stressing that he regarded the program cuts as temporary, lasting only until the budget crisis was resolved, the governor made some concessions to both the Democrats, who opposed reductions in health and social services, and the Republicans, who wanted to see the state government permanently downsized. As for the public, a solid majority of adults (57%) and likely voters (63%) in the January 2004 survey were satisfied with the plan, while only three in ten were dissatisfied. Republicans (86%) and independents (60%) were highly pleased with the proposed budget, while Democrats were divided (44% satisfied, 42% dissatisfied).

Most Californians were happy with the governor's refusal to include tax increases in his plan, with 51 percent of adults and likely voters saying they agreed with his decision. However, four in ten adults (42%) and likely voters (44%) thought the plan should have included tax increases to help close the deficit. Following similar divisions in the legislature, opinions on the tax issue followed partisan lines, with a solid majority of Republicans (67%) saying the governor should not have included tax increases while most Democrats (58%) thought he should have raised state revenues through a tax hike. The fiscally conservative side of independents showed through on this question, with 62 percent opposed to having tax increases in the budget plan.

Still, the public was quite concerned about the effects of the spending cuts outlined in the budget plan. More than one in four (26%) said they were "very concerned," while another 42 percent were "somewhat concerned." Only three in ten residents were "not too concerned" (21%) or "not at all concerned" (9%). Likely voters were similarly worried. The effects of the program cuts were of greatest concern to Democrats, with eight in ten saying they were very (40%) or somewhat (41%) concerned. But two in three independents (68%) and nearly half of Republicans (46%) were also at least somewhat apprehensive about the cuts in the governor's spending plan.

One of the main pillars of Schwarzenegger's budget plan was a $15 billion bond that would go before voters on the March 2004 ballot. Negotiating the bond had been a major accomplishment for the governor in the early days of his administration, showing his ability to work with both Democrats and Republicans in reaching a bipartisan solution. The plan had been rejected by lawmakers the previous December, with Republicans insisting on having the bond accompanied by a spending cap while Democrats staunchly opposed such a move. Schwarzenegger's public approach to the recalcitrant state leaders was a page out of his action hero scripts—threatening to bypass the legislature and take a spending limit measure to voters in the form of an initiative.

But privately, Schwarzenegger was softening his bluster by holding a series of negotiating sessions with legislators on both sides of the aisle, including some over cigars in the tent he had erected outside the smoke-free Capitol building. By all reports, the governor was tough but conciliatory and determined to reach a bipartisan agreement. In the early hours of December

13, 2003, a deal was struck. The compromise plan abandoned the spending cap and linked the bond to a companion ballot measure requiring the state to pass balanced budgets from then on, and set up a "rainy day" reserve fund to hedge against future economic downturns. The $15 billion bond and the companion measure, later given the respective ballot labels Proposition 57 and 58, were headed for the March 2004 ballot.

Schwarzenegger's January budget proposal depended on the public's cooperation in passing the $15 billion bond that March. Without it, the state would be unable to balance its books. The bond, in turn, was dependent on the balanced budget initiative: both measures had to pass for either to take effect. But the public was initially cool toward Proposition 57. The measure, which became known as the Economic Recovery Bond Act, was favored by only 35 percent of voters in the January 2004 poll, while 44 percent were opposed. One in five voters was undecided on the bond at the start of the year. Ominously, the $15 billion bond measure fell well below majority support in all political parties, with only 42 percent of Republicans, 41 percent of independents, and 31 percent of Democrats saying they planned to vote for it on March 2. Proposition 58, called the California Balanced Budget Act, received a better reception in January, when 57 percent of voters said they planned to vote yes. Only 22 percent opposed Proposition 58 in the January 2004 survey, while 21 percent were undecided. This measure, which prohibited the legislature from borrowing to balance future budgets, was supported by majorities of Republicans (62%), independents (63%), and Democrats (52%).

Even though they were being asked to make important fiscal decisions at the ballot box, few Californians had a deep understanding of the state's borrowing process. Only 6 percent of adults and 8 percent of likely voters in the January survey said they knew "a lot" about how state bonds were paid for, while 36 percent of adults and 49 percent of voters described their knowledge as "some." In general, though, residents disliked the idea of the state borrowing money to reduce its structural deficit, with 61 percent of adults and 63 percent of likely voters opposed to this approach.

Schwarzenegger appeared to be unfazed by the early tepid reception for his Recovery Bond by the voters. Dedicating his intense energy to the project and getting some support from across the aisle, he teamed up with the Democratic state controller, Steve Westly, to campaign around the state promoting his "fiscal recovery plan."

ARMAGEDDON AND THE MARCH ELECTION

Schwarzenegger and Westly made for a political odd couple as they toured California in the "Road to Recovery Express" bus and held other campaign events pushing the pair of ballot measures in early 2004. Not only did they contrast politically, but they also cut opposite figures physically, with Schwarzenegger tall, tanned, and muscular while Westly was fair and slightly built. The pair joked that they were like "Twins II"—referring to a film in which Schwarzenegger and the diminutive Danny DeVito played a set of mismatched twins. Using more images from the movies, the former action hero warned that if voters did not support the bond, the state would face "Armageddon" cuts to education and social services (*San Jose Mercury News*, January 21, 2004). Soon after the tour began, the bond measure began to creep up in the polls.

A PPIC survey conducted in early February found support for Proposition 57 at 38 percent, while 41 percent were opposed and one in five were undecided. While this was still short of a majority, it reflected a slight gain from a month earlier. Importantly, favor for the bond measure had risen by three points among Democrats (34%) as well as Republicans (45%), although it had dropped by nine points among independents (32%). Support for the companion measure, Proposition 58, was declining, with 52 percent of voters in the February survey saying they would vote yes on the Balanced Budget Act (down five points from January). The number of "yes" voters had fallen seven points among Democrats (45%) and twelve points among independents (51%) while it remained steady among Republicans (62%). Nonetheless, the measure continued to draw majority support. The task ahead was for a GOP governor to gain the support of Democrats.

Californians continued to give high performance ratings to their new governor: 55 percent of all adults and 61 percent of likely voters in the February survey approved of the way he was handling his job. Supporters outnumbered detractors even among Democrats (44% approved, 32% disapproved), while Republicans highly favored the governor (82% approved, 7% disapproved) and independents were also positive (58% approved, 24% disapproved). A majority of all residents (51%) and likely voters (55%) also approved of the way Schwarzenegger was handling the state budget and taxes, although on this issue, Democrats were divided (39% approved, 43% disapproved) while Republicans (78% approved, 11% disapproved) and independents (49% approved, 33% disapproved) were considerably more positive.

By the March 2 primary election, Schwarzenegger's intense campaigning and his shrewd enlistment of endorsers from both major parties—such as Democratic U.S. senator Dianne Feinstein and delegates to the state's GOP convention—succeeded in overcoming the early resistance of voters and put both measures comfortably over the top (see table 4.4). Proposition 57 won handily, with 63.4 percent of the vote, and Proposition 58 passed with an even larger 71.2 percent of the vote (California Secretary of State, "Statement of the Vote: 2004 Primary Election," 2004).

Table 4.4: March 2004 Vote on Statewide Measures

Proposition 56: State Budget Voting Requirements	
Yes	34.3%
No	65.7
Proposition 57: Economic Recovery Bond Act	
Yes	63.4%
No	36.6
Proposition 58: California Balanced Budget Act	
Yes	71.2%
No	28.8
Registered voter turnout	44.3%

Source: California Secretary of State, "Statement of the Vote," March 2004.

A Los Angeles Times Exit Poll conducted of primary voters found the measures drew solid majorities among all political parties, with 58 percent of Democrats, 59 percent of independents, and 76 percent of Republicans voting in favor of the Economic Recovery Bond and 66 percent of Democrats, 65 percent of independents, and 80 percent of Republicans supporting the Balanced Budget Act. The overwhelming success of both of Schwarzenegger's measures was touted as a demonstration of his ability to cure the state's crippling political polarization by using his powerful negotiating skills to draw both sides toward the center. It also served as a model for the hybrid democracy that was to become a staple of his political agenda—using the populist tool as both a threat and an incentive to gain the cooperation of elected leaders and the buy-in of the voters.

Another measure on the March ballot, meanwhile, demonstrated Californians' ongoing distrust of government and elected officials and their desire to keep state legislators in check. Proposition 56, a citizen's initiative that would have lowered the vote needed to pass a state budget from two-thirds of the legislature to a 55 percent majority, went down to a wide defeat. The number of "no" votes (65.7%) exceeded those in favor of the measure (34.3%) by nearly two to one (see table 4.4). According to the Los Angeles Times Exit Poll, the bid to make it easier for state legislators to pass a budget failed to reach a majority among Democrats (48%), while it had scant support among independents (29%) and Republicans (17%).

THE ART OF COMPROMISE

As demonstrated by the success of his ballot measures, Schwarzenegger's ability to smash through partisan fences with a combination of negotiating skills and direct democracy was in peak form in early 2004 as he worked to put his "year of recovery" plans in place. Ironically, much of his political capital was earned through connections with special interest groups. One of his most trumpeted successes had come in January, when he negotiated a deal with the state's powerful education lobby, getting schools to give up $2 billion in the coming year. The money the schools agreed to forgo amounted to about half of the $4 billion funding increase guaranteed under Proposition 98.

Under the agreement announced with much fanfare at a Sacramento middle school on January 8, the deferred $2 billion would be reinstated when state revenues improved (*Los Angeles Times*, January 9, 2004). It was a coup for the governor, gaining the cooperation of a highly influential, largely Democrat-leaning interest group. But in many ways it was also a coup for the education lobby, allowing them to appear to be doing their part to help repair the budget hole, when otherwise the dictates of Proposition 98 would fatten their budgets while the rest of the state did without. It also avoided the possibility that the legislature would act to suspend the Proposition 98 funding guarantees during the state's fiscal emergency—losing schools the whole $4 billion increase.

Another triumph that showcased Schwarzenegger's skills at the art of compromise was reforming workers' compensation, one of the major goals he had set forth during his election campaign. The state program for compensating employees injured in the workplace was the costliest in the nation and Schwarzenegger portrayed it as a major force driving businesses out of the state. As soon as the March election was behind him, he turned his attention to endorsing a proposition created by business groups that would overhaul the system. The governor and his supporters quickly put together the funding needed to finance a signature drive and gained enough signatures to qualify the measure for the November ballot.

But rather than put the matter before voters, Schwarzenegger used the leverage of having a qualified ballot measure to negotiate a reform plan with Democrats in the legislature. He did so using his by-then-proven approach of publicly threatening to go over legislators' heads while negotiating with them behind closed doors. After weeks of talks, Schwarzenegger and the legislature reached a compromise reform plan, cutting out some of the more restrictive features businesses had wanted, while establishing treatment guidelines, placing a time limit on temporary disability benefits, and increasing payments to employees with the most severe injuries. The legislature passed the bill on April 16, 2004, and the ballot initiative was immediately dropped by its supporters.

The combination of direct democracy and backroom deal making also helped the governor head off a battle with California's cities and county governments. Ever since the passage of Proposition 13 in 1978, California's municipalities and counties had seen their revenues shrink because a primary source of funding—property taxes—was both limited in its growth potential and shifted to the state for distribution. Initially, the state helped cities make up the shortfall by passing surplus money back to local governments. But with the recession of the 1990s, the state started to take back some of those funds and use them for schools. By 2004, the state had diverted more than $33 billion in local property tax funds (*Los Angeles Times*, May 8, 2004). This left cities and counties strapped for funds to pay for local services, such as police, fire, jails, parks, and libraries.

The ongoing funding tug-of-war between state and local governments escalated into major combat in early 2004, as Schwarzenegger announced his intentions to use $1.3 billion in local property tax funds to help reduce the state budget deficit. In response, cities and counties put an initiative on the November 2004 ballot that would amend the state constitution to prohibit the state from taking local government funds without a statewide vote. The measure would apply to vehicle license fees, sales taxes, and local property taxes. It would significantly shift the balance of power over local finances from the state to city and county governments. It would also make it impossible for the governor's budget plan to pass without a statewide vote.

Schwarzenegger spent much of the spring negotiating with city and county officials. He made personal appeals to the League of California Cities, the California State Association of Counties, and other local government groups. The result was a compromise ballot measure announced in early May that would protect local sales and property tax revenues beginning in 2006. The state would not be able to take local funds unless the governor declared a fiscal emergency and two-thirds of the legislature went along with the plan. Until the measure went into effect, the state would take $1.3 billion a year from local governments to help balance the budget. Schwarzenegger offered his personal endorsement to the ballot measure, which he expected the legislature to place on the November 2004 ballot. In return, city and county officials agreed to back away from their original initiative. Although it would still appear on the November ballot, no one would campaign for it—making it an "orphan" initiative.

With yet other key pieces of his fiscal recovery plan appearing to be in place, including agreements with schools and local governments, Schwarzenegger prepared to unveil his updated 2004 to 2005 budget in the traditional May Revise of his January budget.

PARTISAN BATTLES OVER THE BUDGET

As Schwarzenegger revealed his revised budget on May 13, he touted his accomplishments of the past four months, and credited his success to the new age of nonpartisan solidarity in Sacramento.

"By working together with the Republicans and the Democrats and everyone else, we have taken an extraordinary action on my recovery plan," the governor announced at the state capitol in releasing his reworked spending plan that day. "We put the inherited debt behind us and stopped deficit spending and borrowing by passing Proposition 57 and 58 with the biggest bipartisan team ever assembled for a California initiative. We made a huge down-payment on economic recovery by passing workers' compensation reform. We have addressed three of four points in my plan" (Schwarzenegger, "Excerpts of Gov. Schwarzenegger's May Budget Revision Announcement," 2004).

Schwarzenegger went on to outline his revised $103 billion spending plan. Thanks to an improved economy that generated $2 billion more in state revenues than had been anticipated in January, the revised budget did away with the proposed cuts to health services for low-income Californians—a big obstacle for Democratic lawmakers. And true to his promise to GOP leaders, the revised budget did not include any new taxes. Instead, it relied heavily on borrowed funds to close the state's $15 billion budget hole. The budget also was dependent on the funding concessions Schwarzenegger had gotten through his negotiations with the public schools, local governments, and state universities. Now, it was up to the legislature to approve the budget bill.

"I ask the members of the legislature to begin working in earnest with me and with each other, to give the people a budget that is balanced, responsible, and on time," Schwarzenegger said in concluding his May 13 budget revision speech. "I have pledged my leadership to this effort to serve the public interest, and to build a fantastic partnership with our legislators. I am proud, and I'm all pumped up, and I'm ready."

The governor had high hopes of getting the budget passed by the June 30 deadline, a goal that had rarely been reached in recent years. But back in the chambers of the California Senate and Assembly, the harmonious atmosphere that had enveloped the state Capitol at the start of Schwarzenegger's tenure had now begun to sour.

Lawmakers were tiring of the governor's frequent threats to bypass their authority and take his plans directly to the voters through the initiative process if he didn't get his way. They were resentful of his backroom deal making with special interest groups and were generally feeling left out of the legislative process. Senator John Burton, the outspoken president pro tem of the Democrat-controlled Senate, warned after the release of Schwarzenegger's revised budget that state legislators "can't be bypassed. . . . We are the ones who take a budget, work our will up, down or sideways and send it back to the governor," he said, adding that he considered all the separate deals that had been negotiated as merely "a suggestion from the governor" (*Sacramento Bee*, May 14, 2004).

The public, meanwhile, was still generally favorable toward the governor's budget. Half of adults and 52 percent of likely voters in a May 2004 survey said they were satisfied with the May revision, outnumbering the 41 percent in each group who were dissatisfied. But satisfaction with the budget had dropped somewhat since January (57% satisfied, 30% dissatisfied). While a majority of Republicans (74%) and independents (52%) continued to approve of the budget plan, more than half of Democrats (57%) were dissatisfied. Disapproval had risen in all groups.

Despite the governor's refusal to increase taxes, support for using this as a means of balancing the budget had grown since January. In the May survey, half of adults (50%) said some tax increases should have been included in the revised budget, compared to 42 percent in January. The views among likely voters were similar. Opinions remained deeply divided along party lines, with two in three Republicans (64%) opposing tax increases while the same proportion of Democrats (66%) said they should have been included. Among independents, most of whom had opposed tax hikes in January, support had risen to 48 percent in May 2004.

Public anxiety over the spending cuts proposed in the budget had also grown over time. In May, three in four residents were either "very concerned" (33%) or "somewhat concerned" (43%) about the effects of the cuts, up from 66 percent expressing at least some concern in January. Likely voters were similarly apprehensive. While Democrats were most likely to be very (47%) or somewhat (40%) concerned, 60 percent of Republicans and 72 percent of independents also were at least somewhat concerned. Even though the May revised budget proposal included fewer budget cuts than previously suggested, worries about the effects of budget cuts had grown in all political parties.

As for specific fears, residents were most worried about public schools in their local district, with 56 percent saying they were "very concerned" that the state's budget troubles could cause severe cuts in this area. Nearly half (46%) were also very concerned about funding for local health and human services, while 38 percent were similarly concerned about local services such as parks, police, and roads.

Where were they willing to have budget cuts made? The only area in which support for cuts exceeded opposition was prisons and the state correctional system, with 49 percent of residents favoring reduced spending in this area while 44 percent were opposed. Objections were loudest when it came to public K–12 schools, with 81 percent opposing cuts in this area. However, more than two in three Californians also opposed spending cuts on public colleges and universities (73%) and health and human services (68%). Republicans (49%) were more likely than Democrats (17%) or independents (27%) to favor cutting funds for health and human services, while strong majorities in all parties objected to reducing state spending on K–12 or higher education.

Despite their concerns about the state's budget crisis and their antipathy to borrowing money to reduce the state's deficit, most Californians believed that the ballot measures the voters passed in March had improved the fiscal situation. Six in ten adults and 64 percent of likely voters said they thought that Proposition 57, the $15 billion bond measure, was helping "a lot" or "somewhat," with a majority in all parties sharing this favorable view. Californians were even more positive about Proposition 58, the "Balanced Budget Act." Two in three adults and nearly three in four likely voters thought passage of this measure helped the state's fiscal climate at least some degree. Again, a majority in all political parties gave a favorable assessment to the measure.

Even though the previous year had been filled with news reports about the California budget deficit, and voters had just taken a major step to help resolve the problem, the public's understanding of the budget process had changed little over that time. In the May 2004 survey, 73 percent of adults and 80 percent of likely voters called the budget gap a "big problem" for the people of California—identical to the number giving this response to Governor Davis's revised budget in the survey conducted a year earlier. Six in ten adults (61%) in May 2004 said they followed news about the California budget closely, although only 17 percent said they did so "very closely." This response was also similar to the survey in May 2003. And nearly six in ten adults in May 2004 said they were at least somewhat familiar with how their state and local governments raised and spent money, while four in ten knew little or nothing about the process. Californians' responses to this question were identical in the June 2003 survey.

Residents' economic confidence, meanwhile, was improving. Californians were now as likely to expect good economic conditions (42%) as to expect bad times for the state (44%). This was a significant turnaround from the June 2003 survey, when only 32 percent thought economic conditions would be good during the next twelve months, while 58 percent predicted bad times ahead. Economic optimism was not evenly distributed, however. Republicans were much more likely than Democrats to expect good financial conditions (57% to 33%) in the coming year. The outlook was also more positive among whites than Latinos (45% to 37%) and among men than women (46% to 37%).

As for their view of Schwarzenegger, the public's ratings had reached a new high in the May 2004 survey. Nearly two in three adults (64%) approved of the way he was handling the governor's job—a nine-point jump since the February survey—while only 26 percent disapproved. His ratings were even higher among likely voters, with 69 percent giving him a thumbs-up—an eight-point gain since February. Schwarzenegger drew rave reviews in all political parties, including 87 percent of Republicans, 63 percent of independents, and even 53 percent of Democrats. Approval among Democrats had risen nine points since February. The one group that expressed significant disapproval for the governor was Latinos, of whom 44 percent gave him a negative job review. Among whites, by contrast, 72 percent approved.

A majority was also positive about Schwarzenegger's handling of the budget issue, with 55 percent of adults approving and 32 percent disapproving of his performance in this area. Approval had grown four points since February. Likely voters were even more favorable, with 61 percent saying the governor was doing a good job on the state budget and taxes. On this issue, however, Republicans (80%) and independents (56%) were considerably more approving than were Democrats (42%).

Residents were not nearly so generous toward the state legislature in the May survey, with only 40 percent of adults approving and 43 percent disapproving of the way this body was doing its job. Likely voters were even more negative, with 52 percent disapproving and only 35 percent approving. Detractors outnumbered supporters in all political parties. Nonetheless, the legislature's ratings reflected a four-point improvement among all residents since January and a twelve-point rise since August 2003.

As for the state budget, residents were even more negative about the legislature's performance. A majority of adults disapproved (53%), while 32 percent approved. The ratings gap widened among likely voters, of whom 58 percent disapproved and only 30 percent liked the way state legislators were handling this issue. A majority of Democrats (56%), Republicans (53%), and independents (62%) gave a negative assessment. Again, however, the general public's ratings of the legislature's fiscal policy performance showed improvement from PPIC surveys in January 2004 (up four points) and August 2003 (thirteen points).

After two seasons of playing supporting roles in a Schwarzenegger star vehicle, state legislators began to reassert their power and partisanship re-emerged when it came time to pass the budget. Almost immediately after the release of the May Revise, Democrats threatened to block a pay raise for the state's prison guards that was included in the package, claiming that the 11 percent hike was out of line, given the state's fiscal troubles (*Los Angeles Times*, May 19, 2004). Not long after, another group of primarily Democratic state lawmakers announced their intention to fight the deal Schwarzenegger had negotiated with local governments, in which cities and counties agreed to two years of funding cuts in exchange for the governor's endorsement of a constitutional amendment initiative preventing the state from taking local revenues in the future. Opponents maintained that the initiative would encourage localities to approve commercial developments for their sales tax revenues—resulting in miles of sprawling strip malls and big-box stores, while discouraging the development of affordable housing (*Sacramento Bee*, June 11, 2004).

Meanwhile, Schwarzenegger continued to hammer out backroom deals with special interest groups that stood to help, or hurt, the state budget situation. In early June, he defused a lawsuit filed by the Howard Jarvis

Taxpayers Association against his plan to pay for state employee pensions with a $1 billion bond measure by working out a reform that included reducing benefits and increasing employee contributions (*Sacramento Bee*, June 5, 2004). A few weeks later, the governor and five Indian tribes announced they had signed agreements to have the tribes secure a $1 billion bond for the state and make annual payments to the state's general fund. In exchange, the tribes would be allowed to add slot machines and Schwarzenegger promised to campaign against two November initiatives that posed a threat to Indian gaming (*San Francisco Chronicle*, June 22, 2004).

But in the state Assembly and Senate, Schwarzenegger was finding himself suddenly unable to work his deal-making magic. Democrats balked at the cuts to public employee pensions and continued to oppose the deal with local governments (*Los Angeles Times*, June 27, 2004). As the July 1 new fiscal year approached, Democrats took advantage of Schwarzenegger's eagerness for an on-time budget by getting him to back off some of his spending cuts and weaken his state employee pension reform plan. Republicans complained that the governor was making too many concessions to Democrats and threatened to block any budget bill that emerged from the process (*Los Angeles Times*, July 1, 2004). Special interest groups, such as the racetracks and card rooms that lobbied hard against the Indian gaming agreements, joined the fray as lawmakers considered the issue.

By mid-July, the governor and state legislators had abandoned their cordial tone. Schwarzenegger took to the road in a populist effort to appeal directly to the public. Campaigning in a Sacramento-area restaurant, Schwarzenegger referred to himself as the "kindergarten cop," calling state legislators "120 children." The state's elected representatives, he later told patrons at a pizza place, "want to take the money away from you and rob you blind" (*Washington Post*, July 10, 2004). A few days later, he described the state of the budget talks as "chaos" and began threatening to campaign against Democrats running for reelection in November. "Judgment Day is in November," he declared during a campaign stop in Long Beach on July 16. "I want the people to know that in November is the election. If they're not satisfied with the budget, then there will be a lot of new faces after the November election" (*Los Angeles Times*, July 17, 2004). The next day came the infamous "girlie men" speech, in which he accused Democratic lawmakers of obstructing the budget and catering to special interests.

"If they don't have the guts to come up here in front of you and say, 'I don't want to represent you, I want to represent those special interests, the unions, the trial lawyers, and I want them to make the millions of dollars' — if they don't have the guts, I call them 'girlie men,'" Schwarzenegger told a crowd gathered for a July 17 campaign rally at the Ontario Mills mall (*Sacramento Bee*, July 18, 2004). The line "girlie men" was from a skit on the comedy television show *Saturday Night Live*, in which comedians Dana Carvey and Kevin Nealon lampooned Schwarzenegger's persona as a professional bodybuilder

The Democrats' response was swift and hostile. "I think we're seeing the real Arnold Schwarzenegger," said assemblywoman Sarah Reyes (D-Fresno), calling the remark "sexist" and maintaining that it confirmed claims made during the recall race that the actor had behaved inappropriately toward women (*Sacramento Bee*, July 18, 2004). Others charged that the comment was a slur on homosexuals and that it showed the governor as a GOP bully, rather than a bipartisan negotiator.

Negotiations were dead for nearly a week, then gradually began to ease back to life. By the end of July, just in time to avoid having to delay state payments to schools as the 2004 to 2005 academic year approached, a new budget was signed.

In contrast to Schwarzenegger's grand plans, the $105 billion budget was a month late, was $1.2 billion higher than his May proposal, and had stirred up a hornet's nest of partisan conflict. It also had given in to demands by special interest groups in several areas, including backing off from cuts in state payments to home health care aides, abandoning a bid to overturn a state law limiting school districts' ability to contract out some services, and eliminating about $200 million in fee increases for water and timber industries (*San Francisco Chronicle*, July 28, 2004). And despite the governor's promise to deliver a balanced budget, it leaned heavily on borrowing and pushed a $4 billion deficit into the future.

Schwarzenegger's ratings had stumbled somewhat during the budget standoff in July. Although a majority of adults (57%) and likely voters (64%) in a July survey still approved of the way he was doing his job, these ratings reflected a drop from May. However, by August, with the budget turmoil resolved, the governor's job approval ratings had returned to the stratosphere. Two in three adults (65%) and 69 percent of likely voters in an August 2004 survey approved of his performance in office, including majorities of Republicans (89%), independents (66%), and Democrats (57%).

On the issue of the budget, Schwarzenegger's ratings were lower, but still positive—58 percent of adults and 63 percent of likely voters approved of the job he was doing in this area. But while solid numbers of Republicans (84%) and independents (57%) approved of his performance on the budget, Democrats fell short of a majority (49%). Californians were generally satisfied (52%) with the new budget, although likely voters were less approving (49%) in August. More than half of Republicans (69%) and independents (53%) favored the spending plan, while a majority of Democrats (51%) were dissatisfied.

CALIFORNIA PERFORMANCE
REVIEW AND VOTER DISTRUST

Shortly after he signed the 2004 to 2005 budget, Schwarzenegger released the results of his California Performance Review. He had announced this audit of the state government in January as a way to cut costs and increase its effectiveness. The recommendations outlined on August 3, 2004, included: eliminating 119 boards and commissions that had overlapping responsibilities; collapsing dozens of separate agencies and departments into fewer, larger entities; replacing the fifty-eight county school superintendents with eleven regional superintendents; raising money for education by joining a multistate lottery; sharply increasing tuition fees for out-of-state students; requiring students in public colleges and universities to perform community service; selling off underutilized state properties; and privatizing roadside rest stops, among more than 1,200 others (California Performance Review Report, 2004, vol. 4). The authors claimed the recommendations could save the state up to $32 billion over five years.

Analysts' reaction to the proposals was mixed, with some lauding its innovative approaches and others characterizing many of the ideas as things that had been tried before, without success. Legislators worried that the reorganization of state government concentrated too much power in the governor's office. Democrats were dubious about its claims to save money and its impacts on government employees and the public interest.

The public, however, was highly enthusiastic and hopeful about the governor's plans for the reorganization of state government. In May, before the results were released, nearly eight in ten Californians in the PPIC Survey said they expected the review to help the state's fiscal situation "a lot" (27%) or "somewhat (52%). Likely voters expressed similar hopes, reflecting the widespread populist view that the government was inefficient and wasteful. After the Performance Review's findings were made public, 65 percent of adults and 71 percent of likely voters in the August 2004 survey said they favored the proposals for changing state government. Support was especially strong among Republicans (84%) and independents (69%); however, a majority of Democrats (59%) also approved of the California Performance Review recommendations.

While Schwarzenegger was hitting the right notes with the California public that summer, emphasizing reform and vowing to cut out waste in government, the state legislature was not faring so well. Although its performance ratings had risen from 40 percent in May and 36 percent in January 2004, more Californians continued to disapprove (45%) than approve (42%) of the job state legislators were doing that August. Among likely voters, a majority (52%) disapproved of the legislature, and only 37 percent gave a positive

Table 4.5: Ballot-Box Budgeting

"Generally speaking, do you think it is a good idea or a bad idea to protect local government revenues, even if it means less funding for state programs?"

	Likely Voters	Democrats	Republicans	Independents
Good idea	63%	56%	72%	66%
Bad idea	23	30	16	20
Don't know	14	14	12	14

"Generally speaking, do you think it is a good idea or a bad idea to have a specific tax tied directly to a specific service?"

	Likely Voters	Democrats	Republicans	Independents
Good idea	55%	56%	51%	63%
Bad idea	34	33	39	29
Don't know	11	11	10	8

Source: PPIC Statewide Survey, August 2004.

rating in the May 2004 survey. Approval was below 50 percent among Democrats (48%), Republicans (32%), and independents (36%) alike. Similarly, a majority of adults (53%) and likely voters (58%) in the August survey said they disapproved of the way the legislature was handling the state budget and taxes, while only one in three approved. Again, approval was low in all political groups.

Two ballot measures set to appear on the November 2004 ballot capitalized on voters' desire to limit the legislature's leeway in budget matters. Proposition 1A, the protection of local government revenues initiative, was the constitutional amendment Schwarzenegger had promoted in exchange for local government agreeing to two years of reduced funding. The measure was a major sticking point in the just-ended budget impasse, with Democrats grudgingly voting at the last minute to place the initiative on the ballot. However, the measure curtailing the state's ability to dip into local tax revenues when funds got tight was a hit with voters. Six in ten in the August survey said they would vote yes on the measure, while only 25 percent were opposed. Proposition 1A drew majority support among Democrats (57%) and Republicans (61%) alike, and was especially appealing to skeptical independents (66%). The reason for this support was shown by a follow-up question in the August survey, which asked likely voters whether they thought it was a good idea or a bad idea to protect local government revenues at the possible expense of state programs. A resounding 63 percent said they thought it was a "good idea"—including solid majorities in all political parties (see table 4.5).

Another piece of ballot-box budgeting legislation also on the November ballot was Proposition 63, the mental health services expansion and funding initiative, which proposed adding 1 percent to the income tax on the wealthiest Californians, with the revenues used to expand mental health services in the state. This measure, sponsored by Democratic legislators who felt they were otherwise unable to increase funding for the state's mental health system, drew favor from two in three voters in August, including majorities of Democrats (78%), independents (72%), and even Republicans (51%).

A follow-up question showed that most likely voters thought the current funding for state mental health services was inadequate (63%). However, while solid majorities of Democrats (76%) and independents (70%) held this view, only 43 percent of Republicans agreed. Nonetheless, a majority in all parties liked the idea of tying a specific tax to a specific service—one of the few ways to make a tax hike acceptable to most Californians (see table 4.5). Overall, 55 percent of likely voters said this approach was a "good idea," including majorities of independents (63%), Democrats (56%), and Republicans (51%).

PARTISANSHIP RETURNS
WITH THE NOVEMBER ELECTION

"America is back," Schwarzenegger told delegates attending the Republican national convention on August 31, 2004. "Back from the attack on our homeland, back from the attack on our economy, and back from the attack on our way of life. We are back because of the perseverance, character and leadership of the 43rd president of the United States, George W. Bush" (*Los Angeles Times*, September 1, 2004). Schwarzenegger's speech endorsing Bush as the GOP nominee for president was broadcast to a prime-time television audience nationwide. It was the talk of New York, where the 2004 convention was being held, and widely viewed as the highlight of the convention. It was also a noteworthy step away from Schwarzenegger's carefully crafted image as a nonpartisan outsider.

This public declaration of praise of Bush was a risky move for the governor of a state that held little love for the president. In the August survey, 56 percent of Californians said they disapproved of the way Bush was handling his job, while only 40 percent approved. California residents were even more critical of the president's performance on Iraq, with 63 percent disapproving of his actions and only 34 percent approving. Likely voters were similarly critical of the president, and Californians were considerably more negative toward him in these two areas than was the rest of the nation. The only area in which Californians were at least equivocal toward Bush was his handling of terrorism and homeland security, with half of adults and likely voters disapproving and 47 percent approving of his performance in this area. While California Republicans were highly favorable toward Bush, strong majorities of Democrats and independent voters gave him negative approval ratings in all three areas.

Schwarzenegger followed up his August foray into national party politics by campaigning for GOP candidates around the state that fall. In the wake of the "girlie men" comments and the governor's efforts to intimidate legislators to do his bidding, Democrats in Sacramento appeared to have become more defiant. As the 2004 legislative session came to a close that August, Democrats had defied the governor on several fronts, including voiding a deal he had made with one Indian tribe to build a Las Vegas–size casino in a Bay Area city, going against his wishes in approving Assembly speaker Fabian Núñez's plan to regulate utilities' ability to build power plants, and expanding the number of state boards and commissions, in opposition to the recommendations of his California Performance Review.

One of the Democratic-controlled legislature's last acts of the session had been to reinstate driver's licenses for undocumented immigrants—the suspension of which had been one of Schwarzenegger's first acts on taking office (*Los Angeles Times*, August 29, 2004). Schwarzenegger, in turn, cut a wide swath with his veto pen, rejecting the driver's license for illegal immigrants law and nearly 25 percent of the more than 1,200 other bills the legislature had approved that year. Among the casualties was a Democrat-sponsored bid to help Californians purchase prescription drugs at lower-priced Canadian pharmacies over the Internet, five bills aimed at discouraging California businesses to relocate jobs overseas, and a law aimed at protecting car buyers by capping car loan interest rates (*Los Angeles Times*, October 1, 2004). Then, with the legislative session reaching a rancorous end, Schwarzenegger made good on his threat to "terminate" Democratic legislators who did not go along with his plans, by endorsing a slate of forty-nine Republican candidates (*San Francisco Chronicle*, October 18, 2004).

Initially, it seemed like it would be an easy task for the immensely popular Republican governor to use his political influence with voters to help change the balance of partisan power in the state Senate and Assembly. While Schwarzenegger continued to enjoy a 61 percent approval rating in a September survey, more Californians disapproved (46%) than approved (40%) of the job the legislature was doing—just as they had throughout the year (see table 4.6). Likely voters were even more negative in September, with 51 percent disapproving of the legislature's performance and only 37 percent approving. Moreover, disapproval topped approval of the legislature in every political group, making it appear possible for the governor to attract independents and influence Democrats to cross party lines—just as he had in the recall election.

Californians' ratings of their state lawmakers reflected the persistent belief that legislators did not have the public interests in mind. Only 22 percent of adults rated the state legislature as "excellent" (3%) or "good" (19%) in working for the best interests of people like themselves, while four in ten

Table 4.6:   Attitudes toward the State Legislature

"Overall, do you approve of disapprove of the way that the California Legislature is handling its job?"

	Adults	Democrats	Republicans	Independents
Approve	40%	41%	38%	39%
Disapprove	46	46	52	46
Don't know	14	13	10	15

"How would you rate the California Legislature when it comes to working for the best interests of people like you?"

	Adults	Democrats	Republicans	Independents
Excellent/good	22%	24%	20%	20%
Fair	43	45	38	41
Poor	31	28	38	34
Don't know	4	3	4	5

Source: PPIC Statewide Survey, September 2004.

rated it as "fair" and fully three in ten said "poor" (see table 4.6). Likely voters were similarly mistrustful, with only 20 percent rating the legislature as excellent (1%) or good (19%), while nearly four in ten rated it as "poor" at representing the public's best interests. Similarly low numbers in all political parties felt that state lawmakers were performing well in this area.

Meanwhile, Schwarzenegger's populist approach and use of the ballot box in his first year in office had been fairly successful in making Californians feel he had their best interests at heart—46 percent of adults rated him as excellent (13%) or good (33%) in this area. Likely voters were similarly positive (15% excellent, 33% good), and sizeable numbers of Republicans (73%) and independents (45%) rated him as good or better at working for their best interests, although only 29 percent of Democrats shared this view.

The public's ongoing mistrust of state government was further reflected in their solid support for term limits, which had been in place since 1990. Six in ten adults and 65 percent of likely voters in the September 2004 survey said term limits were a "good thing" for California. Only 17 percent of adults called them a "bad thing," while 18 percent said they had made "no difference." Likely voters expressed similar views. Majorities in all political parties were positive about the effects of California's term limits law (Democrats 57%, Republicans 75%, independents 59%). Favor for term limits had remained as high as it was when we first asked this question in 1998, two years after the first state legislators were termed out of office.

Although they expressed relatively little confidence in their state leaders, Californians were cool to a number of legislative reforms being discussed around the time of the September 2004 survey. A proposal to change from a full-time to a part-time legislature—something that had been suggested by

Schwarzenegger during the budget standoff that summer—was called "a bad thing" by a majority of adults (53%) and likely voters (54%). The prospect of increasing the number of state representatives so that each would serve a smaller district also did not trigger a great deal of enthusiasm among Californians—nearly half (49%) said they thought this change would make "no difference" in the quality of representation for people in their district.

Voters were also divided on another legislative reform that was receiving a lot of public attention at the time—the redistricting process. The state's current legislative map had been drawn up by a Democrat-controlled legislature in 2001, resulting in a convoluted system of districts that created "safe" party seats. Schwarzenegger had begun mentioning redistricting reform as part of his next set of priorities, taking the power away from the political parties and placing it in the hands of an independent body. Four in ten adults in the September 2004 survey opposed the proposal to have an independent state commission draw up legislative districts, while 39 percent were in favor and 21 percent were not sure. And despite their suspicions about the influence of special interests in state politics, a majority (57%) of adults in the September 2004 survey were opposed to establishing public campaign funding for state offices even if it cost taxpayers only a few dollars a year. Only 35 percent favored this proposal. The earlier PPIC polls had found support for public campaign funding briefly climbed in the wake of the record spending during the November 2002 gubernatorial election (50% favor, 46% opposed), but fell back to below a majority a year later.

GOVERNOR TAKES SIDES ON BALLOT MEASURES

Schwarzenegger further flexed his political muscles during the fall 2004 campaign season by taking sides on fifteen of the sixteen pieces of direct legislation appearing on the November ballot. In contrast to his partisan focus in backing Republican candidates, however, his slate of initiative endorsements spanned the political map—reinforcing the perspective among voters that he was more populist than partisan in his politics.

The governor followed GOP lines in supporting a measure that proposed to expand the collection and use of DNA samples from accused felons (Proposition 69) and another that curtailed litigants' ability to file "shakedown" lawsuits against businesses (Proposition 64). He also showed his Republican and pro-business roots in opposing Proposition 72, a referendum on legislation passed the previous year requiring all large and medium-sized California employers to provide health care coverage for their workers. The referendum, sponsored by state businesses seeking to overturn the 2003 Health Insurance Act that had been signed by Governor Davis two days before his recall, would be repealed in November if a majority of voters did not vote yes.

But the governor crossed his party in supporting Proposition 71, a bond measure dedicating $3 billion to stem cell research in California. Republicans and religious conservatives opposed the measure because the research used human embryos. He also campaigned vigorously in a bipartisan mode against Proposition 66, an initiative seeking to weaken California's "three strikes" law requiring mandatory life sentences for third-time offenders. When polls late in the campaign showed Proposition 66 ahead, Schwarzenegger teamed up with former Democratic and Republican California governors to spearhead a charge against it.

Schwarzenegger also spent considerable time and money campaigning against two measures to expand casino gambling in the state, in keeping with the pact he had negotiated with several Indian gaming tribes. Proposition 68 would have allowed slot machines at card rooms and race tracks, while Proposition 70 would have increased state taxes on Indian casinos. Both would have cut into the gambling profits of the tribes with whom Schwarzenegger had negotiated a profit-sharing deal to help balance the state budget during the spring—and he worked hard to make sure they did not succeed.

Faced with a ballot loaded with sixteen propositions, Californians hung on to their support for direct legislation. Asked in the September survey who or what should have the most influence over setting state policy, adults (37%) and likely voters (38%) both chose initiatives over the government's other branches (see table 4.7). These results were similar to a December 1999 survey, in which 42 percent preferred initiatives, 30 percent chose the legislature,

Table 4.7: Initiative Reform

"In California state government today, which of the following would you prefer to have the most influence over public policy?"

	Adults	Democrats	Republicans	Independents
Initiatives on the state ballot	37%	36%	38%	36%
The legislature	31	38	22	34
The governor	23	18	31	21
Other/don't know	9	8	9	9

"Do you think the citizens' initiative process in California is in need of major changes or minor changes or that it is basically fine the way it is?"

	Adults	Democrats	Republicans	Independents
Major changes	35%	38%	28%	36%
Minor changes	33	37	34	32
Fine the way it is	21	16	28	22
Don't know	11	9	10	10

Source: PPIC Statewide Survey, September 2004.

and 21 percent opted for the governor. Support for initiatives having the most influence on state policy was nearly identical in all parties in the September 2004 survey. However, Democrats and independents tended to favor initiatives and the legislature about equally, while Republicans gave the greatest role to initiatives, with the governor coming in second.

Despite their enthusiasm for setting state policies at the ballot box, most Californians (68%) also felt the system was in need of some changes (see table 4.7). Thirty-five percent in the September survey said "major changes" were needed, while another 33 percent wanted "minor changes." Only one in five thought the process was fine the way it was. These attitudes were also fairly consistent across time—when we last asked this question in October 2000, 32 percent of Californians said major changes were needed and 43 percent called for minor changes in the initiative process.

MAKING HEALTH POLICY AT THE BALLOT BOX

One of the most far-reaching uses of the initiative process was being played out that season with a group of five ballot measures aimed at establishing policies on health issues. In addition to Proposition 72, the referendum on requiring employers to provide health care coverage, and Proposition 71, the bond measure funding stem cell research, Californians were considering expanding mental health services by raising the income tax on the wealthy (Proposition 63), state funding for children's hospital projects (Proposition 61), and a state tax for emergency medical services (Proposition 67). Propositions 63, 71, and 72 attracted the most interest in the fall 2004 election.

Proposition 72 was well short of a majority in an October 2004 survey. Only 41 percent of likely voters supported the measure, with 38 percent opposed and one in five still undecided. The referendum drew a majority among Democrats (53%), but fell short among Republicans (25%) and independents (47%). Related questions found ambivalence in voters' opinions on the subject. While support for Proposition 72 fell short of the majority needed to keep the law in place, an overwhelming 64 percent of voters in a follow-up question said it was "very important" that large and medium employers give their workers health care benefits.

Voters were giving tepid support to Proposition 71, the $3 billion bond to fund stem cell research, in the October 2004 survey. A scant 50 percent of likely voters said they would vote yes on the measure in November. The measure was strongly supported by Democrats (65%) and drew a slight majority among independents (52%), while 56 percent of Republicans were opposed. Californians' opinions on federal funding for stem cell research were similarly polarized. While 53 percent of all voters thought too little was being spent by the federal government—most Democrats (70%), but few Republicans (30%), held this view.

However, a third initiative dealing with health policy was drawing solid support in October. Six in ten voters said they planned to vote yes on Proposition 63, the mental health services expansion and funding initiative. As in the previous surveys, Proposition 63 had more support from Democrats (76%) and independents (67%) than Republicans (46%). Most voters (66%) continued to say that the current level of state funding for mental health programs was not sufficient. Democrats (79%) and independents (73%) were more likely than Republicans (51%) to hold this perception.

THE NOVEMBER ELECTION—A MIXED MESSAGE

In the end, California voters handed Schwarzenegger a mixed message in the November election. On the direct democracy front, they tended to follow his lead: passing Proposition 1A (Schwarzenegger's deal with local governments), Proposition 59 (increasing public access to government records), Proposition 64 (limiting lawsuits against businesses), Proposition 69 (expanding DNA evidence collection in felony arrests), and Proposition 71 (the stem cell research bond) (see table 4.8). Voters also sided with the governor in rejecting Proposition 65 (the competing local government money protection measure which was abandoned after Schwarzenegger's deal), Proposition 66 (softening the "three strikes" law), Proposition 67 (funding emergency care through a hike in phone taxes), Propositions 68 and 70 (expanding gambling in California at the expense of Schwarzenegger's Indian tribe allies), and Proposition 72 (mandating employer-sponsored health coverage).

However, voters approved two spending measures Schwarzenegger had opposed: Proposition 61 (a bond providing funds for children's hospitals)

Table 4.8: November 2004 Vote on Statewide Measures

Proposition 1A: Protection of Local Government Revenues (Schwarzenegger backed)	
Yes	83.7%
No	16.3
Proposition 66: Limitations on "Three Strikes Law" (Schwarzenegger opposed)	
Yes	47.3%
No	52.7
Proposition 71: Stem Cell Research Funding Bonds (Schwarzenegger backed)	
Yes	59.1%
No	40.9
Proposition 72: Health Care Coverage Requirements (Schwarzenegger opposed)	
Yes	49.2%
No	50.8

Source: California Secretary of State, "Statement of the Vote," November 2004.

and Proposition 63 (the special tax on the wealthy for mental health services). They also veered away from his endorsements on two measures dealing with the state's primary elections, passing Proposition 60 (preserving the current party primary system) and rejecting Proposition 62 (creating an open primary) (California Secretary of State, "Statement of the Vote: 2004 General Election," 2004). Even with these losses, Schwarzenegger's victories on November 3 amounted to the nation's most sweeping and successful use of direct legislation to push a governor's political agenda. It was also the most expensive ever, with spending on ballot measures topping $206 million (*Los Angeles Times*, February 1, 2005).

It was a vastly different story with the legislative races. Despite Schwarzenegger's threatening to "terminate" Democrats and his endorsing and campaigning for GOP candidates, Republicans did not gain a single state seat in the November election (see table 4.9). In the twenty California Senate seats that were up for election in 2004, voters elected eleven Democrats and nine Republicans—keeping the Democrats at a twenty-five- to fifteen-member advantage. In the state Assembly, where all eighty seats were up, voters elected forty-eight Democrats and thirty-two Republicans: the same party ratio as before the election. Clearly, the governor's involvement in partisan races had no effect.

Similarly, California's U.S. Congressional delegation saw no change in its partisan makeup. California voters sent thirty-three Democrats and twenty

Table 4.9: November 2004 Vote on Candidates

U.S. President	
John Kerry, Democrat	54.4%
George Bush, Republican	44.4
Other	1.2
U.S. Senate	
Barbara Boxer, Democrat	57.8%
Bill Jones, Republican	37.8
Other	4.4
U.S. House of Representatives Seats	
Democrats	33
Republicans	20
California Senate Seats	
Democrats	11
Republicans	9
California Assembly Seats	
Democrats	48
Republicans	32
Registered voter turnout	76%

Source: California Secretary of State, "Statement of the Vote," November 2004.

Republicans to the U.S. House of Representatives: the same as before the election. Californians also reelected U.S. senator Barbara Boxer, whose term was up that year—keeping two Democrats in the U.S. Senate (California Secretary of State, "Statement of the Vote: 2004 General Election," 2004).

The fact that no federal or state seats changed hands raised questions about how much to blame Schwarzenegger for the lack of GOP success in the state legislative races. Some saw the legislature's redistricting plan, in which the district maps drawn up after the 2000 Census limited partisan competition, as the force behind the status quo vote. The lack of partisan turnover in 2004, particularly in Schwarzenegger's inability to gain seats for Republicans, would be revisited in the call for legislative districting reform in 2005.

Nonetheless, Schwarzenegger declared the results of the 2004 legislative elections "a good beginning" and vowed to continue working to further a Republican agenda in the Democrat-controlled California legislature. "I think it's very important that we helped the party, and that we got a good, strong theme," he told reporters. "And I will lead the way, I will create the theme for which way we're going to go in this state. It will be me from this office here" (*Sacramento Bee*, November 4, 2004).

The turnout—76 percent—was the highest seen in a California general election since 1976. Of course it was also a presidential election. Although George Bush won reelection nationwide, and despite their governor actively campaigning for the Republican incumbent (including an appearance in the swing state of Ohio during the final days of the race), California voters chose Democratic U.S. senator John Kerry over Bush by a substantial 54 percent to 44 percent margin.

"KICKING THEIR BUTTS" IN SACRAMENTO

As Schwarzenegger's first-year anniversary as governor approached, the reviews of his tenure were generally favorable. "Arnold Schwarzenegger is the celebrity governor who made Californians—and Wall Street—feel good again," wrote one journalist, pointing out that the state's job market, tax revenues, and credit rating had all shown improvement since he took office (*San Jose Mercury News*, November 15, 2004). Another described him as "maddeningly competent" (*Sacramento Bee*, November 14, 2004).[1]

The retrospectives over Schwarzenegger's first year in office credited his upbeat attitude with pulling the state out of the fiscal, economic, and psychological doldrums that had led to the recall. Analysts praised his tenacity in sticking with efforts to work out some of the state's most deeply entrenched problems, such as workers' compensation reform. They admired his negotiating skills in striking funding deals with interest groups such as the state's teachers, local governments, and Indian tribes. And they lauded his ability to build bipartisan coalitions that bridged the wide schism in the state legislature.

As for his accomplishments, pundits pointed out that Schwarzenegger had not brought about the overhaul of state government that he had promised. This was reflected in the fact that voter distrust of state government was still a widespread public attitude. "He has brought glitz and charm, but not fundamental transformation," wrote one political analyst. Another gave him a "B for baloney." Political columnists pointed out that much of the governor's efforts to balance the state budget relied on selling bonds, which added to the state's long-term debt. His fiscal strategies of borrowing money and taking away funds from other entities, such as local governments, "look remarkably like those of previous governors, only more so." Critics also accused him of too often siding with business in setting state policy.[2] And, in contrast to his vow of immunity from the influence of special interests, analysts noted that Schwarzenegger had received millions of dollars in political donations during his first year in office—much of it from special interests with stakes in the 2004 ballot measures.[3]

Nonetheless, Schwarzenegger was generally seen as having avoided the partisan pigeonhole that had trapped his predecessor. The governor was credited as having chosen advisors from all parts of the political spectrum and with drawing Sacramento Democrats and Republicans alike into his smoking tent. Moreover, his folksy, "outsider" style was immensely successful with Californians. In the October 2004 survey, 61 percent of adults—and 69 percent of likely voters—approved of the way he was handling his job. A majority of Republicans (90%), independents (62%), and even Democrats (51%) were pleased with the governor's performance. Eight in ten said Schwarzenegger had met (41%) or exceeded (40%) their expectations for his first year in office. Among likely voters, nearly nine in ten said he had performed better (46%) or about the same (43%) as they had expected. While Republicans were the most effusive about Schwarzenegger's first year in office (53% better, 42% same as expected), many independents (38% better, 47% same as expected) and Democrats (38% better, 42% same as expected) also gave him favorable reviews. It seemed as if the "Populist Governor" would go down as Schwarzenegger's best role.

But the harmony was to be short-lived. On December 6, 2004, Schwarzenegger fired the opening salvo in what was to become an all-out war during his second year in office. Speaking at the California Governor's Conference on Women and Families, organized by his wife, Maria Shriver, Schwarzenegger was interrupted by a handful of nurses who had sneaked into the hall and rolled out a banner reading "Hands off our ratios." It was a reference to the governor's decision to delay implementation of reductions in the nurse-to-patient staffing ratio that had been mandated by state law that January. In November, the Schwarzenegger administration had announced it was delaying the reductions because of a nursing shortage. Angered members of the California Nurses Association attended the conference to protest the action. "Pay no attention to those voices over there. They are only the special interests, and you know what I mean," Schwarzenegger told the 10,000-plus women attending the conference at the Long Beach Convention Center. "Special interests don't like me in Sacramento because I am always kicking their butts" (*Los Angeles Times*, December 8, 2004).

It was the beginning of a political struggle with groups Schwarzenegger characterized as problematic for the state, under the general label of "special interests." Soon, this term would be extended to an array of groups that Schwarzenegger deemed as standing in the way of his plans for his upcoming "year of reform"—including teachers' unions and the public school teachers they represent, the public employee unions whose members include fire fighters, police, state and local government workers and prison guards, and Democratic legislators, who were the political allies of these interest groups.

CONCLUSION

Schwarzenegger began his first year in office in 2004 with populism in full display, while partisanship and special interests were held at bay. The public greeted their new governor with a warm welcome in the January poll, offering glowing reviews of his performance in office, his State of the State speech, and his new budget plans. As he steered a course of bipartisan legislative cooperation in solving some of the problems that he had inherited, such as a multibillion-dollar deficit and a troubled workers' compensation system, most voters across the political spectrum gave him positive marks. The bitter partisan feelings generated during the recall appeared to be in the past. Legislators, apprehensive about their own political fate since the recent expanded use of direct democracy, responded quickly and positively when the governor threatened to bypass them and go directly to the voters for approval of his plans.

Schwarzenegger also called on voters to be active participants in solving the state's budget problems, making good on his populist themes of the recall. He asked them to support a package of bond measures and spending limits on the March primary ballot. In response to a bipartisan campaign that featured the governor and high-profile Democratic leaders, with little organized opposition from interest groups or partisan campaigns, voters turned out to support his fiscal recovery measures by wide margins. The governor also used the threat of the citizen's initiative over contentious discussions about workers' compensation reform, and the parties eventually agreed to a legislative package rather than face off against their popular governor and certain defeat at the hand of voters. Direct democracy seemed to be entering a new phase in California, with a populist governor stepping outside of his role of party leader allied with special interests, and calling on legislators to act alongside the voters in making public policy decisions.

However, the budget debates during the summer marked the end of this brief era of legislative bipartisan cooperation. In an unexpected turn of events for the governor, the legislature balked at his spending plans and the budget was passed late, after an unpleasant and public episode of name-calling on both sides. Schwarzenegger and the legislature turned their attention to their partisan priorities—the presidential election and winning legislative seats—and both called on special interests to help them gain political advantage through the fall election. The results were mixed. Voters sided with Schwarzenegger on the ballot measures and with the Democrats in their choice of elected representatives; emboldening both entities to end their cooperation and act alone. The governor turned away from his populist approach and began to side with partisans and special interests: characterizing Democratic lawmakers and their supporters as the enemy of government reform.

Despite the legislative successes of 2004, voters remained as distrustful of their government as ever during the year of recovery. Opinions of the governor had improved dramatically, but the legislature was still held in low esteem. No doubt, the governor's colorful, negative characterizations of them damaged public support for state legislators. But voters also lacked confidence in the legislative process and in state government's ability to handle issues effectively, respond to average people rather than to special interests, and manage the state's money in an efficient manner. In this context, voters rejected an initiative on the March ballot that would have made it easier for legislators to pass state spending plans by reducing the two-thirds vote majority to a simple majority. The governor also announced a "California Performance Review" that was intended to reduce fraud, waste, and abuse in government. In doing so, he once again reinforced the perceptions of distrustful Californians. The subsequent lack of action on this plan and the governor's struggles with the legislature furthered the public's belief that government and representative democracy could not be trusted. These events strengthened their belief that an alternative to elected representatives was needed for making public policy. Throughout the year, Californians continued to express their faith in direct democracy and the initiative process. The year ended with Governor Schwarzenegger planning to put the public's trust in direct democracy to a further test in 2005.

NOTES

1. See, for example, Ann E. Marimow, "Capitol Gain: Schwarzenegger's First Year in Office," *San Jose Mercury News*, November 15, 2004, A1; Margaret Talev, "Flair for Surprise Keeps Him in the Catbird Seat," *Sacramento Bee*, November 14, 2004, A1.

2. See columns by George Skelton, "Capitol Journal: Student Governor Needs to Buckle Down and Work," *Los Angeles Times*, November 15, 2004, B4; Peter Schrag, "Meeting Your 'New Day in California' Governor," *Sacramento Bee*, November 17, 2004, B7; Daniel Weintraub, "Arnold: Year One. Twelve Months in the Life of California's Celebrity Governor," *Sacramento Bee*, November 14, 2004, E1.

3. Schwarzenegger raised $23.07 million in 2004, according to the California Secretary of State's year-end campaign finance report released January 30, 2005. The biggest single donor was Orange County billionaire Henry Nicholas, who contributed $1.5 million to defeat Proposition 66. The next-highest donation was $1.054 million from Ameriquest Capital Corporation, a mortgage lender with major interests in the state. See Dan Morain, "Schwarzenegger a Big Fund-Raiser in 2004," *Los Angeles Times*, February 1, 2005, B1; Christian Berthelsen, "Governor Sets Money-Raising Record: $26.6 Million in His First Year—Most of It from Special Interests," *San Francisco Chronicle*, November 17, 2004, A1.

5

The Year of Reform: Partisan Conflict and the 2005 Special Election

By 2005, Schwarzenegger's populist tone and independent style of leadership was no longer in evidence. In its place, he had resorted to name-calling of Democratic lawmakers and hurling insults at interest groups, including teachers, nurses, and labor unions. He increasingly adopted a Republican, pro-business approach to policy making. He raised campaign funds constantly, surpassing the war chest of his predecessor despite his prior avowal that he would not take money from donors. Democrats in the legislature with whom he worked successfully early in his term had now deserted his tent. Meanwhile, interest groups were spending millions of dollars on political advertising to sway voters' opinions against the governor and his proposed actions on school spending and political reforms. In the public's view, Schwarzenegger's agenda had been hijacked by partisan politics and the influence of special interests. His sky-high approval ratings at the start of the year fell sharply within the space of a few months, signaling that disappointed voters had found new reasons to distrust their state government and elected representatives.

Schwarzenegger failed to convince the legislature to adopt his overhaul of state government, which included reforming public employee pensions, imposing spending caps on the state budget, changing teachers' pay from a seniority-based to a merit system, and stripping Sacramento lawmakers of the authority for drawing the state's legislative districts. Rebuffed by legislative Democrats, he sought solace with conservatives and pro-business interests, who helped convince him to call a special election and financed his efforts to place the reform measures on the ballot as initiatives. Voters were unenthusiastic about the special election, and the governor's proposed reforms faced spirited opposition from labor unions. Schwarzenegger was forced to withdraw an initiative to change the public employee pension system because of the outcry that it would eliminate benefits for the families of police and fire-fighters killed in the line of duty. His teachers' merit pay proposal foundered and instead he shifted his support to a measure promoted by the pro-business group, lengthening the time required for teachers to earn tenure. He also adopted an initiative placed on the ballot by GOP and conservative interests that sought to restrict unions' ability to engage in political campaign funding.

A nasty, protracted battle between partisan and special interest groups ensued. On one side was a coalition of Republicans, conservatives, and business leaders who had formed a campaign committee to fund and promote the governor's measures. On the other side was an alliance of Democratic officials and labor unions who had joined forces to fight his reform agenda. Both sides spent record amounts on the initiative campaigns. Schwarzenegger's special election strategy failed: under heavy opposition from Democratic and independent voters, all of his measures were defeated in the special election. Its aftermath left voters even more cynical and alienated from their state government than before. In the end, Schwarzenegger apologized to Californians and signaled that he had learned an important lesson from the 2005 special election. He promised to work with the legislature and reach bipartisan compromises, rather than asking voters to settle the parties' and elected officials' differences at the ballot box through the initiative process.

DECLARING WAR
IN THE STATE OF THE STATE ADDRESS

"In every meeting I attend in Sacramento, there's an elephant in the room," Governor Schwarzenegger told state lawmakers assembled to hear his second State of the State address on January 5, 2005. "The elephant in the room is a budget system that has removed our ability to make the best decisions for California," he continued. "It has taken away the freedom and the responsibility of legislating. We can change that. My colleagues, I say to you, political courage is not political suicide. Ignore the lobbyists. Ignore the politics. Trust the people" (Schwarzenegger, "Governor Schwarzenegger's 2005 State of the State Address," 2005).

The governor had just announced that he was calling the legislature into a special session to work on overhauling the state government. He outlined a plan of four reforms he wanted to place on a special election ballot in the coming year, the first of which was doing away with the system of formulas that dictated how much the state must spend on certain programs in its annual budget. Schwarzenegger proposed a constitutional amendment that would override the formulas and impose across-the-board spending caps when state revenues fell short. It was a bold and risky move, taking on allocations for popular causes such as public schools, which had been put in place when voters passed the ballot-box budgeting Proposition 98 more than a decade earlier.[1]

The second reform outlined in Schwarzenegger's address involved the pension system for the state's public employees. Citing costs that had risen to $2.6 billion for the current year, the governor proposed changing from a defined benefits plan, which guaranteed a high level of retirement payments, to one in which benefits were matched to contributions, similar to private 401(k) plans. The change was proposed for new state employees and would not affect current workers. Nonetheless, it was certain to draw the anger of the state's sizeable public employee unions.

Schwarzenegger's third reform was to tie public school teachers' pay to their performance, giving bonuses to "excellent" teachers and making it easier to fire "ineffective" ones. This attempt to eliminate the tenure system that currently guaranteed teachers' jobs and based their pay on length of service, rather than merit, was seen as an affront to educators and a direct attack on the California Teachers Association. The governor also proposed increasing the number of charter schools and expanding vocational programs.

Rounding out his reform agenda, Schwarzenegger urged that the authority to draw legislative districts be taken away from state legislators and handed over to a panel of retired judges. This redistricting plan, he said, would result in "honest district lines" that would make "politicians of both parties accountable to the people." It was an obvious attempt to remove the gerrymandered borders that had kept Republicans from gaining any seats in the 2004 election. It was also a declaration of war on Democrats.

"I know the special interests will oppose all the reforms I have mentioned," Schwarzenegger declared during his annual address to legislators. "Any time you try to remove one dollar from the budget, there are five special interests tugging on the other end. Anytime you try to make something more efficient, there are a half-dozen special interests trying to prevent it. . . . The result is that nothing changes in Sacramento. This place is in the grip of the special interests."

Schwarzenegger went on to outline a series of reorganizations to state government, beginning with the corrections system, which he described as "an agency in which there has been too much political influence, too much union control and too little management courage and accountability." He also announced his intention to eliminate nearly a hundred state boards and commissions and "abolish over 1,000 political appointments in the process."

The governor concluded his address with what had become his characteristic challenge to California lawmakers, threatening to bypass them and go directly to the public in a special election if the legislature did not go along with his plans. "If we here in this chamber don't work together to reform the government, the people will rise up and reform it themselves," he warned. "And I will join them. And I will fight with them."

The tone of Schwarzenegger's 2005 State of the State address was a marked change from his speech given a year earlier. In contrast to the populist, "we're all in this together" approach of 2004, the governor's latest remarks were widely seen as partisan and divisive. Instead of portraying state leaders as working together to solve California's problems, he depicted a dysfunctional government in dire need of an overhaul. His unilateral agenda was a provocation to Democrats, who were still irate over his campaigning solely for Republicans in the previous November's election. To many, the governor's 2005 address was a signal that the era of bipartisan cooperation was over.

"Deep down inside, at the end of the day, I don't think we're going to be able to come to agreements," said then assemblyman Joe Canciamilla, (D-Pittsburg), generally considered a moderate (*San Francisco Chronicle*, January 7, 2005). In response, Democrats began preparing their own set of initiatives that brought up pieces of legislation Schwarzenegger had vetoed in the previous legislative session, such as prescription drug cost reform and increased rights for car buyers. Unions also gathered forces to challenge the perceived attack on their hegemony. The battle lines were being drawn.

Table 5.1: Reactions to 2005 "State of the State" Speech

"Overall, do you have a favorable or an unfavorable impression of the plans and policies for California that Governor Schwarzenegger presented in his 'State of the State' speech?"

	Adults	Democrats	Republicans	Independents
Favorable	42%	28%	68%	44%
Unfavorable	32	47	11	33
Don't know/didn't hear speech	26	25	21	23

"How would you vote on limiting the amount that the state could spend each year equal to the amount of revenue it receives, which would include across-the-board cuts when spending grows past revenues?"

	Adults	Democrats	Republicans	Independents
Yes	59%	49%	77%	65%
No	32	41	16	29
Don't know	9	10	7	6

"How would you vote on a legislative redistricting reform measure that requires an independent panel of three retired judges, instead of the state legislature and governor, to adopt a new redistricting plan?"

	Adults	Democrats	Republicans	Independents
Yes	44%	34%	56%	47%
No	41	53	30	41
Don't know	15	13	14	12

Source: PPIC Statewide Survey, January 2005.

As for the public, response was mixed. While four in ten Californians (42%) had a favorable impression of the overall plans laid out in Schwarzenegger's State of the State address, a sizeable 32 percent had an unfavorable impression (see table 5.1). Compared to his 2004 address, a similar proportion was favorable (44%), but nearly twice as many residents had a negative response now than in the previous year (18%). Likely voters were more enthusiastic about the governor's 2005 agenda, with 52 percent favorable, while 33 percent were unfavorable. However, the plans were much better received by Republicans (68%) and independents (44%) than by Democrats (28%), an indication that they were conjuring up a partisan division. What's more, disapproval of Schwarzenegger's plans among Democrats had grown twenty points since the previous January (27% to 47%).

The public's initial reaction to the fiscal reforms Schwarzenegger called for in his State of the State address was quite positive. Nearly six in ten adults (59%) and 64 percent of likely voters supported his proposal to impose spending caps and override funding mandates when revenues fell short (see table 5.1). Support was near a majority among Democrats (49%) and was considerably higher among independents (65%) and Republicans (77%). His proposal to change the defined benefit pension system for public employees was similarly favored, with 61 percent overall and 64 percent of likely voters saying they would vote yes. Support for this reform topped 50 percent in all political groups, with favor especially high among Republicans (72%).

However, opinions were divided on the topic of redistricting reform. Nearly equal numbers of adults supported (44%) and opposed (41%) the proposal to hand redistricting power to a panel of retired judges (see table 5.1). Likely voters were somewhat more inclined to vote yes than no (46% to 40%). While Republicans and independents tended to support the proposed redistricting reform, a majority of Democrats opposed it.

PROPOSED BUDGET FUELS
PARTISAN, INTEREST GROUP WRATH

On January 10, 2005, Schwarzenegger unveiled his proposed 2005 to 2006 state budget. The $109 billion spending plan included deep cuts in health and social services, lowered funding for schools, and a diversion of money from transportation projects into the general fund (Legislative Analyst's Office, 2005–06 Overview of the Governor's Budget," 2005).

"This budget is not everything I want," Schwarzenegger said in releasing his budget, "but the fact is, it's a budget forced on us by a broken system" (Schwarzenegger, "Governor's Remarks at the Release of his 2005–06 State Budget," 2005). The governor described his budget as "balanced" and pointed out that it did not raise taxes. But he admitted that the allocations for some programs proposed in his plan did not meet California's budget formula requirements, because to do so would have increased the state's debt. "Now those who want to keep on spending more money than we actually have will try to make you believe that this is a spending 'cut,'" he said. "It's not; we are increasing our spending by 4.2 percent." He outlined the budget's proposed increases over the previous year for education and social services, adding, "Of course we would like to spend more on these important services, but that's all the revenue we have and we must be fiscally responsible." He then launched into a diatribe on the "lunacy" of the current budget system and called for an end to the state's "autopilot" spending mandates. "I propose we fight fire with fire," he said, once again pushing for his plan of budget reform and spending caps. "Instead of a formula that forces us to spend more money, we should have a formula that forces us to live within our means."

Democratic lawmakers again took umbrage, maintaining that the budget unfairly targeted middle-class Californians by limiting funding for schools, transportation, and social services. The education community also jumped into the fray, accusing the governor of reneging on his agreement to restore the funds he "borrowed" to help balance the 2004 to 2005 budget. "Gov. Schwarzenegger has not only broken his promises to public school children, he proposes breaking the promise of California voters to provide a minimum amount of state funding to support public schools," said Jack O'Connell, state superintendent of public instruction. "This is unconscionable, not to mention a bad example for California's schoolchildren" (*Los Angeles Times*, January 11, 2005).

The public also took a dim view of the proposed 2005 to 2006 budget. In contrast to January 2004, when a majority (57%) of Californians were satisfied with the governor's 2004 to 2005 budget plan, a majority (55%) in a January 2005 survey were displeased with the current plan (see table 5.2). Only 38 percent of adults said they were satisfied with the 2005 to 2006 budget proposal. Likely voters were similarly negative (54% dissatisfied, 40% satisfied). Strong majorities of Democrats (74%) and independents

Table 5.2: Reactions to 2005–2006 Budget Proposal

"The governor recently proposed a budget that includes withholding money from education, reducing certain health and human services and general government spending, transferring a portion of gasoline sales tax, and using state bonds. In general, are you satisfied or dissatisfied with this budget plan?"

	Adults	Democrats	Republicans	Independents
Satisfied	38%	21%	62%	38%
Dissatisfied	55	74	32	54
Don't know	7	5	6	8

Source: PPIC Statewide Survey, January 2005.

(54%) disapproved of the new budget plan, while most Republicans (62%) were satisfied. However, compared to the previous year, significantly more Democrats (up thirty-two points), independents (up thirty-seven points), and even Republicans (up twenty-two points) were dissatisfied with the current budget proposal.

This frustration was echoed in residents' ratings of the way Schwarzenegger was handling the budget and taxes. Despite continued high marks for his overall performance in office (60% approving), ratings for the governor's actions on state fiscal issues slipped below a majority in the January 2005 survey, down six points from the previous year (54% to 48%). The percentage disapproving of the way Schwarzenegger was handling the budget and taxes rose to 41 percent—up fifteen points from one year earlier.

Concern over the effects of the budget cuts had also climbed. In January 2005, nearly three in four residents said they were either "very" (31%) or "somewhat" concerned (42%) that the proposed spending cuts would hurt state programs. Likely voters expressed similar levels of concern. One year earlier, two in three Californians were "very" (26%) or "somewhat" concerned (42%) about proposed cuts in the 2004 to 2005 budget. Apprehension over the 2005 to 2006 budget cuts was high among Democrats (88% very or somewhat concerned) and independents (72% very or somewhat concerned), and even 56 percent of Republicans were at least somewhat worried about the effects.

The January poll demonstrated that Californians still had major concerns about state spending and finances. Overall, seven in ten adults and 76 percent of likely voters called the budget gap a "big problem." Concern was high in all political and demographic groups. As for their preferred approach to the budget gap, 40 percent of adults and 43 percent of likely voters said the government should implement a mixture of spending cuts and tax increases, while 34 percent of adults and 37 percent of likely voters advocated spending cuts alone. Only 11 percent in either group thought the state's budget shortfall should be made up mostly through tax hikes. While Democrats (54%) and independents (41%) tended to opt for a mixture of spending cuts and tax increases, a majority of Republicans (55%) wanted the gap to be closed primarily with spending cuts.

Nonetheless, the public objected to funding reductions for most of the programs that make up the bulk of state spending. In fact, a majority of Californians favored increased state spending on K–12 public schools (62%) and pluralities wanted funding for health and human services (47%) and higher education (44%) to also be expanded. Fewer than one in five supported spending cuts for any of those areas. While Democrats and independents tended to be more supportive of increased spending overall, only one in three or fewer Republicans favored cuts for K–12 public education (18%), health and human services (34%), or public colleges and universities (25%).

As for where to raise taxes, Californians strongly favored increasing the tariff on cigarettes and alcohol (74%) and taking a greater portion of the income earned by the state's wealthiest residents (69%), with likely voters expressing similar support. Solid majorities in all parties favored boosting so-called sin taxes, while more than seven in ten Democrats (84%) and independents (73%)—and nearly half of Republicans (45%)—approved of raising the income tax rate on top earners. However, when it came to higher taxes on "ordinary" Californians, the attitudes voiced in the January 2005 survey sharply shifted. By a two-to-one margin (64% to 32%), residents opposed raising the state sales tax. A majority of Democrats (58%), Republicans (71%), and independents (62%) alike objected to this possible move. Once again, Californians expressed their desire to fund programs that benefited large numbers of residents with revenues raised from relatively few people.

Residents' seemingly contradictory tax and spending preferences were bolstered by their widespread belief that state government was wasting money. Nearly two in three (64%) in the January 2005 survey said they thought the government could spend less and still provide the same level of services. Of those who held this view, four in ten thought state spending could be cut between 10 and 20 percent and a quarter thought even greater cuts could be made without reducing public services. Meanwhile, voters were deeply divided along partisan lines on fiscal issues, with six in ten Democrats willing to pay higher taxes for a state government that provided more services and seven in ten Republicans preferring a state government with less services and lower taxes. Independents were split on this issue, with 49 percent preferring a larger, more comprehensive government and 43 percent wanting a leaner one. All political groups agreed on one point: two in three said that the voters should be making the long-term fiscal policy decisions, rather than the governor and legislature.

FALLING STAR

It wasn't long before the interest groups angered by Schwarzenegger's budget plan and reform proposals launched a counterattack on the governor. On January 18, 2005, a parade of black coffins followed by 1,500 nurses converged on the state capitol, accompanied by a band playing a death march. They were protesting Schwarzenegger's suspension of the nurse-to-patient ratio reductions announced at the end of 2004. Moreover, they were still irritated by the governor's "kicking their butts" comment the previous December. Meanwhile, the California Teachers Association began running ads on dozens of radio stations, accusing the governor of breaking his funding promise to schools. State workers started appearing around Sacramento in purple shirts, protesting the governor's plan to change their retirement system. And parents and schoolchildren sent stacks of letters to the governor's office, urging him to restore school funding to the level stipulated under Proposition 98.

Schwarzenegger responded by ratcheting up his tough-guy rhetoric and inching closer to political conservatives in attacking what he characterized as special interests and state bureaucracy. Telling the *Sacramento Bee* editorial board that his lean budget plan was designed to "starve the public sector" by cutting state spending and closing the budget deficit without raising taxes, Schwarzenegger declared that "we don't want to feed the monster" (*Sacramento Bee*, January 19, 2005). In the same interview, the governor referred to California attorney general Bill Lockyer, treasurer Phil Angelides, and superintendent of public instruction Jack O'Connell as "the Three Stooges" for criticizing his proposed budget. He blasted legislative Democrats for not joining his efforts to stand up to "special interests." With his characteristic self-assurance, he vowed: "This is going to be the year where things will change very drastically."

Like fuel to a fire, Schwarzenegger's hard line with his critics inflamed the opposition and helped it to spread. By March, his public appearances were routinely picketed by nurses and firefighters who were protesting his suspension of lowered patient ratios and his proposed changes to the retirement system for public employees. Democratic attorneys, meanwhile, were mounting a legal challenge to his prolific campaign fund-raising (*Los Angeles Times*, March 16, 2005). And teachers' unions were continuing to air ads accusing him of breaking his promise to California schools. More than a thousand protesters showed up at a Schwarzenegger fund-raiser at a Los Angeles hotel in March and as many as 2,500 paraded outside his appearance in San Jose two weeks later.

Over at the legislature, meanwhile, relations between Schwarzenegger and state lawmakers had cooled considerably. Three weeks into the special session the governor had called in January, he publicly berated legislators as having done little more than make "a lot of excuses, a lot of complaints, and a lot of finger pointing," and effectively gave them a March 1 deadline for acting on his proposals before he took the measures directly to the public. "I want to let everyone know that we are going to move ahead according to our plan," the governor told reporters gathered at a Sacramento Press Club luncheon that day, vowing that "when comes the beginning of March . . . we're going to go out and start gathering signatures. And I will be doing again what we did last year. You will see me at Costcos, you will see me at different shopping malls, and I will be out there gathering the signatures and helping, and making sure that we get all of those things on the ballot" (Schwarzenegger, "Governor's Remarks at the Sacramento Press Club Luncheon," 2005).

But this time, the leaders of the Democrat-controlled legislature did not respond to Schwarzenegger's threat. March 1, the deadline he had given legislators to act on his measures before he took them directly to the voters, came and went with no movement on either side. The governor did not even meet publicly with Senate and Assembly leaders to discuss his reform proposals until mid-March—well after he had begun touring the state in a Humvee called "Reform 1," pitching his initiatives. The evening before he was to have his first meeting to discuss his plans with state legislators, the governor announced on national television that he planned to call a special election "very soon" (*San Francisco Chronicle*, March 15, 2005). By the time Schwarzenegger and legislative leaders did meet, there seemed to be little interest in compromise on either side, despite the governor publicly planting a kiss on the cheek of Assembly speaker Fabian Núñez.

Meanwhile, Schwarzenegger's initiatives were advancing toward a special election ballot with the help of coalition of state business leaders, who endorsed the measures and donated funds toward signature-gathering efforts. The group, called Citizens to Save California, included the presidents of the California Chamber of Commerce and the California Business Roundtable, as well as Republican and conservative activist Joel Fox, a former president of the anti–property tax group, the Howard Jarvis Taxpayers Association. On March 1, the campaign committee announced its endorsement of an initiative to change the public employee pension system to a 401(k) type plan, one of Schwarzenegger's four main reform proposals outlined in January.

The initiative petition, written by Jon Coupal, then president of the Howard Jarvis Taxpayers Association, was to begin circulating for signatures immediately. The business group also announced that it would help promote signature-gathering for a measure seeking to lengthen the time required for public school teachers to earn tenure, although it did not address the "merit pay" provision advocated by Schwarzenegger (*Sacramento Bee*, March 1, 2005). Two weeks later, the group did add its endorsement to a teachers' merit pay measure, pledging to spend "whatever it takes" to qualify it and another measure requiring unions to get written permission from their members before using dues on political campaigns.[2] In addition, the group drafted and endorsed the "Live within our Means Act," a ballot measure inspired by Schwarzenegger's budget reform plan to limit state spending increases and give the governor new powers to cut the state budget. The initiative put forward by the business group would limit increases in state spending to the average of state revenue growth over the previous three years. The group also endorsed a version of the governor's proposed initiative to give the job of redistricting to a panel of retired judges (*Sacramento Bee*, March 17, 2005).

Although he continued to maintain that he was open to discussion and negotiations, Schwarzenegger seemed to be spoiling for a fight during the spring of 2005. When asked by a *Washington Post* reporter if he would be disappointed if a compromise solution denied him the chance to face off with his opponents in the legislature, he agreed, "There's something very attractive about it" (*Washington Post*, March 28, 2005). In that same interview, he reiterated his populist view of the conflict boiling down to "special interests" versus "the people," predicting that "They're going to fight for the status quo and for their power, and the people in the end will make the decision: Do we want to be ruled by the unions and by the special interests of California, or do we want to go and take the power back?"

The public, however, was losing confidence in their governor and seemed little inclined to join him in his partisan and special interest conflict. The April 2005 PPIC survey found Schwarzenegger's job approval rating had taken a twenty-point plunge since January, and now fewer than half of California adults (40%) liked the way he was performing in office (see table 5.3). One in two said they disapproved. While likely voters were slightly more favorable (45% approving, 47% disapproving) toward Schwarzenegger, their ratings still reflected an eighteen-point drop since January. Significantly, the governor's approval had taken a tumble in all political groups. While the drop-off was steepest among Democrats (43% to 24%) and independents (60% to 40%), even Republicans had lost considerable faith in the state's chief executive (88% to 71%). The governor now faced dismally high levels of disapproval in many key groups, including Democrats (68%), independent voters (49%), blacks (72%), Latinos (69%), and residents of the state's populous Los Angeles (55%) and San Francisco Bay Area (56%) regions.

The governor's ratings dropped even further when it came to the front-burner issue of the state's educational system. Only 28 percent of adults and 30 percent of likely voters approved of the way he was handling the matters

Table 5.3: Governor's Ratings in April 2005

"Do you approve or disapprove of the way that Arnold Schwarzenegger is handling . . . "

His Job as Governor of California

	Adults	Democrats	Republicans	Independents
Approve	40%	24%	71%	40%
Disapprove	50	68	20	49
Don't know	10	8	9	11

The State's K–12 Public Education System

	Adults	Democrats	Republicans	Independents
Approve	28%	14%	50%	28%
Disapprove	51	69	29	50
Don't know	21	17	21	22

Source: PPIC Statewide Survey, April 2005.

involving public schools, while a little more than half disapproved (see table 5.3). Democrats (69%) and independents (50%) took an especially dim view of the governor's performance in this area, while half of Republicans said they approved. Disapproval was also higher among blacks (69%) and Latinos (61%) than among the state's Asians (38%) and white residents (46%).

As further indication of declining public confidence in Schwarzenegger's approach to the state's most pressing issues, more Californians said that when it came to budget choices on taxes and funding for K–12 schools, they preferred the approach of legislative Democrats (38%) to that of the governor (24%) or that of Republicans in the legislature (15%). Likely voters had similar views. Significantly, while Democrats preferred that budget decisions be made by legislators from their own party (68%) and the governor was the top choice of Republicans (40%), independents sided with the legislature's Democrats (32%) more than with the governor (25%). And for setting policies on this issue that figured so prominently in the public's priorities, large majorities of residents and voters in all parties said they preferred major, long-term changes in the state's educational system to be made by voters at the ballot box (66% of adults, 65% of likely voters), rather than by the governor and legislature (21% of adults, 25% of likely voters).

FAILED NEGOTIATIONS

By the spring, declining public confidence, a well-organized opposition, and lack of cooperation from the legislature were knocking holes in Schwarzenegger's plans. In early April, he was forced to scrap one of the main pillars of his "year of reform." Shortly after another of his public appearances drew thousands of protesters—this time in San Francisco, where a crowd of largely union members blocked streets and flew an airplane with a banner proclaiming "Arnold, California is not for sale"—the governor announced that he was dropping his bid to reform the government pension system (*Sacramento Bee*, April 8, 2005). The rhetoric surrounding the measure had been ratcheted up by an advertising campaign launched a few days earlier, featuring tearful widows of police officers and firefighters killed in the line of duty. The ads maintained that Schwarzenegger's pension reform plan would eliminate death and disability payments for the families of fallen public safety officers. Although the governor attempted to reassure police and firefighters that the new pension system would not affect these payments, irreversible damage had been done by the measure's ballot summary, which stated clearly in the second sentence that the initiative "eliminated" such benefits.[3]

Meanwhile, the measure that was supposed to be the main engine of Schwarzenegger's year of reform—the balanced budget plan that was later put on the ballot in a somewhat different form by the Citizens to Save California—was also running into difficulty. Instead of the governor's proposal for automatic spending cuts that would be triggered whenever state revenues fell short, the initiative that was ultimately put forward limited budget growth to the average of the amount that state revenues had increased over the previous three years. The measure sparked divisions among Republicans and business leaders, with one prominent group having written and sponsored the initiative while others criticized it as not doing enough to control state spending and putting up a rival measure. In addition, the budget reform measure was suffering a ballot label woe similar to that which had doomed the pension reform plan. The title that attorney general Bill Lockyer assigned to the measure, as it began to circulate for signatures, focused on the narrower and more controversial issue of school funding and state spending, and the ballot summary dealt with how the measure would change the minimum school funding requirements imposed by Proposition 98. With K–12 education repeatedly emerging in PPIC surveys as the public's top budget priority, the implication that the measure would cut money for schools was certain to draw fire.

The governor's touted education reform, in the shape of merit pay for teachers, was also foundering. The plan to tie teachers' compensation to their performance, rather than seniority, had drawn such acrimony from the powerful teachers union that Schwarzenegger had backed away from it. Instead, he shifted his school reform plans to stretching new teachers' probationary periods from two to five years—an issue that also had limited appeal to voters. And by late April, he had backpedaled on his plan to change the state's legislative districting system, saying he was willing to delay the timetable for its implementation rather than have it go into effect in 2006.

The direct democracy tactic that had worked so well for Schwarzenegger in 2004—threatening to go to the voters to pass initiatives if there was no legislative action on his proposals—seemed to have lost its magic because the governor seemed to have lost the trust of the public. Rather than rushing to the bargaining table when the governor threatened to bypass their authority and appeal directly to voters, the Democratic lawmakers controlling the state legislature now seemed to be calling his bluff. Their change of heart had its roots at the end of the previous year, when the limits of Schwarzenegger's powers with the voters became apparent after his partisan foray in the November election failed to pick up any Republican seats. Now, Democratic legislators were further emboldened when the governor's approval ratings began to drop in response to coordinated attacks by separate, well-organized interest groups.

Schwarzenegger's efforts to portray teachers, public employees, nurses, and other union members as "special interests" fighting for the status quo galvanized these normally disparate groups into a powerful coalition, with enormous resources and energy to fight his proposals. While the unions flooded the airwaves with millions of dollars in ads criticizing the governor and dogged his campaign efforts with protesters, Democratic legislators worked with their long-time political allies behind the scenes to derail his year of reform. Publicly declaring their desire to collaborate with the governor, Democratic legislators privately turned him a deaf ear. The public seemed to side with the groups who described the governor's motives as partisan and favoring conservative interests.

Finding no partner for negotiations on the Democrats' side of the table, Schwarzenegger withdrew into the fold of pro-business groups and political conservatives that had allied to promote his reform agenda. His rightward drift had begun the previous year, in response to suggestions by his political advisors, themselves long-time partisan Republicans, that he increase his political clout by allying himself more closely with the Republican Party. In a series of meetings in August 2005 described by political commentator Bill Bradley, Schwarzenegger's advisors capitalized on his impatience with the slow pace of change in Sacramento by counseling him to align himself more closely with the Republican Party.[4] As the governor's political shift continued throughout the spring of 2005, his rhetoric grew increasingly conservative and partisan. On a conservative talk radio program in April, for instance, he taunted Democrats and angered Latinos by lambasting illegal immigrants and praising the efforts of the "Minutemen"—a private citizens' militia that patrolled the Mexican border. Schwarzenegger told the hosts of the talk radio program that he was troubled by a recent Fox News television broadcast showing "hundreds and hundreds of illegal immigrants coming across the border" and went on to criticize the federal government for not doing enough to stop the flow. Asked how he would like to address the problem, the governor said, "The most important thing is what they're doing with the Minutemen now . . . have more people controlling it."[5] Schwarzenegger had requested the radio appearance to protest television station billboards advertising the station's news coverage of "Los Angeles, Mexico," which he maintained was encouraging illegal immigration. It was a jarring departure from his moderate and independent reform agenda, and recalled the tactics of former Republican governor Pete Wilson, who had exploited the immigration issue to drum up GOP support for his reelection in 1994. In particular, Wilson had run television ads showing shadowy figures running across a freeway, with a voice-over saying, "They just keep coming." The campaign led to the passage of Proposition 187, which denied public services to undocumented aliens, and helped Wilson overcome sagging ratings and win the race.

Now it appeared that Schwarzenegger was trying the same strategy of raising hot-button conservative issues in an effort to divert attention from his own flailing campaign. The partisan divide was becoming a ravine, interest groups had taken center stage for and against the governor, and his populist theme was on hold. For voters, this return to "politics as usual" was reinforcing their feelings of distrust in state government.

INITIATIVES QUALIFY

In early May, Schwarzenegger began to turn in the signatures needed to qualify his measures for a ballot. The first to be handed in were for his initiative to lengthen the probationary period for teachers. On May 4, echoing the theme from his successful Proposition 49 campaign three years earlier, schoolchildren pulling little red wagons helped deliver petitions with 26,000 signatures to the Sacramento County registrar of voters. This time, however, the mood was shattered by the shouts of union protesters from the sidelines.[6] The rest of the 350,000 signatures were delivered to other counties around the state. In the next few days, supporters delivered petitions for Schwarzenegger's "Live within Our Means" act and his measure seeking to strip legislators of the power to draw legislative and congressional districts.

The prospect of a November special election drew several other initiatives that had qualified for placement on the next available ballot. These included the measure requiring public employee unions to obtain members' written permission every year to use their dues for political campaigns. The measure, written by Lewis Uhler, a well-known and highly active antitax advocate, had not yet received Schwarzenegger's endorsement. But unions, whose political clout would be decimated by the measure, vowed to blame the governor if it made the ballot (*Los Angeles Times*, May 6, 2005).

By May 10, the unofficial deadline for submitting signatures for a possible November 8 election, eight measures had been put forward. In addition to the Schwarzenegger and Uhler initiatives, elections officials had received petitions for a union- and consumer group–backed measure to lower prescription drug prices, as well as another sponsored by a coalition of pharmaceutical companies aimed at defeating the first measure. The ballot was rounded out by an initiative requiring parental notification when minor girls sought an abortion and another seeking to reregulate the state's electricity utilities (*Los Angeles Times*, May 11, 2005).

With the signatures submitted for verification, the action now shifted back to the legislature, where lawmakers had about a month-long window to negotiate with the governor and avoid a special election. Schwarzenegger said he would make his decision on whether to call a November election by the middle of June.

THE MAY BUDGET REVISIONS

With his initiative petitions now in the hands of state election officials, the governor turned his attention to the budget. On May 13, a Friday, an upbeat Schwarzenegger released a revised budget proposal that included an extra $4 billion in state revenues. The unexpected funds were part of what he said was a more than $6 billion increase in state revenues over the previous year, demonstrating the success of his economic programs. "In just one year we have gone from the brink of bankruptcy to the strength of success," he said in his presentation to the legislature. Schwarzenegger described his revised $115.7 billion spending plan for the 2005 to 2006 fiscal year as "a budget that will rebuild California." He went on to call it, "a responsible budget that pays down our debt and contains no new borrowing." His goal, he said, was a "prudent budget that uses one-time revenues for one-time expenditures and it does not make long-term commitments the state can't keep" (Schwarzenegger, "Governor's Remarks at May Budget Revise," 2005).

The new budget proposal contained more funding for prisons and a restoration of $1.3 billion in Proposition 42 gasoline tax funds for transportation that had earlier been appropriated into the general fund. It included an early payback of money owed to cities and counties under the deal the governor negotiated the previous year. It restored funds for health and social services that had been cut under his January proposal. And it would give nearly $50 million in grants to help the lowest-performing schools recruit and retain teachers and principals (California Department of Finance, "Governor's Budget, May Revision 2005–06," 2005).

As for schools, the governor announced that funding for K–12 education would increase by nearly $3 billion from 2004 to 2005 and maintained that schools were receiving nearly $500 million more than the allocation stipulated by Proposition 98. But the legislative analyst's report concluded that the revised budget contained little change from January in the amount of Proposition 98 funding (Legislative Analyst's Office, "Overview of the 2005–06 May Revision," 2005).

Education officials immediately denounced the governor as continuing to renege on his promise to restore the $2 billion they believed they were owed from the previous year. And Democrats dug in for a battle. "The governor has broken his promise to public education once again," Assembly speaker Núñez said after the revised budget release. "He's clearly not listening to our teachers and certainly not listening to our children" (*Sacramento Bee*, May 14, 2005).

In response to the governor's revised budget, some Democratic lawmakers proposed placing a tax increase for schools on the ballot if a special election were called in November. And the Senate budget subcommittee on education, in an act of open defiance to the governor, voted to put an additional $2 billion into the education budget.

PARTISAN FALLING-OUT

The atmosphere in Sacramento became even more poisoned the following Monday, when Schwarzenegger advisor Mike Murphy hinted that the governor was planning to endorse the Uhler initiative requiring unions to get members' permission to use their dues for political campaigns. Until that point, the governor had not taken a position on the so-called paycheck protection initiative, although speculation was that he supported it because it was being promoted by Joel Fox, a major player in the Citizens to Save California. His endorsement of the measure would amount to a direct attack on legislative Democrats, for whom unions provided a major source of campaign funds. "Arnold has not touched the legislature with a feather yet compared to what the real campaign will be," Murphy told reporters at the state capitol. "It's a referendum on the governor versus the legislature, and he will win" (*Los Angeles Times*, May 17, 2005). The Democratic reaction was an immediate attack on the governor's actions.

"It is no more about putting an end to bipartisan bickering in Sacramento; it's now about let's see who is tougher, who can punch harder," said Assembly speaker Núñez, insisting that the possibility of compromise was "now behind us" (*San Francisco Chronicle*, May 18, 2005). Democrats charged Schwarzenegger with lying to them about his involvement with the union dues measure. The governor countered that education officials, and by implication the Democratic lawmakers allied with them, were distorting the truth about his fateful promise to schools. "I did not break a promise like they keep saying," he said during an appearance at a Sacramento-area school (*San Francisco Chronicle*, May 18, 2005). Schwarzenegger maintained that his agreement was to pay back the $2 billion over several years, not the current year, as education activists and many Democrats were now claiming.

The prospect of successful budget negotiations and a state spending plan in place by the start of the new fiscal year July 1 had become remote and a special election was now all but certain. All the acrimony in Sacramento had soured Californians' mood about the state of the state. In a May 2005 survey, more than half of residents (57%) said things were headed in the wrong direction. Only 35 percent thought things were going well in the state, which was the lowest this measure had been since Schwarzenegger took office. The percentage with a negative assessment of the state's direction had climbed sixteen points since the beginning of the year (41% to 57%). While Republicans still tended to have a positive outlook (50%), two in three Democrats (68%) and 57 percent of independents thought things were not going well. This view was shared by a majority of residents in all regions of the state, although those in the urban coastal areas of San Francisco Bay Area (60%) and Los Angeles (60%) regions tended to be more negative than those in the Central Valley (53%) and other Southern California counties (53%).

Economic confidence also had plunged. Half of residents now expected bad financial times in the year ahead, while only 39 percent forecast good times. Gloomy predictions had risen ten points since January (39% to 49%). Likely voters were somewhat more positive than the general public in May, with 44 percent anticipating good times and 45 percent expecting bad times for the state's fiscal conditions. But while a majority of Republicans were optimistic (58%), most Democrats (57%) and independents (50%) took the opposite view. And pessimism was higher in the governor's home region of Los Angeles (52%) than elsewhere in the state.

Schwarzenegger's ratings, meanwhile, remained at the low point they had reached in April, with only 40 percent approving of the way he was handling his job as governor, while nearly half (49%) disapproved. This was a twenty-four-point drop from the proportion giving him a positive evaluation one year ago (64%). Likely voters in May 2005 were slightly more favorable, with 45 percent approving and 46 percent disapproving of the governor's overall performance in office. As in April 2005, a majority of Republicans approved (72%), while Democrats (68%) and independents (48%) tended to have a negative view of the governor's job performance.

While the governor's overall job performance ratings were negative, the legislature's approval ratings were even worse. Only 26 percent of Californians in May 2005 liked the way the state lawmaking body was doing its job, while 58 percent disapproved. This was an eleven-point drop in approval since January 2005 (37%) and the lowest point measured in PPIC surveys since August 2003 (28%). Likely voters were even more disapproving, with 63 percent giving the legislature a thumbs-down and only 24 percent favorable about its performance. A majority of Republicans (69%), independents (61%), and Democrats (54%) were now disapproving of the legislature's job performance.

As for specific issues, the governor's ratings in May 2005 were lower than his overall evaluation in all but one area. Fewer than three in ten adults approved of the way he was handling transportation (28%) and public schools (29%), and only 31 percent gave him positive marks for handling illegal immigration. On the state budget and taxes, 37 percent approved of his performance. Schwarzenegger's highest ratings in May were for his efforts at government reform. On this topic, 40 percent approved of his performance—the same as his overall job approval ratings.

The May 2005 ratings reflected precipitous drops since the January survey in approval for the governor's handling of government reform (down eighteen points) and the state budget (down eleven points). His approval ratings also declined for handling transportation (down seven points) and public schools (down five points). Likely voters in May were slightly more favorable about the governor's performance in all these areas (government reform 47%, state budget 42%, illegal immigration 36%, public education 33%, transportation 29%), but fewer than half gave him positive ratings in any area.

While Republicans remained generally favorable about their governor in all these areas, Democrats were strongly disapproving across the board. Independent voters also were more negative than positive about the governor's job performance in all but one area—government reform—where nearly half said they liked the job he was doing.

CALLING AN UNPOPULAR SPECIAL ELECTION

In late May, Schwarzenegger gave further indications of his intentions when he embarked on a three-state fund-raising tour to collect money for a special election. At events in Florida, Texas, and Illinois, the governor met with business leaders and GOP luminaries, hoping to raise an estimated $30 million for his reform plans (*Sacramento Bee*, May 20, 2005).

Democrats fumed. While the governor was away, actor Warren Beatty jumped into the escalating acrimony, declaring at a UC Berkeley commencement speech that Schwarzenegger was "bullying labor and the little guys," while endorsing "the reactionary right wing." Beatty went on to hint that he might consider his own run for governor, saying, "I'd do a hell of a lot better job than he's done" (*San Francisco Chronicle*, May 22, 2005). Meanwhile, foes of Schwarzenegger's reform plans continued their vociferous protests, with thousands of nurses, teachers, firefighters, police officers, students, and public employees showing up at rallies in Sacramento and Los Angeles.[7]

In the legislature, the Democratic majority was so angered by Schwarzenegger's special election that virtually all of his attempts at enacting legislation were automatically rejected. Among the governor's proposed programs that were eliminated during May budget hearings was a nonpartisan plan to have local farms provide fresh fruit for schoolchildren, a Democrat-friendly initiative to help lower prescription drug costs for senior citizens, and plans to fund nurse training programs at community colleges. The legislature's out-of-hand rejection of such programs was widely seen as an effort to prevent the governor from accomplishing anything that would increase his standing with the public. "Partisanship poisoned the waters," said a disappointed spokesman for the American Association of

Retired Persons, which had championed the discounted prescription drug plan (*Los Angeles Times*, May 31, 2005).

The governor countered with a television ad accusing Democrats of catering to unions and planning to raise taxes. Earlier, he had lambasted legislators for raising their own salaries, even though the pay increase was decreed by an independent state commission, rather than by the legislators themselves. As the rhetoric heated up, the budget remained stalled in the legislature and Sacramento had reverted to its customary partisan gridlock. But emboldened by the success he had enjoyed with his ballot measures in 2004, when distrustful voters had supported his populist appeals to send legislators a message, Schwarzenegger was undeterred in his path to a special election.

The governor's march toward a ballot showdown was further propelled by pressure from Republican conservatives, who warned him that a retreat on his reform agenda could be the death of his political career. "If it doesn't happen, the governor has a credibility issue," said Jon Fleishman, author of the conservative weblog FlashReport (*San Francisco Chronicle*, June 7, 2005). Conservative Republicans and political action groups, such as the national antitax group Club for Growth, were pushing for Schwarzenegger's three reform initiatives on state spending caps, teachers' tenure, and redrawing legislative districts. The groups were also actively supporting the "paycheck protection initiative" restricting the political use of union members' dues, even though the governor had still not publicly endorsed that measure.

As the president of the Club for Growth's California chapter, former state assemblyman Tony Strickland, put it, a special election would send a message to the nation. "Arnold Schwarzenegger is a good salesman for our message," Strickland told club members at a June meeting. "With Arnold Schwarzenegger's success, we will be able to make sure we will win California in 2008 and send [Democratic U.S. senator from New York] Hillary Clinton packing" (*San Francisco Chronicle*, June 7, 2005).

On Friday, June 10, the last of Schwarzenegger's initiatives were certified by the California Secretary of State as qualified for a November ballot. That same day, Democratic lawmakers abruptly changed their tone and made conciliatory efforts toward the governor's budget. In dropping their demand for an extra $3 billion in education funding and accepting a version of the budget similar to Schwarzenegger's proposal, Democrats were hoping to avoid being seen as obstructionists. "We're not going to delay the budget simply because Republicans and the governor are turning their backs on the will of the people of California," Assembly speaker Fabian Núñez told reporters at a press conference that day (*Sacramento Bee*, June 11, 2005).

But it was too late for compromise. On June 13, the governor held a televised press conference announcing that he was calling a special election for November 8. In an odd twist of fate, Schwarzenegger's proclamation was upstaged by the news that a Los Angeles jury had acquitted singer Michael Jackson of child molestation charges that day. Every major Los Angeles station, and several others around the state, chose to go with coverage of the Jackson verdict, rather than broadcast the governor's speech live.

Schwarzenegger soldiered on with his vision of a people's revolt. "In my state of the state speech in January, I said that if the Legislature did not act on reforms this year, the people of California would," Schwarzenegger announced in his capitol address that day. "The people are the ones who wield the power. The people are the ones who can cut through the chains of politics and the past. It is from the people that a democracy gets its strength." Buoyed by what he perceived was a flood tide of populism, the governor declared, "With those millions of people who signed petitions standing behind me, today I signed a proclamation calling for a special election." In concluding, he promised that, "With the people's help, there will be reform" (Schwarzenegger, "Governor Schwarzenegger's Address," 2005). The statewide special election called by Schwarzenegger was the fifth in California history. Previous special elections had been held in 1973, 1979, 1993, and 2003, the recall in which Schwarzenegger himself was elected.

In tying his political future to a special election, Schwarzenegger was playing a risky game. Gambling on legislating by initiative had not always paid off for previous governors. Two notable attempts—by former governors Ronald Reagan and Pete Wilson—had opposite outcomes. In 1973, the Republican Reagan called a special election on a spending and tax-limiting initiative. The complicated measure was staunchly opposed by Democrats and it lost by a margin of 54 to 46 percent.[8] Two decades later, Wilson scored a victory with a special election he called on a measure to help fund public safety with a state sales tax extension. This time, the Republican governor reached across the aisle and lined up bipartisan support before the election. The measure passed in 1983 with a 58 to 42 percent vote.

In contrast to Wilson, whom Schwarzenegger often referred to as his mentor, this governor was heading into a special election in a bitterly partisan environment. His months of muscle flexing and name-calling had alienated Democrats and his proposed reforms threatened their allies. The rival party was in no mood to support this Republican's plans.

Schwarzenegger had also failed to warm the public to his special election. By nearly a two-to-one margin, Californians in the May survey thought it was better to wait until the next scheduled election in June 2006 (61%) than to call a special election in November (33%) (see table 5.4). The views of likely voters were similar: 33 percent favoring a November special election and 62 percent preferring to wait until the following year. The climate for the special election had changed considerably since Schwarzenegger first promoted it in January, having dropped twelve points from the 45 percent favoring the idea

Table 5.4: Special Election Plans

"Governor Schwarzenegger is considering a special election in fall 2005 to vote on budget, educational, and governmental reform measures. Do you think it is better to have a special election later this year, or is it better to wait until the next scheduled statewide election in June 2006?"

	Adults	Democrats	Republicans	Independents
Special election in 2005	33%	24%	46%	37%
Wait until 2006 scheduled election	61	72	49	58
Don't know	6	4	5	5

Source: PPIC Statewide Survey, May 2005.

in January. Even more ominous was the special election's failure to draw majority support from any political party. Only 24 percent of Democrats, 37 percent of independents, and 46 percent of Republicans thought it was better to call a special election right away than to wait.

THE INITIATIVE CAMPAIGNS

Governor Schwarzenegger launched the campaign for his roster of initiatives on the special election ballot with an effort to cast them as protection for Proposition 13. Speaking to a group of elderly homeowners in Santee, a small town near San Diego, he warned that Democrats were plotting to weaken the landmark measure's restrictions on property tax increases. "I tell them, 'Don't you dare touch Proposition 13, because the people of California voted to protect their homes,'" Schwarzenegger told an audience of about twenty-five people on June 14, the day after he announced he was calling a special election in November. Democratic legislators, driven by their union allies, are overspending state funds, he maintained, and "There's no way to pay for that spending without huge tax increases. That's why the state needs a fundamental change like the governor's budget initiative" (*San Francisco Chronicle*, June 15, 2005).

Democratic leaders were outraged, countering that the governor's initiatives had nothing to do with Proposition 13, and accused him of trying to scare voters. In reality, Proposition 13's caps on property tax increases could not be changed without a public vote.

A few days later, the governor appeared to be making an effort at conciliation with Democratic legislators, admitting that he deserved some of the blame for the divisive atmosphere in the state capitol. "I guarantee you that all of us in this building can share blame," Schwarzenegger said at a June 21, 2005, press conference called in an effort to restart stalled negotiations on the state budget, "All of us, including myself" (*Sacramento Bee*, June 22, 2005).

But the budget, then a week past the legislature's constitutional deadline for passing a spending plan for the upcoming fiscal year, remained stalled. Although Democratic legislators had earlier dropped their demands for more education funding and had put forth a budget bill similar to what the governor had proposed, Republican lawmakers defeated that bill in a June 15 vote, calling for further spending cuts (*Los Angeles Times*, June 16, 2005). Nearly a month of partisan rancor would ensue before the budget was finally signed on July 11, 2005, eleven days into the new fiscal year.

"No single budget can fix a broken system scheduled to put our state into a deficit year after year," Schwarzenegger said after signing the new budget. "We need budget reform to fix our broken system. Let's keep our momentum going by working together to reform the budget once and for all" (*Los Angeles Times*, July 12, 2005). It was still Schwarzenegger's hope that Democratic legislators would take up his call for budget reform and place compromise measures on the special election ballot. They had until the August 15 ballot deadline to do so. If a deal could be reached in time, the governor promised to drop his original initiatives and campaign in bipartisan unity for the new ones.

Meanwhile, another of the governor's reform proposals was running into trouble. The previous Friday, attorney general Bill Lockyer had filed suit to block Proposition 77, the redistricting measure. The suit charged that Proposition 77 violated the state constitution because the wording on the version circulated for signature-gathering was different from the text that had been approved by the attorney general's office (*Associated Press*, July 9, 2005). Lockyer's suit asked that the measure be stricken from the November ballot. Schwarzenegger's staff members and leaders of the campaign promoting the measure admitted that a clerical error had sent the wrong version of the initiative to the printer. Ted Costa, head of the antitax group, People's Advocate, which had put up the measure with the help of Citizens to Save California, said that his office manager had made the mistake. He maintained that the differences in the two versions were minor and would not mislead voters. But on July 21, 2005, a Sacramento County Superior Court judge ruled that the initiative should not be allowed on the November ballot (*Los Angeles Times*, July 22, 2005).[9] With Democrats now feeling victorious in derailing a second item on Schwarzenegger's reform agenda, the prospect of compromise on the remaining measures receded.

While the fate of Schwarzenegger's initiative was being decided in the courts, other interest groups were seizing the opportunity provided by the special election to advance their own causes. A coalition of pharmaceutical companies had amassed more than $53 million to fight Proposition 79, the prescription drug discount measure put up by the unions (*San Francisco Chronicle*, July 13, 2005). The group's strategy was to campaign heavily for Proposition 78, a rival initiative it had placed on the ballot, in hope of either getting their less restrictive measure passed or confusing voters into voting no on both propositions.

In addition to the dueling drug initiatives was Proposition 73, a measure sponsored by antiabortion groups that would require parents be notified when their minor child was seeking an abortion and prohibit the procedure from taking place until forty-eight hours after the notification had been made. Proposition 80, backed by consumer groups, sought to partially reregulate California's electricity. And Proposition 75, which the governor still had not officially endorsed, would force unions to get written permission from their members before using money paid in dues for political purposes. Added to Schwarzenegger's three initiatives—Proposition 74, the teachers tenure measure, Proposition 76, imposing spending caps, and Proposition 77, the redistricting measure—a total of eight ballot measures were beginning to fire up their campaign machines and aim for voters' attention in the November 8 election (California Secretary of State, "Initiative Update," 2005).

Shortly before the August 15 deadline for the legislature to place a compromise measure on the ballot, Schwarzenegger made a last, desperate attempt to reach a deal with Democratic lawmakers.[10] The governor called on former Assembly speaker Bob Hertzberg, a Democrat, to serve as a negotiator, and the two met several times with Assembly speaker Núñez and finance director Tom Campbell to hammer out compromise measures. But despite a three-day extension on the ballot deadline, the two sides were unable to close the partisan gap and on August 18, Schwarzenegger conceded that the talks had failed and his measures would stand in November.

The campaigns for and against the measures on the special election ballot began in earnest. But the governor appeared to be outflanked from the start. By mid-September, when Schwarzenegger officially kicked off the campaign for his reform initiatives, a coalition of public employee unions and teachers had already earmarked more than $52 million toward defeating Schwarzenegger's measures. This was twice the amount that had been raised to support the measures (*Los Angeles Times*, September 13, 2005).

Schwarzenegger's performance ratings had reached a new low in an August 2005 survey, with 34 percent of Californians approving and 54 percent disapproving of the way he was handling his job. This was a six-point drop in approval since May. Similarly, 35 percent of Californians in the August survey liked the way he was handling the issue of reforming the state government, while 50 percent disapproved. This was a five-point drop from May. Likely voters were somewhat more favorable toward the governor on both measures, but still, about half disapproved.

But Californians continued to be even more negative toward the state legislature than the governor. In the August survey, only 27 percent overall approved of the way the legislature was doing its job, while 56 percent disapproved. These approval ratings were as low as they had been in August 2003, just before the recall, when 28 percent gave the legislature a positive job rating. In the August 2004 survey, by contrast, 42 percent approved of the way the legislature was doing its job. The legislature's approval dropped even lower among likely voters in August 2005, with only 23 percent positive and 64 percent giving negative ratings. Approval was low in all political groups.

The months of bickering in Sacramento had done little to restore Californians' faith in their government. In the August 2005 survey, only three in ten said they trusted the state government to do what is right always or most of the time (see table 5.5). Confidence was even lower among likely voters (24%) and was similar across political party groups. When they voted to recall Governor Davis in October 2003, 27 percent of Californians expressed trust in Sacramento. Public confidence in state government had been significantly higher in January 2002 (47%) and January 2001 (46%), before the decline that began during the 2002 election.

Most Californians also continued to think that their state government was in the sway of a few big interests (65%), rather than benefiting all the people (26%). This perception had held steady since the days of the recall (65% in January 2004) and was markedly higher than in January 2002 (54%) or January 2001 (60%). Likely voters in August 2005 were even more inclined than all adults to think the government was being run by special interests (71%). Sizeable majorities across party groups held this view.

The clash between special interests reached a new level in mid-September, when the governor officially endorsed Proposition 75. This measure, restricting public employee unions' ability to use member dues for political purposes, had long been a goal of Republicans and business groups seeking to remove a major source of funding for Democrats, and a similar initiative failed at the ballot a few years earlier (see Broder 2000). Playing on Californians' perceptions of state government being in the clutch of special interests, Schwarzenegger characterized himself as a political outsider crusading against the power of corrupt "union bosses" (*Los Angeles Times*, September 18, 2005).

Table 5.5: Trust in State Government

"How much of the time do you think you can trust the government in Sacramento to do what is right?"

	Adults	Democrats	Republicans	Independents
Just about always/most of the time	30%	27%	28%	27%
Only some of the time	62	65	64	64
None of the time (volunteered)	5	5	6	9
Don't know	3	3	2	0

Source: PPIC Statewide Survey, August 2005.

Unions responded to the governor's endorsement by firing up three new television ads featuring a teacher, a nurse, and a firefighter maintaining that Proposition 75 would stifle the voices of the people who work to protect the state. They also announced they were preparing a counterinitiative that would prohibit corporations from using funds for political causes without getting shareholders' approval (*Los Angeles Times*, October 3, 2005). According to reports filed with the California Secretary of State, as of September 24, 2005, unions and their Democratic allies had amassed more than $21 million to fight the union dues initiative, while the Yes on 75 committee had raised a little over $1 million (*Sacramento Bee*, October 1, 2005).

While Schwarzenegger and the unions were the headline bout, the same report showed that special interest groups promoting the other initiatives on the November ballot had also been busy. Since the beginning of the year, the group of abortion opponents supporting Proposition 73 had raised a total of $1.2 million, while their opponents had raised $1.3 million to fight the parental-notification measure. The war chest of the pharmaceutical companies fighting Proposition 79 and promoting their own rival measure had swollen to more than $80 million. Teachers had dedicated $5.5 million to fight Proposition 74, the tenure initiative, and unions and Democrats had gathered more than $14 million to defeat Proposition 76, the spending reform initiative. And Schwarzenegger had written a check for $1.25 million out of his own funds to promote Proposition 77, his redistricting measure (*Los Angeles Times*, September 24, 2005).

VOTERS' VIEWS ON THE SPECIAL ELECTION

As the campaign for the initiatives on the special election ballot proceeded, even though most did not approve of this specific use of the initiative process, Californians expressed considerable confidence in their system of direct democracy. Nearly six in ten adults (57%) and likely voters (58%) in the August 2005 survey said they thought public policy decisions made through the initiative process were probably better than those made by their elected leaders. Only one in four said such decisions were probably worse. This belief had been fairly consistent in PPIC surveys for the past five years and did not reflect influence by the events of the spring and summer. Faith in the initiative process was high in all political parties, as well as all age, income, education, and racial groups.

In fact, the public wanted the role of initiatives in setting state policy to increase. In the August 2005 survey, most respondents thought the governor (34%) or state legislature (35%) had the greatest power in making policy decisions, while only 19 percent said that initiatives had the biggest influence. However, asked in a September survey what their preferred balance of power would be, 39 percent said they wanted initiatives to have the most influence over public policy in California and 32 percent opted for the legislature. Only 18 percent said they wanted the governor to play the biggest role in the state's public decisions. Thus, there was a twenty-point gap between the public's preferences and perceptions on the role of initiatives in governing California.

Likely voters were even more adamant about setting policy at the ballot box, with 42 percent saying initiatives should have the greatest influence, 35 percent opting for the legislature, and only 16 percent choosing the governor. Support for the governor's influence on state policy had actually declined by five points among adults in the previous year, at a time when approval of Schwarzenegger had declined sharply. In a September 2004 survey, 23 percent preferred to have the governor wield the most power. Even Republicans were not their governor's staunch supporters in the fall of 2005—46 percent preferred policy to be decided by initiatives over the governor (21%) or the legislature (24%). Democrats (13%) and independents (20%) showed even less support for the governor, but favored the legislature over initiatives by a slight margin. Californians clearly considered initiatives as a way to compensate for what they saw as a state government that was failing to focus on the issues they considered most important. In the September 2005 survey, 74 percent of adults and 79 percent of likely voters said that initiatives brought up important public policy issues that the governor and legislature were not addressing adequately. This perception was shared by more than three in four in all political groups and solid majorities across demographic categories. Nonetheless, Californians acknowledged that the system of citizens' legislation was not perfect. Only about one in ten adults and likely voters in the August survey said they were "very satisfied" with the way the initiative process was working, while most (58% of adults, 60% of likely voters) were "somewhat satisfied." Twenty-six percent in each group said they were not satisfied with the process at the time. Again, these views did not seem to be affected by the impending special election—Californians were as satisfied with the initiative system at the time as they had been for the past five years. However, Republicans in August 2005 expressed greater satisfaction with the process (78% very satisfied or somewhat satisfied) than did Democrats (61%) or independents (66%).

Californians' awareness of the flaws in their system of direct democracy continued to be apparent in the September 2005 survey, with 29 percent of adults and 28 percent of likely voters saying major changes were needed. Another 34 percent of adults and 36 percent of likely voters said minor changes were needed. However, the number saying the system was fine the way it was had actually increased over the past year—rising from 21 percent in a September 2004 survey to 29 percent in September 2005. Democrats (69%) and independents (64%) were more likely than Republicans (58%) in 2005 to see a need for change.

One of the problems for Californians was that their state ballots were often crowded with initiatives. More than six in ten adults (62%) and likely voters (61%) in the September survey said there generally were too many propositions on the state ballot. A majority in all parties agreed. An even bigger problem was the wording for citizens' initiatives, which more than three in four adults (77%) and likely voters (82%) said was often too complicated and confusing for voters to understand a measure's impact. Again, solid majorities in all parties held this view, and the perception rose with age, education, and income. Californians also were very concerned about special interests exerting their influence over the initiative process. A majority of adults (56%) and even more likely voters (65%) believed that special interests had "a lot" of control over initiatives—a perception that had risen four points since January 2001. Nonetheless, more than six in ten adults and likely voters in the September 2005 survey also felt that initiatives fulfilled their populist purpose by reflecting the views of ordinary Californians. Majorities in all political parties agreed.

Even though they continued to have faith overall in their state's system of direct democracy, most California voters were skeptical about the special election in the months leading up to it. A majority of likely voters (53%) in the September 2005 survey said the special election was a "bad idea," while four in ten supported it (see table 5.6). This echoed opinions expressed in May and August PPIC surveys, in which approximately twice as many residents said it would have been better for the governor to wait until the next regular election to put his measures on the ballot than said he was right to call a special election. Only Republicans were approving of the special election in the September survey, with the proportion calling it a good idea outnumbering detractors by more than two to one (63% to 29%). But the governor's plan

Table 5.6: Opinions of the Special Election

"Governor Schwarzenegger has called a special election in November 2005 to vote on budget, educational, and governmental reform measures. In general, do you think the special election is a good idea or a bad idea?"

	Voters	Democrats	Republicans	Independents
Good idea	40%	23%	63%	36%
Bad idea	53	73	29	56
Neither (volunteered)	1	—	1	2
Don't know	6	4	7	6

Source: PPIC Statewide Survey, September 2005.

was clearly out of favor with Democrats and independents, among whom solid majorities called the special election a bad idea.

VOTERS' INTEREST IN THE SPECIAL ELECTION

The special election and its roster of eight initiatives consumed California newspapers and airwaves during the fall of 2005. Ads featuring teachers, nurses, firefighters, and police officers continued to assail the governor's initiatives and, more pointedly, Schwarzenegger himself. The union-sponsored advertising accused the governor of taking millions of dollars from business-oriented special interests and using the upcoming election to promote their agenda. In response to this direct attack on the governor, the campaign for his initiatives backed away from their damaged spokesman and pulled his image from some of their television ads. Meanwhile, the pharmaceutical industry continued its well-funded barrage of advertisements and campaign mailers. And wealthy individuals, such as Silicon Valley executive Steve Poizner,[11] Stockton developer Alex Spanos, and Univision (Spanish-language television) CEO Jerry Perenchio, pumped in millions of their own dollars to promote the reform agenda.

By the end of October, the various campaigns for and against the November initiatives had raised more than $250 million, making it by far the most expensive election in California history (*San Francisco Chronicle*, November 2, 2005). Schwarzenegger attempted to reprise his role as "man of the people" with a series of staged events portraying himself as an outsider, rather than a politician. Appearing at televised "town hall" style forums around the state, the governor attempted to contrast himself with state legislators, whom he portrayed as being under the influence of "union bosses."

It was hard for voters to avoid the deluge of information about the special election. In an October 2005 survey, more than eight in ten likely voters (83%) said they had seen television ads about the November ballot measures. This advertising awareness was similar to levels seen during the 2003 recall and the 2002 gubernatorial election. Democrats (84%), Republicans (84%), and independents (87%) were equally likely to have noticed advertising about the special election initiatives.

Voters' interest in the November ballot was equally high in the October survey. Eight in ten likely voters said they were following the election news "very" (31%) or "somewhat" (50%) closely. Interest had grown markedly in the past month—in the September and August 2005 surveys, one in five voters was following the election news very closely. Voters in all political, demographic, and regional groups were paying a similar amount of attention to the initiative campaigns in October.

But familiarity with the November election and its propositions was not making voters any more favorable toward it. A majority (54%) in the October survey continued to call the special election a "bad idea," while only 41 percent had a positive assessment. Opinions on the special election were virtually unchanged since September. As the election approached, only Republicans were approving, with 70 percent calling it a "good idea." A majority of Democrats (76%) and independents (57%) thought the upcoming election was a bad idea.

Nor had any of the measures on the November ballot captured voters' support as election day neared. In fact, the intense campaigning around the initiatives seemed to have turned off many distrustful voters. Most importantly, the measures triggered a sharp, partisan split, indicating that Schwarzenegger's reform agenda was perceived as a political battle among party officials and special interests. He had fallen short in efforts to pitch his proposals in nonpartisan and populist terms.

Proposition 74, the governor's reform measure that lengthened the probationary period for teachers, had voters evenly divided in the October 2005 survey, with 46 percent in favor and 48 percent opposed. The number planning to vote "no" had risen six points since the August survey. The measure was favored by a majority of Republicans (71%) in October, while most Democrats were opposed (69%) and independents were divided (49% yes, 43% no).

Proposition 75, the bid to limit public employee unions' ability to use member dues for political purposes, had also slipped over time. In October, only 46 percent of likely voters said they planned to cast their ballot in favor of this measure, while an equal 46 percent intended to vote no. Support for Proposition 75 had fallen 12 points since the August survey (58% yes, 33% no). While Republicans favored it in large numbers (74%), a majority of Democrats (63%) and independents (51%) were opposed in October.

Proposition 76, the governor's effort to reform the state budget, was trailing by more than two to one in the October survey. Six in ten likely voters were planning to vote no on this measure, while only 30 percent were in favor. Opposition had held steady since August (61%) and September (63%). Proposition 76 was opposed by large numbers of Democrats (81%) and independents (70%) in the October survey. Among Republicans, a less than overwhelming majority (56%) favored Proposition 76 as the election neared.

And Proposition 77, the third of Schwarzenegger's original reform measures, was far behind in October. Half of likely voters said they were going to vote no on this proposal to change the way legislative districts were drawn, while only 36 percent supported it. Like the governor's other initiatives, favor for Proposition 77 remained low throughout the campaign, with 34 percent in August and 33 percent in September expressing support. It too had failed to draw bipartisan backing—while 60 percent of Republicans in the October survey said they would vote yes on the redistricting initiative, 66 percent of Democrats and 57 percent of independents planned to vote no.

Instead of rallying around their governor's reform measures, Californians had turned against their state leaders. Only 33 percent of adults and 38 percent of voters approved of the governor's performance in the October survey, while nearly six in ten disapproved. These results were virtually identical to the September survey and reflected a twenty-seven-point drop in Schwarzenegger's approval since the beginning of the year. Republicans remained faithful in October, with 69 percent giving Schwarzenegger a favorable rating. But his divisive approach to governance had soured other voters, with eight in ten Democrats and 58 percent of independents now disapproving of his job performance.

Moreover, Schwarzenegger had alienated most Californians on his entire reform agenda. A majority (57% of adults, 56% of likely voters) disapproved of the way he was handling government reform, while only 31 percent of adults and 37 percent of likely voters approved. Once again, his partisan approach pleased the state's Republican minority (66%), but triggered significant opposition among the much higher numbers of Democratic voters (79%), as well as the sizable group of independent voters (59%).

As his second year in office drew to a close, Schwarzenegger's political fortune had shrunk and his populist image was fading. When asked how well the governor was meeting their expectations for his performance, only 13 percent of Californians in the October 2005 survey said he was doing better than they had expected, 42 percent said it was about the same, and 39 percent said he was performing worse than they had anticipated. In October 2004, four in ten said he was doing better than they had expected and another four in ten said he was meeting their expectations. Only 17 percent toward the end of Schwarzenegger's first year in office said he was doing a worse job than they thought he would—a number that had climbed twenty-two points as the public expressed its disappointment with the "year of reform."

The state legislature fared no better in the bitter partisan climate surrounding the special election. Californians were as disapproving of the job state lawmakers were doing (56%) in October as they were of the governor (58%). Only one in four adults approved of the legislature's performance. Likely voters were even more negative, with 65 percent disapproving and only one in five giving the legislature a favorable job rating. Since October 2004, Californians' positive assessments of their legislature had fallen eighteen points, sliding back to the low point they had been at in August 2003, just before the governor's recall (28% approval). As voters prepared to exercise

California's direct democracy provisions yet again, in the context of a special election called by the governor, majorities of Republicans (68%), independents (63%), and even Democrats (53%) were unhappy with the way the state legislature was functioning in October 2005.

THE SPECIAL ELECTION VOTE

Accompanied by a vampire-costumed staffer dubbed "Count Cartaxula," Arnold Schwarzenegger held a Halloween campaign rally at an Ontario junkyard in one of his final attempts to drum up voter support for his reform initiatives before the special election. Sacramento politicians, he said, "wrecked the state of California. . . . The people finally said 'We're mad as hell, we're not going to take it anymore,' and you organized a recall election and you sent me to Sacramento" (*Los Angeles Times*, November 1, 2005). Attempting to invoke the popularity of his first act after taking office—repealing the increase in vehicle registration fees instituted under Governor Davis—Schwarzenegger insinuated that the so-called car tax might have to be raised again if voters did not pass Proposition 76. His point was illustrated by a black Ford Fairlane rising from a giant mock grave, driven by a skeleton symbolizing a resurrected car tax.

But in this special election, Schwarzenegger's populist appeal and success with direct democracy deserted him. All three of his original reform measures went down to resounding defeat on November 8, as well as the fourth ballot measure that he had endorsed. Each failed to attract sufficient support outside of his GOP base. In fact, all eight of the initiatives on the special election ballot ended up on the losing side.

The biggest loser among the governor's initiatives was Proposition 76, the spending cap measure, which drew only 38 percent support (see table 5.7). Proposition 77, his redistricting initiative, did not do much better, with only 40 percent voting yes. The governor's attempt at school reform (Proposition 74), which lengthened the time required for a public school teacher to earn tenure, garnered the favor of 45 percent of voters. The most successful of the reform measures was Proposition 75, restricting the use of public employee union dues for political purposes, which the governor endorsed but was not one of his original proposals. Proposition 75 came in with 47 percent approval. Proposition 73, which would have required parental notification for minors seeking abortions, also had a 47 percent yes vote. The negative mood of the electorate extended to both prescription drug discount measures, with Proposition 78, sponsored by the pharmaceutical industry, gaining 42 percent of the vote, while the consumer- and labor-backed Proposition 79 drew 39 percent. And Proposition 80, a complicated measure put up by consumer

Table 5.7:   November 2005 Vote on Governor's Measures

Proposition 74: Public School Teachers Waiting Period	
Yes	44.8%
No	55.2
Proposition 75: Public Employee Union Dues Employee Consent	
Yes	46.5%
No	53.5
Proposition 76: School Funding State Spending	
Yes	37.6%
No	62.4
Proposition 77: Redistricting	
Yes	40.2%
No	59.8
Voter turnout	50.1%

Source: California Secretary of State, "Statement of the Vote," November 2005.

advocates seeking to reregulate the state's electricity industry, was supported by only 34 percent of special election voters. Voter turnout was 50.1 percent, even lower than the 50.6 percent of registered voters casting ballots in the 2002 governor's contest but higher than past experiences with special elections outside of the 2003 recall (California Secretary of State, "Statement of the Vote," 2005).

Just about the only winner in the 2005 special election was the initiative campaign industry. The yes and no campaigns for several of the initiatives were heavily funded by special interests such as business and labor groups. According to filings with the California Secretary of State, a record $317 million was spent on the eight ballot measures. The previous record for spending on initiatives was November 2004, when approximately $250 was spent on the sixteen statewide measures (*San Jose Mercury News*, February 1, 2006). The campaigns for the initiatives in the 2005 special election outstripped the $241 million spent by John Kerry and the $306 million spent by President Bush in the 2004 presidential contest (*San Francisco Chronicle*, November 9, 2005). The bulk of the money spent on the special election, about $165.6 million, went to television advertising for the various ballot measures. Another $23.1 million went to campaign mailings, while $17.6 million was spent on gathering signatures to qualify measures for the ballot and $12.5 million ended up in the wallets of political consultants, according to campaign finance reports filed with the California Secretary of State and compiled by the *Sacramento Bee* (*Sacramento Bee*, February 4, 2006).

The coalition of nurses, teachers, and public employee unions that opposed Schwarzenegger's reform measures spent $148.5 million, the analysis by the *Sacramento Bee* showed—outspending the $72.7 million put up by the yes campaigns by more than two to one. The Pharmaceutical Research and Manufacturers Association spent another $83.6 million to fight the Proposition 79 drug discount measure and promote their own initiative, Proposition 78.

Much of the money used to fight the governor's measures came from the California Teachers Association, which spent about $58 million in funds raised through a temporary increase in member dues. On the yes side, the California Recovery Team—the main committee promoting the governor's measures—spent about $45.5 million. Schwarzenegger contributed $7.7 million out of his own pocket (*San Jose Mercury News*, February 1, 2006). The state of California, meanwhile, spent about $50 million in public funds to conduct the special election.

THE POLITICAL AFTERMATH OF THE SPECIAL ELECTION

"If I would do another Terminator movie, I would have Terminator travel back in time to tell Arnold not to have a special election," a contrite Governor Schwarzenegger told reporters at a televised news conference on November 10, 2005. "Believe me, I should have also listened to my wife, who said to me, 'Don't do this'" (Schwarzenegger, "Governor Schwarzenegger's Press Conference," 2005). The governor took full responsibility for calling the special election to push his slate of defeated reform measures and said he had gotten the message that voters were tired of going to the polls to vote on partisan and special interest initiatives. "I think that's the thing that I've learned from this election here is that the people said, 'Initiatives are fine, but go and work it out with the legislators,'" he said. "The people sent a message to us that, 'Don't come to us with all your stuff . . . but work it out at the Capitol.' And so that's exactly what we're going to do."

As all the initiatives headed into oblivion and the governor and state legislature publicly kissed and made up after the 2005 special election, voters appeared somewhat shaken by the experience. In mid-November, PPIC conducted a survey of voters who had participated in the special election, to examine the effects on their confidence in state government, views of direct democracy, and desires for initiative reforms. Asked if the special election made them feel better or worse about California politics, 38 percent of those who had cast ballots said it made them feel worse, while only 21 percent said it made them feel better. Another 38 percent said the event did not affect their views. Republicans were especially hard-hit by the special election, with nearly half (46%) saying it made them feel worse about their state government, compared to 33 percent of Democrats and 39 percent of independents. Older, more affluent and more educated voters were also more likely to say they felt worse about state politics in the wake of the special election. One issue on which the parties agreed was their opinion of the way the governor and state legislators were

Table 5.8:   Role of Representative Democracy

"Overall, do you approve or disapprove of the way that the California Legislature and the governor are working together in making public policy?"

	Voters	Democrats	Republicans	Independents
Approve	14%	12%	20%	14%
Disapprove	76	78	70	77
Don't know	10	10	10	9

Source: PPIC Statewide Survey, November 2005, special election voters.

working together to make public policy. Fully three in four special election voters in a November 2005 survey disapproved of the way the two branches of government were getting along, and only 14 percent were satisfied (see table 5.8). Strong majorities in all political and demographic groups held this view.

The election appeared to have taken a further toll on Californians' already diminished trust in state government. Only 17 percent of special election voters said they trusted their state leaders to do what is right "just about always" (2%) or "most of the time" (15%), while 73 percent said "only some of the time" and 8 percent volunteered that they never trusted the state government. In the August 2005 survey, 24 percent of likely voters said they trusted the government in Sacramento always or most of the time. Trust among the November special election voters was low in all political parties. Evaluations of elected officials were also negative. Job approval ratings for both the governor (39% approve, 56% disapprove) and the legislature (20% approve, 66% disapprove) in November remained at the record low levels we had seen in October.

With a turnout of just over half of California's registered voters, who were the hardy citizens who bothered to trudge to the polls in November 2005? They were not representative of the adult population, since they were predominantly white (71%), college graduates (53%), affluent (35% had annual incomes of $80,000 or more), and homeowners (78%)—but they were similar to the profile of frequent voters in elections. Special election voters were somewhat older, with 88 percent aged thirty-five or older, compared to 82 percent of likely voters overall. An equal number of men and women voted in the special election and Democrats (43%) outnumbered Republicans (36%) and independents (15%), which reflects the makeup of all registered voters in California.[12]

In addition, special election voters were well-informed, with 85 percent in the November survey saying they had closely followed the news about the propositions, including 44 percent saying they followed it "very closely." They were pessimistic, with 68 percent saying things in the state were going in "the wrong direction" and only 23 percent saying "right direction." And they were cynical, with 61 percent believing that state government wasted "a lot" of the money they paid in taxes and 78 percent perceiving that the government in Sacramento was being run by a few big interests looking out for themselves, rather than for the benefit of all of the people (15%).

Majorities of special election voters in all political parties expressed these negative, cynical views of state leadership in November 2005. Compared to likely voters in the PPIC preelection surveys, special election voters were better informed (44% in November versus 31% in October following election news "very closely"), more pessimistic about California (68% in November versus 62% in October saying state was headed in the "wrong direction"), and more distrustful of their state's representative government (78% in November versus 71% in August saying state government was "run by a few big interests").

Although they rejected all the governor's reform measures in the special election, voters in the November survey did feel the initiatives touched on some of the major issues facing the state. For instance, while Proposition 74, the public school teachers waiting period initiative, went down by a 55% to 45% vote, seven in ten special election voters said that major changes in the state's school system were still needed. The top reasons given for voting no on Proposition 74 were the opinion that five years would be too long to wait for tenure decisions, the belief that it would hurt teachers, and that it would discourage people from taking teaching jobs in California. Proposition 74 was opposed by a majority in all age, education, and gender groups, and by voters with and without children in the public schools. While most Republicans supported it (78%), majorities of Democrats (82%) and independents (53%) were opposed.

Proposition 75, the public employee union dues employee consent initiative, lost by an eight-point margin (46% to 54%). But six in ten special election voters polled in November 2005 said major changes are needed in the way campaigns are financed in California. The main reasons given for opposing Proposition 75 were the perception that it was unfair in singling out unions for the restrictions, the belief that the measure's passage would silence some political voices, and the position that the measure was unnecessary because union members can already opt out of having their dues used for political purposes. Among Republicans, 78 percent said they voted for the initiative, while 83 percent of Democrats were opposed and independents were divided (52% no, 48% yes). It also drew greater opposition among younger voters, the less affluent, Latinos, and women.

Proposition 76, the school funding state spending initiative, was opposed by 62 percent of voters in the special election. Yet seven in ten in the November survey believed major changes in state spending were still needed. Those who cast ballots against this measure cited the belief that its passage would take money away from schools, that it gave too much power to the governor, and that they did not like the idea of spending caps. This measure was favored by 71 percent of Republicans, but opposed by 87 percent of Democrats and 63 percent of independents. It failed in all demographic groups, with opposition especially high among women, Latinos, and younger and less affluent voters.

As for Proposition 77, the redistricting initiative, 60 percent of voters said no in the special election and only 49 percent in the November survey agreed that major changes in the redistricting process were needed. Top reasons given for rejecting this measure included the belief that judges are not impartial, that midterm redistricting is not necessary, and that the initiative would hurt Democrats' chances of getting elected. Seven in ten Republicans voted yes on Proposition 77, while 84 percent of Democrats and 59 percent of independents voted no. Although it failed to gain a majority in any demographic group, it was favored somewhat more by men, whites, older, and more affluent voters.

After rejecting all his measures, only one in three special election voters in the November survey approved of the way the governor was using the initiative process to make public policy. Six in ten disapproved. Similarly, six in ten said it was a bad idea for Schwarzenegger to have called the special election. Voting in the special election was a mixed experience for those who turned out on November 8. Forty-six percent in the November 2005 survey said they were happy to be able to vote on the initiatives, while 51 percent were unhappy. Republicans were much happier about voting in the special election (66%) than were Democrats (31%) or independents (44%). However, whites were more likely than Latinos to say the experience made them unhappy (52% to 43%).

Overall, two in three special election voters still believed that the initiatives on the November ballot addressed important issues that their elected leaders had not adequately addressed. A majority in all political groups agreed, although Democrats (62%) were less enthusiastic than Republicans (72%) or independents (69%).

As for specific complaints about the special election, the vast majority of voters in the November survey felt that the initiative campaigns spent too much money. More than eight in ten held this view, including 69 percent saying they "strongly agreed" (see table 5.9). Majorities in all parties said that too much money was spent on the initiatives. Women, whites, and those with higher levels of education were also more likely to hold this view. Most voters also felt that the initiatives' wording was too complicated and confusing. Fifty-five percent agreed with this statement, including 28 percent who strongly agreed (see table 5.9). A majority of Democrats and independents, and nearly half of Republicans, had this opinion of the ballot wording. Latinos, women, and those with less education were most likely to agree.

However, in keeping with their fundamental belief in direct democracy, most special election voters did not think there were too many propositions

Table 5.9: Perceptions of the Special Election Ballot

	Voters	Democrats	Republicans	Independents
"There was too much money spent by the initiative campaigns."				
Agree	83%	88%	76%	81%
Disagree	13	8	18	14
Don't know	4	4	6	5
"The wording of citizens' initiatives on the state ballot was too complicated and confusing."				
Agree	55%	61%	49%	55%
Disagree	43	36	48	43
Don't know	2	3	3	2
"There were too many propositions on the state ballot."				
Agree	41%	52%	30%	38%
Disagree	57	46	68	60
Don't know	2	2	2	2

Source: PPIC Statewide Survey, November 2005, special election voters.

on the November ballot. Only four in ten said the ballot was too crowded with initiatives, while 57 percent disagreed (see table 5.9). Republicans (68%) and independents (60%) were especially likely to say the number of initiatives in the special election was not excessive, while a majority of Democrats said there were too many (52%).

And in reflecting on the California special election, voters who had gone to the polls held their own judgment in higher esteem than that of their elected leaders. Forty-eight percent said that public policy decisions made by voters through the initiative process were probably better than those made by the governor and state legislature, while 30 percent said voters' decisions were probably worse, and 22 percent either said both were about the same (9%), or were unsure (13%). But while Democrats (52%) and independents (50%) tended to express faith in their fellow voters' decisions, Republicans, disappointed in the special election's outcome, were noticeably less confident (42%).

CONCLUSION

In early 2005, Governor Schwarzenegger sought to use his populist image and high approval ratings to bend the political will of Democratic legislators and their special interest allies. In his annual address in January, he laid out an ambitious platform of political, fiscal, and education reforms and gave legislators an ultimatum: either approve his agenda in a special session or he would take his proposals to the voters for their endorsement in a special election. It was a risky strategy for a GOP governor who depended on the support of independents and moderate Democrats to view him as a populist, nonpartisan figure, unfettered by ties to the political establishment or special interests.

The governor's budget and reform agenda were interpreted by Democratic legislators and the special interest groups who were their allies as a turn away from his politically independent stance and his efforts the previous year to seek bipartisan compromise. They went on the attack, and spent millions of dollars in advertising designed to rally Democrats and independent voters against the governor. The governor's political rhetoric and harsh tone in response to these attacks offered the material that was needed to persuade distrustful voters that he had changed from moderate to conservative. By the spring, a governor who was once viewed as an independent-minded populist was perceived as just another politician under the sway of partisanship and special interests.

Nonetheless, the governor continued to collect signatures for his initiatives, and was determined to call a special election. This would be California's fifth special election since 1910, but the first time a governor had tried to enact virtually his entire legislative agenda for the year through the direct democracy process. In pursuit of his goal, Schwarzenegger collected money from special interests and took sides with partisan causes that, in turn, rallied Democrats and their labor allies to defeat his initiatives.

Voters were not enamored with the governor's use of special elections for this purpose. Most said that the reform initiatives could have waited until the following regular election for consideration. After a costly and bitter campaign, all the governor's reform initiatives failed to attract sufficient support outside of his party. Voters rejected all eight initiatives on the November ballot. Governor Schwarzenegger's standing with voters and their trust in state government were casualties of this unpopular special election. For voters, being called to the ballot box reinforced their belief that state government was dysfunctional.

The 2005 California special election illustrates that direct democracy is prone to use by powerful actors as well as average citizens: the partisans and special interests who goaded Schwarzenegger into promoting conservative and pro-business legislation through the initiative process; the coalition of labor unions that spent millions of dollars to blast away at the governor's leadership; and the corporate and religious interest groups that used the opportunity of a special election to advance their own agendas. This use of the initiative process to circumvent the orderly process of bipartisan compromise fueled a new round of voter distrust of representative government. Still, voters continued to support the initiative process as a populist tool to counter the influence of partisanship and special interest groups. The failure of the special election initiatives served as an important lesson on the potential for misuse of direct democracy by elected officials. It was a lesson that Schwarzenegger seemed to take to heart, as, late in 2005, he promised to work with the legislature and reach bipartisan agreements before taking proposals to the voters again.

NOTES

1. See chapter 1. Also, see Peter Schrag, *Paradise Lost: California's Experience, America's Future* (New York: New Press, 1998), 163–67.

2. Although Schwarzenegger hadn't formally endorsed the union dues initiative at the time, he privately supported the idea and later made it a centerpiece of his reform agenda.

3. The ballot label and summary were prepared by the state's attorney general, according to California elections law. The attorney general at that time was Bill Lockyer, a Democrat, who was then a potential challenger to Schwarzenegger in the 2006 gubernatorial election. See article by Robert Salladay, "Lockyer's Statement under Fire," *Los Angeles Times*, March 8, 2005, B3.

4. See political blog by Bill Bradley, "Wrong Turn Right: Inside Arnold's Fateful 2004 Shift," *New West Notes*, December 23–29, 2005, www.newwestnotes.com (December 29, 2005).

5. See reports by Carla Marinucci and Mark Martin, "Governor Endorses Minutemen on Border," *San Francisco Chronicle*, April 29, 2005, A1; Gary Delsohn, "Governor: No Political Aim in Border Remarks," *Sacramento Bee*, April 30, 2005, A1.

6. See description by Delsohn, "Schwarzenegger Hands in First Petitions," *Sacramento Bee*, May 5, 2005, A3.

7. See description of protests in Dion Nissenbaum, "Capitol Heats Up: Rhetoric Intensifies as Fall Vote Grows More Likely," *San Jose Mercury News*, May 26, 2005, A1.

8. For an in-depth description of Reagan's tax-limitation initiative (Proposition 1) and its failed campaign, see Lou Cannon, *Governor Reagan* (New York: Public Affairs, 2003), 368–79.

9. That ruling was reversed by the California Supreme Court on August 12, 2005, and Proposition 77 was reinstated on the November 8 ballot.

10. See detailed account in Joe Mathews, *The People's Machine: Arnold Schwarzenegger and the Rise of Blockbuster Democracy* (New York: Public Affairs, 2006), 370–77. Also see Andrew LaMar and Kate Folmar, "Democrat Is Drafted to Broker Ballot Talks: Many Issues Still Unresolved," *San Jose Mercury News*, August 18, 2005, A9; and Aaron C. Davis and Mark Gladstone, "Governor, Democrats Unable to Settle Ballot: Special Election to Decide Three Measures," *San Jose Mercury News*, August 19, 2005, A10.

11. Poizner, a Republican, was picked by Schwarzenegger to head his Redistrict California committee promoting Proposition 77, the redistricting initiative. At the time, Poizner was intending to run for state insurance commissioner the following year, but did not then hold public office. He had lost a bid for the state Assembly the previous year, which was largely seen as the result of his district being heavily gerrymandered in favor of Democrats.

12. See PPIC report, "Just the Facts: 2005 Special Election Voter Profiles" (San Francisco: Public Policy Institute of California, 2005).

6

The Year of Rebuilding:
Reconstruction and Reconciliation
in 2006

After the resounding defeat of the special election in 2005, Schwarzenegger adopted a humble and introspective tone in 2006. In an effort to reengage the Democrats and independents that had deserted him during his 2005 alliance with partisan and special interests, the governor proposed a bold new policy agenda providing billions of dollars in infrastructure spending and involved the legislature in the process. The "year of rebuilding" he outlined as his vision for the state was also an attempt to repair his public image as a populist leader. At the same time, he once again called on voters to make the big decisions about the state's future at the ballot box.

In his State of the State speech in January, the governor outlined a $222.6 billion plan to rebuild California's decaying roads, schools, prisons, ports, and levees. His budget plan released a few days later included hefty increases for education and transportation—using a greater-than-expected budget surplus and no tax increases. The infrastructure and budget proposals initially received a cool reception by both parties in the legislature. But they eventually reached agreement on a $37 billion package of state bonds for infrastructure projects to put before voters on the November ballot. The governor and legislature also managed to pass a state budget on time—a rare event in light of the state's perennial partisan gridlock over tax and spending policy.

A bitter and divisive Democratic gubernatorial primary in June ended with the lowest voter turnout in state history and the selection of a liberal, party-insider, and union-backed candidate. This set the stage for a test of voters' opinions about partisanship, special interests, and populist beliefs in the fall contest. Voters rejected both propositions on the primary ballot, adding to the string of defeats since the special election—only to face thirteen measures on the November ballot.

In November, California voters sent a clear signal that the "year of rebuilding" was a political success. Governor Schwarzenegger was reelected in a "blue" state on a day that the GOP lost considerable ground nationwide. Voters sifted through a crowded ballot to ratify the infrastructure bond measures, while defeating citizens' initiatives increasing taxes and spending on other areas that were favored by special interests. His Democratic challenger's efforts to rally California voters with partisan appeals fell flat, and the special interest groups that had been such a potent force against the governor a year earlier now failed to deliver on election day.

While distrust in government and the legislative process remained high at year's end, Schwarzenegger had experienced a remarkable rebound in his approval ratings. In contrast to his divisive tactics during the year of reform, the governor had used the legislative process to pass laws and endorse his ballot measures before submitting them to voters in 2006, gaining success by returning to his populist themes and centrist, bipartisan policies while steering clear of special interests.

A NEW BEGINNING

On January 5, the governor delivered an annual State of the State address that took a radically different tack from the one he had given a year earlier. This time, in place of the confrontational tone of the 2005 address, calling the state's political system "broken" and its schools and other public institutions a "disaster," Schwarzenegger's persona was apologetic and conciliatory. His new approach to governing California outlined a decade-long plan for massive rebuilding of the state's infrastructure, which had been badly overwhelmed by age, neglect, and a huge boom in population.

Schwarzenegger's ambitious proposal called for a $222.6 billion rehabilitation of the state's freeways and roads, school facilities, prisons and courts, and levees and commercial seaports. The project would be financed in large part by a series of multibillion-dollar state bond issues, with the first to be placed before voters in 2006, and a combination of federal grants, existing state and local funding sources, and yet-to-be specified user fees and public-private partnerships. It was a virtual about-face from his budget-cutting, government-reforming, Democrat-baiting agenda of the past year. On the other hand, in the spirit of the populist belief that state government had all the funds it needed—which had pervaded California since the Proposition 13 tax revolt—it was a major spending plan with no new taxes to fund it.

"I have absorbed my defeat and I have learned my lesson," Schwarzenegger said in his annual address to lawmakers in the state Assembly chamber. "And the people, who always have the last word, sent a clear message—cut the warfare, cool the rhetoric, find common ground and fix the problems together. So to my fellow Californians, I say—message received" (Schwarzenegger, "Governor Schwarzenegger's 2006 State of the State Address," 2006). The plan he outlined was the state's most ambitious endeavor since the 1960s, when Democratic former governor Edmund G. "Pat" Brown led a decade-long effort that expanded the university system with the addition of eleven new campuses, created a network of freeways spanning the state, and built the massive California Water Project, providing water to the arid south while protecting northern cities from floods. Schwarzenegger's plan called for the largest amount of state spending ever proposed by a Republican governor. And it included something to please almost every major interest group in the state.

About half of the proposed funding over the next decade ($107 billion) would be spent on transportation, which had long been a top concern for Californians enduring lengthy and frustrating commutes every day. The key transportation projects were judiciously divided in a way that would address the interests of road, mass transit, and environmental advocates: 750 miles of new highway lanes, 600 miles of new commuter rails, 550 miles of new high-occupancy vehicle lanes, and 8,500 miles of new bicycle and pedestrian paths.

Over one-fourth ($59.9 billion) of the infrastructure funding would be dedicated to education, a policy area that typically leads the list of public concerns in PPIC polls. The governor's plan had promised to deliver 9,700 new classrooms, the modernization of 38,800 existing classrooms, twenty-nine new and renovated buildings on the University of California campuses, fifteen new and renovated buildings on the California State University campuses, and fifty-eight new and renovated buildings on community college campuses.

With issues raised about emergency preparedness planning in the wake of Hurricane Katrina in late 2005, Californians were expressing concerns about the capabilities of federal, state, and local governments to prevent a similar catastrophe in their state. The governor's plan thus also called for $35 billion in spending on flood control and water supply projects. This part of the long-range plan had funds for levee strengthening and repairs and flood-control system improvements, as well as water conservation, supply management, and new water storage.

To address the public's concerns about law and order and public safety issues, the governor's plan also included about $17.4 billion for construction or expansion of jails, prisons, and juvenile detention facilities. Finally, about $3.3 billion was dedicated to the renovation of court facilities, seismically retrofitting state buildings, and health and safety improvements at state parks.

Schwarzenegger's new script unveiled in his State of the State address included a number of other measures that signaled a sharp return to the middle in his political orientation. Increasing the minimum wage, augmenting funding for schools by $4 billion, allowing residents to buy prescription drugs at reduced prices abroad, freezing tuition at the state's colleges and universities—these all put the governor closer to his liberal Democratic and labor union opponents in the special election than to the conservative Republican and business interests he had championed in the previous year.

Democrats were cautious, publicly expressing mild approval for the governor's new agenda, while privately complaining that he had appropriated their ideas and claimed them for his own. Analysts speculated that despite Schwarzenegger's advancement of causes they supported, the Democratic majority in the state legislature would block his efforts so as to make him look bad to voters in the November 2006 election. In his response immediately following the State of the State address, Senate leader Don Perata complained that "The governor is proposing a lot more spending than we are" (*Los Angeles Times*, January 6, 2006).

As for Republicans, Schwarzenegger's move was seen as treason. He had already riled them by appointing Democrat Susan Kennedy, a key advisor to former governor Gray Davis, as his new chief of staff less than three weeks earlier. Now, Republicans were outraged at his spending plan. Staffers tried to sell Republicans on Schwarzenegger's plan by portraying it as part of his strategy to continue pushing his reform agenda. As conservative blogger Jon Fleischman reported in his January 6 Internet column, *FlashReport*, he and a colleague met with the governor's staff shortly before the speech on January 5 and were told the following:

> They expressed four general reasons why Republicans should support this plan. First was the notion that this kind of huge spending would take place with Democrats in power anyway, but with too much emphasis on social programs instead of infrastructure needs such as ports, roads, schools and access to technology. They said they would much rather have a "Republican stamp" on the spending. Their second point was that we currently experience what they called a "Christmas Tree Ornament Approach" to bonds, where various narrow interest groups place their pet issues on the ballot, leading to debt without long-term planning. Another point was that economically we have to address these infrastructure needs as a state. Their last point was that they could use this plan to negotiate and achieve some of the reforms the Governor tried to pass on that ballot last November. (Fleishman 2006)

Other conservatives were less generous. Most conservative talk radio commentators declared the governor a "sellout." The mainstream media in California were also skeptical, such as *Sacramento Bee* columnist Dan Walters, who described the plan as "ginned up as a vehicle to restore Schwarzenegger's popularity" (*Sacramento Bee*, January 6, 2006).

In the days that followed, Schwarzenegger had an unfortunate brush with the law. Riding his motorcycle with his twelve-year-old son in a sidecar near his Brentwood home in Los Angeles, he collided with a neighbor backing her car out of her driveway. No one was seriously hurt, but Schwarzenegger ended up with fifteen stitches — and a citation for driving without a license to operate a motorcycle. Two days later, he delivered his 2006 to 2007 budget proposal with a swollen lip and a joke about how his accident was a metaphor for California's partisan pitfalls: "A car pulled out in front of me . . . I just couldn't make a decision which way to go," he quipped at the January 10 press conference. "I knew if I would turn left that the Republicans will get mad, and I knew if I turned right, my wife will get mad. So I just crashed right into the car. This was the safer thing to do" (Schwarzenegger, "Governor Schwarzenegger's Remarks at Release of 2006–07 Budget," 2006).

Schwarzenegger began this new year by moving far away from the partisan and interest group politics that had dominated his agenda in 2005. He steered clear of conflict with the Democrat-controlled legislature and their political allies and moved back to policies that placed him in the independent, moderate, and crowd-pleasing mode that had served him so well during and just after the recall. Once again, he invoked Californians' populist impulses by calling on voters to ratify his policies at the ballot box. But this time, he also asked the legislature to join in and offer its own solutions. He had learned that legislative bipartisanship was the safest and most effective way of maneuvering through California's amalgam of representative government and direct democracy.

STATE BUDGET SURPLUS: SOMETHING FOR EVERYONE

The governor's $126 billion budget unveiled a few days later followed the plans outlined in his State of the State address. With a surplus in hand, this included a $4.3 billion increase over the previous year's spending for K–12 schools and community colleges ($1.7 billion more than required by Proposition 98), a $1.2 billion increase in health care spending, and an early payback of $920 million in money borrowed from transportation funds (California Department of Finance, "Governor's Budget Summary 2006–07," 2006).

The proposed budget would funnel $1.4 billion in gasoline taxes, which in previous years had been used to cover general state expenses, into transportation-specific projects. It would substantially increase spending on corrections and enable hiring more prison guards. A planned increase in tuition at California's public universities would be eliminated with the allocation of an extra $129 million in funding. The budget also included $428 million in new spending to fund after-school programs—the result of Schwarzenegger's Proposition 49 that passed in November 2002. The only major group of constituents that did not see increased funds in the governor's budget proposal was welfare recipients, who would not get a cost-of-living increase in their benefits and whose child care services for parents in job-training programs would be eliminated. All together, accounting for all expenses and cuts, the proposed 2006 to 2007 budget would increase state government spending by $4 billion over the past year.

In marked contrast to his "live within our means" mantra for 2005, Schwarzenegger's 2006 to 2007 budget included a $6.4 billion gap between state expenses and revenues. The governor maintained that the shortfall would be made up with surplus funds created by increased tax revenues from the improving economy. In the previous six months, California's economic performance had shown marked gains and the state took in $2.6 billion more than anticipated, largely through growth in personal and business income tax receipts. The governor's balance sheet showed the 2004 to 2005 fiscal year ending with a reserve of $9.1 billion. It did not dwell on the fact that some of this projected surplus was actually debt, having been generated by the deficit-financing bonds Schwarzenegger convinced voters to pass in the spring of 2004 (Legislative Analyst's Office, "2006–07: Overview of the Governor's Budget," 2006). Schwarzenegger was banking on continued economic growth to fill in the gap and maintain the state's coffers at an adequate level.

However, California legislative analyst Elizabeth Hill, the chief nonpartisan examiner of the fiscal impact of state policies, panned the governor's budget. In her preface to the Legislative Analyst's Office's (LAO) analysis of the budget, Hill wrote that it "moves the state in the wrong direction in terms of its long-term goal of getting its fiscal house in order" (Legislative Analyst's Office, "2006–07: Overview of the Governor's Budget," 2006). The report warned that the proposed budget would push debt into the future, with a structural deficit of a $6.6 billion gap for the 2007 to 2008 fiscal year climbing to $9.7 billion in 2008 to 2009. The LAO analysis also pointed out that, because of the funding mandates created by ballot measures such as Proposition 98 and Proposition 49, many of the spending increases would become permanent expenditures. "Given the state's current structural budget shortfall," Hill warned, "we believe that the 2006–07 budget should focus more on paying down existing debt before making expansive new commitments."

REBUILDING WITHOUT RAISING TAXES

No one disagreed with the governor that the state's infrastructure was in dire need of funds. For nearly a decade, studies from a variety of sources, including the LAO, the California Business Roundtable, the Center for the Continuing Study of the California Economy and the California Commission on Building for the 21st Century had warned that facilities, including the K–12 public schools, water systems, and transportation networks, were overburdened and in need of major repairs.[1]

Most of the state's major building projects had been undertaken during the 1950s, 1960s, and 1970s, when the public universities, highways, and water projects were developed. Since then, California's population had grown by more than 10 million residents, drastically overwhelming the existing systems. And though the state had been undergoing tremendous population growth since the 1970s, public spending had dropped sharply in the wake of Proposition 13 and its legacy of citizens' initiatives limiting the government's revenue from taxes (de Alth and Rueben 2005).

So the issue was not whether investment in the infrastructure was needed, but how to pay for it, and perhaps most important, how to navigate the minefield of competing needs and interests in bringing such a project to life. In contrast to the homogenous California of the 1960s and 1970s, the state had become sharply fragmented along regional, racial/ethnic, and political lines. The infrastructure needs of the populous coastal cities were at odds with the growing inland regions. Latinos, who were projected to number half of the state's residents by 2025, had different priorities than whites. And Republicans and conservatives found little common ground with Democrats and liberals on the subject of taxes and spending.

One of the most factionalized issues was the environment. The environmental effects of major building projects, such as reservoirs or highways, were much more widely recognized in 2006 than in 1967. Every project triggered an onslaught of reviews and regulations as a result of Proposition 65, the California Environmental Quality Act (CEQA), passed by voters in 1986. The required reviews would assess whether transportation, water, or other public works projects would have any major effects on areas such as air and water quality, wildlife habitats and ecological systems, population distribution, land use, and scenic beauty (CEQA 2005). This process added greatly to the project's cost and time frame. Moreover, the environment was among the most fractious issues in California public opinion, triggering strong emotions and hard-to-resolve conflicts among a host of competing interest groups.

Still, by outlining a long-term, massive rebuilding plan with no new taxes and presenting a budget for the coming year that increased funding for education and other major state programs without asking more from taxpayers, the governor had sidestepped the most contentious issues in planning for the state's future. There were no direct costs to voters and no apparent losers among the state's current expenditures. With the help of new revenues from an improving economy and debt deferred by the 2004 bond issues, he escaped the need to raise taxes or make unpopular choices in cutting the state budget.

In the place of partisan conflict, Schwarzenegger had managed to re-create his populist role as an outsider who had come to fix a broken state system and was calling on voters to join in the effort. This time, they would be summoned to the ballot box to endorse his plans for seemingly cost-free rebuilding of the state infrastructure systems that Californians noticed most in their daily lives—education, transportation, and water.

THE PUBLIC'S SHORT MEMORY

Californians seemed to be in a forgiving mood as they embraced the governor's populist rebuilding plan and new budget proposal. In a January 2006 survey, more than six in ten adults (68%) and likely voters (64%) approved of his proposal to spend more than $222 billion in infrastructure improvements over the next ten years. Six in ten adults (60%) and likely voters (58%) said they were satisfied with the governor's recently released 2006 to 2007 state budget—a substantial increase from the four in ten adults (38%) and likely voters (40%) who were satisfied with the state budget one year earlier (see table 6.1).

And though their elected representatives in Sacramento had been quick to divide into partisan factions in their response to the governor's budget and infrastructure proposals, California voters' solid support for his newly announced plans cut across party lines. Schwarzenegger's $222.6 billion infrastructure plan was favored by solid majorities in all parties, including

Table 6.1: Support for Infrastructure and Budget Plans

"Do you approve or disapprove of the governor's plan to spend $222 billion over ten years on infrastructure projects including surface transportation, education facilities, air quality, water and flood control, jails and prisons, and courts?"

	All Adults	Democrats	Republicans	Independents
Approve	68%	64%	72%	71%
Disapprove	23	26	20	23
Don't know	9	10	8	6

"In general, are you satisfied or dissatisfied with the governor's budget plan?"

	All Adults	Democrats	Republicans	Independents
Approve	60%	51%	72%	62%
Disapprove	28	36	21	29
Don't know	12	13	7	9

Source: PPIC Statewide Survey, January 2006.

72 percent of Republicans, 71 percent of independents, and 64 percent of Democrats. His 2006 to 2007 budget proposal was similarly approved of by all party groups, with 72 percent of Republicans, 62 percent of independents, and 51 percent of Democrats saying they were satisfied with the plan. He seemed to have found his way back into the public's good graces soon after his dismal showing in the 2005 election.

Even Schwarzenegger's job approval ratings saw a modest resurgence in response to his plans, with 40 percent of Californians approving of the way he was doing his job as governor, up from a disappointing 33 percent measured three months earlier in an October 2005 survey. Among likely voters in the January 2006 survey, 45 percent approved and 48 percent disapproved. However, deep partisan divisions remained in assessments of the governor's overall job performance. While more than seven in ten Republicans (72%) gave Schwarzenegger high marks for the way he was handling his job, 40 percent of independents and only 20 percent of Democrats agreed with that evaluation. Moreover, although the governor's 40 percent approval rating was an improvement, it was still well below the 60 percent high marks just one year earlier.

Meanwhile, the legislature's approval ratings remained at historic lows: only 29 percent of adults and 25 percent of likely voters approved of its overall performance. Majorities of Democrats, Republicans, and independents were disapproving. Approval ratings for the legislature had been significantly higher in January 2004 (36%) and January 2005 (37%), indicating that the partisan bickering over the past year had taken its toll on the public's view of their state elected representatives.

The governor's kickoff for his ten-year infrastructure plan—a $25 billion bond proposed for the 2006 ballot that was to be the first of five cycles totaling $68 billion—was enjoying strong early support, with a sizeable 65 percent of adults and 57 percent of likely voters in the January 2006 survey saying they would vote yes on the bond. Support crossed partisan lines, with majorities of Democrats (66%), independents (70%), and Republicans (57%) saying they would vote for it. However, support for a smaller, rival infrastructure bond measure proposed by Senate president pro tem Don Perata, an Oakland Democrat, was even stronger. Nearly three in four adults (73%) and 68 percent of likely voters said they would vote yes on Perata's proposed $10 billion bond issue, including majorities of Democrats (74%), independents (78%), and Republicans (69%) alike.

Despite the overall favorable public response to his infrastructure plan, other results from the January survey pointed to some continued conflicts for the governor. Asked which area of public works projects should have the highest priority for additional state funding, education facilities topped the list (48%). Surface transportation, a primary focus in Schwarzenegger's

Table 6.2: Public Doubts about the Legislative Process

"Do you think that Governor Schwarzenegger and the state legislature will be able to work together and accomplish a lot in the next year, or not?"

	All Adults	*Democrats*	*Republicans*	*Independents*
Yes	43%	41%	48%	39%
No	48	49	46	53
Don't know	9	10	6	8

Source: PPIC Statewide Survey, January 2006.

infrastructure improvement plan, was ranked a distant second, named the top priority by 25 percent of adults. Water systems and flood control, another area slated for considerable attention under the governor's proposal, came in third (17%), while his proposed funding increases for jails and prisons were only seen as a high priority by 3 percent of Californians. Strong partisan differences also emerged, with education a higher priority than transportation among Democrats (54% education, 19% transportation) and independents (52% education, 26% transportation), while Republicans rated the two areas nearly equal (39% transportation, 36% education).

And despite their early approval for state bond sales to finance infrastructure improvements, three in ten voters said their preference would be to increase funding solely through the use of surplus state funds, while only one in four opted for bond sales. Increasing user fees (17%) or taxes (14%) were even less popular choices. These views about preferred funding options were consistent across political groups—pointing to the public's strong and enduring populist belief that reducing government waste would free up enough money to pay for big state projects, making tax increases both unnecessary and unacceptable.

Perhaps most telling in the January 2006 survey were Californians' expectations for their state government. Asked whether they thought the governor and the legislature would be able to work together and accomplish a lot in the coming year, just 43 percent had an optimistic view, while nearly half (48%) did not think the two branches of state government would manage to function cooperatively (see table 6.2). Likely voters were even more dubious, with a majority (51%) having no hope for cooperation between the governor and legislature. Fewer than half in any political party had high expectations for leadership in Sacramento, with Republicans only somewhat more positive (48%) than Democrats (41%) or independents (39%).

BRIDGING THE PARTISAN DIVIDE

The legislature's response to the governor's initiatives almost immediately bore out voters' low expectations. While vowing to work together on rebuilding the state's infrastructure, the two parties were in fact miles apart at the start of the 2006 legislative session. Democratic lawmakers and their allies complained that the governor's plan did not include funding for affordable housing, mass transit, or environmental cleanup. Despite the $72 million in Schwarzenegger's budget to increase access to health care for minors, children's advocates criticized the effort as inadequate. And though the proposed budget would give schools $1.7 billion more than the amount required by Proposition 98, the California Teachers Association characterized it as a "start," maintaining that it was still $3.2 billion short of what they believed was owed to K–12 public schools.

Republicans, meanwhile, saw the governor's plan as an opportunity to weaken the state's environmental laws, long characterized as a bane to business in California. GOP legislators quickly realized that at least some of their votes were needed to reach the two-thirds majority required to place a bond on the ballot, giving them effective veto power on any legislation. Armed with this leverage, Republican lawmakers proposed waiving environmental review requirements on some projects and intimated that limiting the scope of CEQA would be essential to their support for Schwarzenegger's bond. They also suggested that some of the bond's proceeds be earmarked specifically for new dams and reservoirs—sure to trigger the opposition of state environmental groups.

By the end of January, a full-on power struggle was underway. Democrats denounced the governor's infrastructure plan as an attempt to bypass legislative oversight. Under Schwarzenegger's proposal, final decisions on major projects financed by bonds would be made by state agencies, rather than by elected lawmakers. Because the bonds would not be included in the state's general fund, projects financed through this method would not be subject to the legislative review and approval required for the annual budget. Two specific areas that concerned Democrats were the $26 million in bonds for transportation projects, over which the nine appointed members of the California Transportation Commission would have final say, and the $10 million bond for water projects, which would be overseen by state water agencies. Legislators contended that this process would strip them of their ability to make decisions, leaving politically sensitive issues to be resolved by nonelected officials.

Schwarzenegger countered that the process was structured that way so as to avoid pork-barrel projects created by legislators who put their district ahead of the needs of the state. "We're all clear . . . that we should build what is necessary for the state of California, not having each legislator say, 'Well, I need this street to be built in my neighborhood, and I need this little bridge there, and I need this and I need that,'" Schwarzenegger had told reporters at the release of his proposed budget (Schwarzenegger, "Governor Schwarzenegger's Remarks at Release of 2006–07 Budget," 2006).

While the loudest objections were heard from legislative Democrats, Republicans also had complaints about the governor's infrastructure proposal. Opposed to Schwarzenegger's plan to finance the effort with the sale of state bonds, Assembly Republicans put forward their own plan for a "pay as you go" approach. The Republican proposal would dedicate 1 percent of the state's general fund to infrastructure projects beginning with the 2007 to 2008 fiscal year. The rate of funding could grow another 0.5 percent in years when state revenues grew by at least $5 billion. According to state Assembly GOP leader Kevin McCarthy (R-Bakersfield), this approach could generate as much as $35 billion over ten years for infrastructure improvements. However, the proposal would limit spending to projects involving the University of California and the California State University, reservoirs, flood control, levees, and transportation improvements (McCarthy 2006).

After two months with virtually no progress, negotiations began to gather steam as the March 10 deadline for putting a bond measure on the June ballot approached. Democratic leaders, who initially had said they would only approve a $25 billion to $30 billion bond, agreed to compromise on a $48.8 billion borrowing plan—$20 billion less than the governor had initially proposed. Both Schwarzenegger and legislative Democrats made several concessions: on his part, the governor gave up his quest to expand jails and renovate courthouses and agreed with the opposition party's requests for funding affordable housing, public transit, and urban parks. Democrats abandoned their bid to retrofit hospital buildings for seismic safety and gave in to Republican demands for easing environmental regulations on some building projects.

Republicans, however, held fast, refusing to yield the six votes in the Assembly and two votes in the Senate needed to achieve the two-thirds majority required by the state constitution for spending measures. Sticking points for the GOP included objections to including what some called "social engineering," such as affordable housing, advocating instead a focus on roads and other "bricks and mortar" projects. The state's perennial conflicts over water also emerged as a wedge, with Republicans insisting that the plans include constructing new reservoirs and rebuilding a dam—provisions that benefited their party's agricultural interests but were poison to the Democrats' environmental lobby. The $48.8 billion bond measure died on the Senate floor early on the morning of Saturday, March 11, on a vote of 24 to 12, three votes shy of a two-thirds majority. Not a single Republican voted for the governor's proposal.

Nonetheless, negotiations continued for several days past the March 10 deadline, with legislators working through the weekend and late into the night. Several times, it was announced that they were close to reaching a compromise, and the governor's office issued optimistic statements throughout the negotiations. But by midnight on March 15, the time the state printing office said was truly the last chance to get the measure on the ballot in time to be printed and mailed to voters before the June election, the deal was officially declared dead. Earlier that day, Schwarzenegger had pared his wide-ranging $222.6 billion plan down further from the $48.8 billion measure rejected over the weekend. The new proposal—for $4.1 billion—dealt only with shoring up the state's moldering levee system. Negotiations with Assembly speaker Fabian Núñez later that day upped the proposed June ballot measure to $14.5 billion, with $4.1 billion for levee repairs and $10.4 billion for construction of schools and universities. The agreement included an additional $9.1 billion bond for schools to go before voters in 2008.

This time, the stripped-down measures gained the Republican votes needed to pass the lower house on the evening of March 15. But before the bills could be taken to the Senate for approval, the Senate passed its own version—not a bond, but a $1 billion appropriation from the state's general fund to pay for emergency levee repairs—then quickly adjourned until the following week. In gaveling the session to a close, Senate president pro tem Don Perata was making sure that the governor's infrastructure bonds would not go before voters until November at the earliest.

In his day-after autopsy of the stillborn proposal, Schwarzenegger was asked at a news conference about his inability to get members of his party to deliver the votes he needed to put his plan on the ballot. The governor attributed much of the conflict to the issue of water storage. "This is an issue that has become almost a religious issue," Schwarzenegger told reporters, likening it to a "holy war" (Schwarzenegger, "Governor Arnold Schwarzenegger's Remarks at a Press Conference Detailing Bond Negotiations," 2006). Until the end, Republicans had insisted on including provisions to build new dams and create new water-storage reservoirs in northern California. GOP leaders had argued that no new dams had been built in the state in decades and that the water-storage capacity had not kept up with population growth. Democrats countered that dams and reservoirs hurt the environment by diverting water from rivers and flooding plant and animal habitats. The state's water needs, according to Democrats, could be met by conservation and reallocating water from farms to urban areas—a highly contentious proposal that roused the ire of California's powerful agricultural lobby whenever it was mentioned. At the same time, the proposal riled the state's active environmental lobby, with at least one organization issuing an "action alert" during the final efforts to place a measure on the June ballot, telling members to call their legislators and urge them to vote against the infrastructure bond (Planning and Conservation League 2006).

In addition to the thorny and perennial issue of water, however, several other factors played key roles in killing the infrastructure bond that March. One of the most significant was Schwarzenegger's political inexperience in the face of the state's highly charged partisan atmosphere. In his effort to appeal to voters with a goody bag of public works projects, the Republican governor made a strategic mistake. By laying out his infrastructure proposal during his State of the State address and making it known how important the plan's success was to him, Schwarzenegger was in effect handing the rival party the recipe for his defeat. The plan's success was dependent on the support of Democrats, who controlled the legislature and could guarantee its defeat by blocking the governor's efforts to get an infrastructure bond on the ballot. Coming on the heels of his humiliation at the polls the previous November, the failure of Schwarzenegger's infrastructure project would reinforce voters' image of him as ineffectual during his reelection bid, thus helping the Democratic candidate win the state.

Partisanship also worked against the governor within his own party. During the days of intense negotiations to get the infrastructure bond on the June ballot, Schwarzenegger angered Republicans by spending far more time with legislative Democratic leaders than with them. Republicans had been ambivalent to hostile about what they considered a grandiose plan from the start. The amount of spending proposed by the governor so angered conservatives that at the GOP convention in February they had tried to yank the party's endorsement for his reelection bid. Yet Schwarzenegger did little to woo his disaffected party members until a last-minute push to have donors and party activists exert pressure on the governor's behalf. In the end, this effort failed.

Schwarzenegger's populist approach also hindered his initial efforts for the year of rebuilding. In putting forth such a wide-ranging plan, the governor hoped to win broad public appeal by including something to please every element of California's diverse populace. Instead, the proposal turned out to contain something to draw the objections of nearly every interest group and partisan faction. Democrats and Republicans were united for once in complaining about the price tag. Aside from that, the two sides were miles apart, with Democrats calling for more spending in areas such as mass transit, affordable housing, urban parks, and hospitals, while Republicans wanted funding largely restricted to roads, schools, and water projects.

The projects outlined in the governor's plan pitted agricultural interests against environmentalists, business concerns against social programs, rural against urban, north against south, and coastal against inland. It was a stark reminder that populism in the new century was a vastly more complex proposition than it had been a hundred years earlier. Public opinion was also badly splintered on project priorities, once one went beyond the general perception that more funding for public works was needed

Finally, the effort to rebuild California was hamstrung by the measures voters had put in place in the past to fix what they perceived to be a broken system. Once again, the two-thirds vote requirement for passage of virtually all .

fiscal issues made it all but impossible for the legislature to achieve consensus, allowing a minority blockade to thwart the public will. The state's major building projects of the past, which Schwarzenegger called the "foundation of California's prosperity" in his 2006 State of the State address, were built during a time when only a simple majority of votes was required for passing bond issues. The two-to-one vote requirement that had been extended to include bonds in 1962 would have killed efforts such as the California Water Project (approved by the state Assembly on a vote of 50 to 30 in June 1959), if they were put to a vote today.

The rebuilding effort was further stymied by the term limits imposed by voters with Proposition 140. The shorter tenure of elected officials clouded the long-range vision of legislators whose time in office was now capped at less than a decade, and focused their attention on getting their next elected position. Term limits also sapped the legislature of experienced members who could exert the leadership needed to shape the plans into bills and guide negotiations on a project as complex as the infrastructure.

LEGISLATIVE EFFORTS AND VOTER CONFIDENCE

In the end, by failing to take action on the infrastructure bond in March, the legislature reinforced the public's distrust of their state government. In a PPIC Statewide Survey conducted just after the demise of the effort to place a bond on the June ballot, only three in ten Californians believed the governor and state legislature would be able to work together and accomplish much in the coming year, while nearly twice as many—58 percent—expected them to fail. Confidence in their elected leaders had plunged thirteen points since January, when 43 percent of Californians had at least some hope for success in Sacramento. Likely voters were equally negative in their evaluations of the state's elected officials. While Republicans were somewhat more sanguine about the prospects than were Democrats or independent voters, pessimists well outnumbered optimists in every political group. And among the 56 percent of residents who thought the state was headed in the wrong direction, fully three in four did not think the governor and legislature would be able to find common ground and move forward.

Voters focused their disappointment more on the legislature than the governor. While Schwarzenegger's 37 percent job approval rating in March was not stellar, it was virtually unchanged from January. The governor's ratings were significantly better than the legislature's 25 percent approval, which had dropped four points since January and was near its lowest point of the decade. And while opinions of the governor broke down along party lines—seven in ten Republicans approved and the same number of Democrats disapproved of

Table 6.3: Approval of the Governor and Legislature

"Do you approve or disapprove of the way that (Arnold Schwarzenegger is handling his job as governor of California) (the California Legislature is handling its job)?"

All Adults	Governor Schwarzenegger	California Legislature
Approve	37%	25%
Disapprove	52	59
Don't know	11	16

"Do you approve or disapprove of the way that (Governor Schwarzenegger) (the California Legislature) is handling the issue of transportation and other infrastructure projects?"

All Adults	Governor Schwarzenegger	California Legislature
Approve	36%	23%
Disapprove	40	54
Don't know	24	23

Source: PPIC Statewide Survey, March 2006. Adults.

the job Schwarzenegger was doing—a majority in all parties had a negative opinion of the legislature. Californians also were more approving of the governor (36%) than the legislature (23%) on handling the issue of transportation and other infrastructure needs. Still, approval ratings of elected officials were low in general and specifically for their handling of the most publicized issue (see table 6.3).

Despite Sacramento's failure to move forward on the infrastructure bond in March, Californians remained solidly favorable toward the plan. In a March 2006 survey, 69 percent overall said they approved of the governor's $222 billion proposal: statistically unchanged from the support voiced just after the plan was announced in January. More than two in three in all political parties favored the proposal—in fact, both Democrats (up four points) and Republicans (up three points) had warmed toward it in the past three months. Interestingly, while likely voters had been a bit more skeptical toward the governor's plan than the general public in January (64% approving), support within this group had risen seven points by March, with 71 percent of likely voters now favoring the infrastructure proposal. Solid majorities in all demographic groups agreed with the plan.

BACKROOM BIPARTISANSHIP

While publicly the infrastructure bond appeared to be dead, state legislative leaders continued meeting in private throughout the spring to attempt to reach an agreement. The partisanship that had derailed the previous effort was replaced by a new spirit of legislative cooperation, with Assembly speaker Núñez and Senate president pro tem Perata, the Democratic leaders, working alongside Assembly Republican leaders Kevin McCarthy and George Plescia and Senate Republican leader Dick Ackerman to create a compromise plan. Just after midnight on May 5, the new infrastructure bond package passed in the Senate. Three hours later, the plan cleared the Assembly. California's two-thirds vote requirement for placing bond measures on the ballot reportedly posed a stumbling block in the Assembly, where at least six Republican votes were needed. But after the measures passed the Senate, two hours of intense lobbying of Republicans by Plescia, and the reassignment of an obstinate Democratic assemblyman to the tiny office known as the "doghouse," led the plan to victory in the lower house and earned it a place on the November 2006 ballot (*Sacramento Bee*, May 6, 2006). The revamped package included four bonds totaling around $37 billion—more than twice the amount of the eleven-hour proposal left to die on the Senate doorstep six weeks earlier. It was well short of the $68 billion bond the governor had outlined in his ten-year-plan, but more than the $25 billion he had proposed for the June primary ballot.

The infrastructure projects that would be funded under the new plan included: $19.9 billion for transportation; $10.4 billion for construction and renovation of public schools, community colleges, and universities; $4.1 billion for levee repair and flood control measures; and $2.9 billion for development of urban and low-income housing (California Secretary of State, "Propositions That Are on the November 7, 2006 General Election Ballot," 2006). Conspicuously missing were mentions of two projects that had doomed the previous attempt: new dams or water storage facilities (toxic to Democrats) and urban parks (repugnant to Republicans).

Efforts to reach a bipartisan agreement on the bond package were helped along by the looming "May Revise"—the governor's release of his revised state budget plan for the upcoming fiscal year—after which virtually all other legislative business would come to a halt until a new budget was passed. The 2006 May Revise was to begin on May 12 and legislators were eager to reach closure on the bonds in advance of budget meetings.

An even bigger motivation for legislators was an initiative headed for the November ballot that would forbid them from using state gasoline tax revenues to balance the state budget under virtually all circumstances. A citizens' initiative passed in 2002, Proposition 42, had restricted the use of gas tax funds for any purpose other than transportation, but had allowed legislators to raid those funds in a fiscal emergency. They had dipped into it, to the tune of around $2.5 billion, to fund schools and other state programs during the state's recent budget crunch. The pending initiative, being promoted by a coalition of highway construction companies and contractors, threatened to close that loophole for good.

When legislative leaders learned that the initiative had garnered enough signatures to qualify for the November ballot, they took preemptive action.

They did so by placing on the ballot their own proposal, which would permit borrowing of gas tax funds in a state emergency but require repayment within three years. That effort, however, necessitated getting the highway lobby to drop its initiative and support the legislature's version. They agreed, in exchange for being allowed to write the title and ballot wording for the new measure. In addition, the highway group insisted that the measure be placed at the top of the ballot. Thus, November voters would first confront Proposition 1A, labeled "transportation funding protection," followed by Propositions 1B: the transportation bond, 1C: the housing bond, 1D: the school bond, and 1E: the flood-control bond, with the assumption that measures nearest the top had the best chance of passing.

But perhaps the biggest push for lawmakers to drop their partisan differences and work together to craft the state's largest investment in its infrastructure since the 1960s was the drubbing they received after failing to take action in March. The low 25 percent approval rating the legislators in Sacramento received in the March survey was echoed by other surveys PPIC conducted throughout the spring, and the public could now point to the legislature for the sorry state of California's roads, levees, and schools. It was enough to spark the state Assembly and Senate into action and bring about the return of what *Los Angeles Times* columnist George Skelton called a "retro Legislature"—with "legislators doing the legislating" (*Los Angeles Times*, May 8, 2006). Echoing the governor's "message received" statement that January, legislators appeared to be cooling the rhetoric, finding common ground, and working toward fixing the problems together.

A SURPRISE WINDFALL

Shortly after the passage of the infrastructure package, Governor Schwarzenegger delivered a major dose of good news to Californians on May 12. For reasons that were not quite clearly understood at the time but were largely linked to increased personal income tax collections, state coffers were about $7.5 billion richer than had been forecast at the beginning of the year. This allowed the governor to put out a revised budget that included generous increases for education, health care, and law enforcement.

The biggest beneficiaries of the governor's new largesse were K–12 schools, which would receive an additional $2 billion in the 2006 to 2007 budget and an extra $2.9 billion by 2014. The funds were characterized as repayment for the money borrowed from the state's school budget in 2004. It was an effort to mollify the California Teachers Association, which had hounded Schwarzenegger throughout 2005 claiming that he reneged on his promise to pay schools back. The revised budget also included adding $1.6

billion to the state's "rainy day" reserve fund, as well as $400 million to hospitals and public health agencies for emergency preparedness, $500 million for repairing levees, and $23 million for child health care. Under the new plan, the state would spend $3.2 billion to pay down its debts, including early payment on some of the bonds issued to fund the state budget in 2004 (California Department of Finance, "Governor's Budget, May Revision 2006–07," 2006).

But the welcome bonus in state funds carried with it the threat of new spending commitments like those that had contributed to the demise of Governor Davis. Blessed with a $12 billion budget surplus during the high-tech boom in 2000 and 2001, Davis had yielded to pressure from Republicans to cut taxes and from Democrats to increase funding for state programs. When the dot-com economy collapsed a year later, the state was unable to pay for the newly mandated programs with lowered tax revenues. The outcome was a massive deficit, causing the budget crisis that ultimately led to Davis's recall from office.[2]

In his revised budget, Schwarzenegger was working hard to avoid the pitfall that had trapped Davis. Nearly all the proposed funding increases would go to one-time expenditures, characterized as debt repayment, budget reserves, and infrastructure projects, rather than ongoing programs that would have to be funded in perpetuity under the dictates of California's ballot-box budgeting. But whether the new, conciliatory Schwarzenegger would be able to withstand the demands of partisan and special interest groups would determine the success or failure of his effort.

And even if he could resist the pressure to win friends by cutting taxes and raising spending, another danger lurked—Proposition 98—which would automatically funnel about 40 percent of the increased state revenues into education funding. That would be fine, if the state economy stayed healthy. But if the $7.5 billion bonus collected during the 2005 tax year turned out to be a one-time windfall, as many budget experts warned, and revenues declined in subsequent years, the state would be hard-pressed to come up with the increased allocations for education. Yet, under the provisions of Proposition 98, legislators would be required to give schools the same amount they received during the rosiest years—putting a severe strain on their ability to provide for other state programs without taking the highly unpopular step of suspending the funding formula. Schwarzenegger's suspension of Proposition 98 in 2004 had set the stage for the ongoing conflict with the teachers' union that ultimately torpedoed his year of reform.[3]

A similar risk accompanied Proposition 49—the initiative that Schwarzenegger had used to launch his political career four years earlier. Although state budgets had been too lean to trigger implementation of the measure's spending guarantees since its passage in 2002, the increased revenue base for the 2006 to 2007 budget made the measure kick in. Despite its relatively small size—$426 million allocated in the May Revise—the money given to schools to operate after-school programs nonetheless presented the challenge of being a continuous appropriation, meaning that it would be funded with or without the approval of the legislature in the future. Indeed, the citizens' initiative Schwarzenegger had championed was an even more inflexible case of "autopilot spending" than Proposition 98, in that the after-school funding could not be suspended even in a state fiscal emergency (Legislative Analyst's Office, "Analysis of the 2006–07 Budget Bill," 2006).

PUBLIC IS COOL TO OFFICIALS,
POSITIVE TOWARD THEIR PLANS

While the governor's revised budget was an immediate hit, the public remained skeptical about Schwarzenegger's leadership. In a PPIC survey conducted just after the release of the May Revise, 57 percent of Californians said they were satisfied with the new budget plan—considerably higher than the 44 percent approving of the revised 2005 to 2006 budget in a PPIC Statewide Survey one year ago. Californians were especially favorable toward the plans to increase spending for schools (77%), pay down the state debt and add to the reserve fund (76%), and put money into levee repairs (67%). But a majority of adults (52%) and nearly half of likely voters (47%) still said they disapproved of the way Schwarzenegger was handling the budget and taxes.

The governor's overall job approval ratings remained a low 36 percent among all adults and 42 percent among likely voters—virtually unchanged from March. Moreover, when it came to making decisions on taxes and state program funding, Californians expressed more confidence in the leadership of the Democrats (35%) and Republicans (20%) in the legislature than in the governor (19%). This was a sharp drop from a May 2004 survey, when 30 percent preferred the governor's approach to fiscal policy, tying with the number preferring that of legislative Democrats.

As for the legislature, despite the public's preference for having this body set state fiscal policy, the May survey showed that the Assembly and Senate still had a long way to go to regain the people's confidence. Only 26 percent of all Californians and 23 percent of likely voters approved of the way the elected members of the state house were handling their jobs—statistically unchanged from the 25 percent approval in March. Solid majorities in all political groups disapproved of the job the legislature was doing. And though their passage of the infrastructure bond package did improve the legislature's ratings for handling transportation and the infrastructure—30 percent approval among all adults in May, up from 23 percent in March—a majority of adults (51%) and likely voters (57%) continued to dislike the legislature's performance in this specific area.

Nonetheless, people showed considerable enthusiasm for three of the four infrastructure bonds set for the November ballot, with 74 percent of all adults and 68 percent of likely voters in the May survey saying they would vote yes on the $10.4 billion bond for schools and universities, 62 percent overall and 65 percent of likely voters backing the $19.9 billion transportation bond, and 62 percent of both adults and likely voters planning to approve the $4.1 billion levee repair and flood protection bond. However, the fourth bond—raising nearly $3 billion to build new affordable housing—failed to win the support of likely voters (49%), although six in ten adults overall were in favor. All the proposed bonds except for the affordable housing issue were backed by a majority in all political parties. But while a majority of Democrats (66%) and independent voters (58%) supported the housing bond, only 34 percent of Republicans agreed.

Even though state leaders were showing signs of returning to a "retro" legislature, with elected officials forging bipartisan compromises and reassuming responsibility for governing California, several findings in the May survey underscored the public's continued distrust in state government and the strength of the populist urge to weaken the power of their elected leaders.

As the legislature headed into another budget session, which throughout the past two decades had been plagued by chronically late budgets and much acrimony caused by the supermajority vote requirement for passage, a plurality among all adults (46%) and a majority of likely voters (52%) nonetheless said it would be a "bad idea" to change from the current two-thirds of the state legislature to a 55 percent majority vote. This proposal had previously been rejected in March 2004, when only 34 percent of voters cast ballots in favor of Proposition 56 (which also would have lowered the vote requirement for raising taxes). Support for reducing the two-thirds budget vote requirement had actually declined over time—from 46 percent calling it a "good idea" in June 2003, to 44 percent in May 2005, to 42 percent approving in the May 2006 survey. Among likely voters, only 40 percent now favored this change. Fewer than half in any political party approved of lowering the vote requirement for passage of the state budget.

Although the legislature's failure to devise a bond package for the June ballot was at least partly the result of term limits robbing Sacramento of experienced leaders, Californians remained adamantly in favor of restricting elected officials' time in office. Six in ten adults and two in three likely voters in the May survey said term limits were "a good thing," similar to the September 2004 (61%) and October 2005 (57%) surveys (see table 6.4). Term limits were favored by solid majorities in all political groups, with support especially strong among Republicans (74%).

Table 6.4: Term Limits and Campaign Finance

"The California Legislature has operated under term limits since 1990, meaning that members of the state Senate and state Assembly are limited in the number of terms they can hold their elected office. Do you think that term limits are a good thing or a bad thing for California, or do they make no difference?"

	All Adults	Democrats	Republicans	Independents
Good thing	60%	59%	74%	63%
Bad thing	15	21	10	15
No difference	21	17	15	19
Don't know	4	3	1	3

"Do you think that campaign contributions are currently having a good effect or a bad effect on the public policy decisions made by state elected officials in Sacramento, or are campaign contributions making no difference?"

	All Adults	Democrats	Republicans	Independents
Good effect	12%	11%	10%	7%
Bad effect	55	63	57	65
No difference	23	17	21	21
Other	1	1	2	1
Don't know	9	8	10	6

Source: PPIC Statewide Survey, May 2006.

As a further sign of their lingering distrust of state government and on-going concern about the influence of special interest groups, a majority of Californians (55%) and an even larger number of likely voters (64%) said that campaign contributions were currently having a "bad effect" on public policy decisions made by elected officials in Sacramento (see table 6.4). Only a quarter of all adults (23%) and fewer than one in five likely voters (18%) said campaign contributions made "no difference." The number of residents believing that campaign contributions were harming public policy decisions was similar in the October 2005 (53%) and September 1999 (56%) surveys. In this case, independents (65%) and Democrats (63%) were more likely than Republicans (57%) to say that campaign contributions were having a bad effect.

PASSING AN ON-TIME BUDGET

Schwarzenegger scored a major victory on June 30 when he and the legislature delivered California's first on-time budget since 2000, and only the fourth in the past twenty years. The state's general fund budget of just over $100 billion (a total of $131.4 billion from all sources), had plenty of spending increases to mollify the various constituencies that had been upset with the governor's more frugal approach of the previous year. Most important from a political and public opinion standpoint, the budget included a record $55 billion for K–12 and community colleges—up about $3 billion from one year earlier. The budget also added more spending for public health, higher education, transportation, and law enforcement over the previous year. In addition, the budget offered something for the fiscally conservative California voters—the prospects of nearly $5 billion for debt repayment and building a budget reserve (California Department of Finance, "California State Budget 2006–07," 2006). "It's amazing what can be accomplished when Democrats and Republicans work together in Sacramento," Schwarzenegger said on signing the budget (Schwarzenegger, "Office of the Governor press release, June 30, 2006," 2006).

A BITTER PARTISAN PRIMARY

As Schwarzenegger continued to develop his new role as a bipartisan lawmaker, a bitter political contest was taking place in the Democratic primary for governor. Steve Westly, the state controller, and Phil Angelides, the state treasurer, were locked in a nasty campaign for their party's nomination. Each man's independent wealth and business connections—Westly as a former eBay executive and Angelides as a successful developer—gave them the means to skirt the state's campaign contribution caps imposed by a citizens' initiative passed in 2000. That initiative, Proposition 34, limited individual contributions to candidates in the primary and general elections for governor to $22,300 per contest, in an effort to overhaul campaign financing and weaken the influence of major donors. The rules went into effect for the first time during the 2006 primary.

Because of their personal wealth, Westly and Angelides were able to bypass the new limits on donors by financing their campaigns from their own pockets. The wealthier of the two, Westly, spent a reported $34 million of his own money on his campaign. While Angelides spent less in personal funds on his bid to win the nomination, the loophole allowed Angelides's longtime friends, developer Angelo Tsakopoulos and his daughter Eleni Tsakopoulos-Kounalakis, to contribute nearly $9 million through an independent committee called "Californians for a Better Government." While the committee was represented as a coalition of firefighters, police, deputy sheriffs, and developers—its largest contributions by far came from the Tsakopoulos family (*San Francisco Chronicle*, June 1, 2006).

The 2006 Democratic primary clearly demonstrated the flaws in Proposition 34's efforts at campaign finance reform. Rather than limiting the clout of big money donors and special interest groups, it seemed to have intensified it. Thus, the implementation of this measure appeared to have accelerated a trend underway for some time—that it was mostly the independently wealthy candidates, who could draw on their own finances and those of their colleagues to avoid campaign finance rules, who could afford to run for office. This perception stood to further alienate voters who were already distrustful of their state government and the influence of special interests.

Yet, while both Democrats flooded the airwaves with attack ads maligning their opponent's ethics and integrity, the millions spent appeared to have little effect on a disinterested electorate. Burned out by the previous year's special election, and lacking enthusiasm for either the Democratic candidates or the two measures on the ballot, many voters gave the June 6 primary a cold shoulder. The preelection surveys in March, April, and May found just three in ten independents planning to vote in either of the major party primaries, with only one in five expressing an interest in the Democratic primary. About three in four likely voters had actually seen the television advertisements for the Democratic gubernatorial candidates, but apparently these did not make much of an impression. Of all the voters who were likely to cast ballots in the Democratic primary, fewer than half had a favorable impression of either Angelides or Westly, and more than four in ten were undecided in the May survey conducted within weeks of the election.

Angelides's endorsement by the Democratic party and his support from the unions that were key funders of Democratic candidates proved to be crucial to his victory in a low-turnout primary that attracted few but the party faithful. On June 6, Angelides defeated Westly by five points (48% to 43%)—a mere 120,000 votes (see table 6.5). How did Angelides manage to win this close race? According to the Los Angeles Times Exit Poll of voters casting ballots in the June 6 primary election, Angelides won by large margins among liberals and union members, while the race was relatively close among moderates and non–union members. Four in ten Democratic primary voters were liberals, and one in four said they belonged to a union. In this low-turnout election, the influence of interest groups and partisan activists appeared to be the deciding factors for Angelides.

The 33.6 percent voter turnout in June 2006 was the lowest on record—edging out the 34.6 percent turnout in the March 2002 primary, which was the previous low for a California primary. On the GOP side, despite no real opposition and no paid advertising to attract interest in the party's primary,

Table 6.5: Democratic Gubernatorial Primary

Phil Angelides	48.0%
Steve Westly	43.2
Other candidates	8.8
Registered voter turnout	33.6%

Source: California Secretary of State, "Statement of the Vote," June 2006.

Schwarzenegger still received about 1.7 million votes—more than either Angelides (1.2 million) or Westly (1.08 million). But the low turnout raised an important question about the November election: would voters who were too turned off to vote in the Democratic primary show up to vote for the GOP governor and the package of infrastructure bonds that he placed on the ballot with the help of Democratic legislators, or would they simply stay home again in the fall?

Another important, negative feature of the June primary for voters were the "down-ticket races" for the other executive branch offices—lieutenant governor, California secretary of state, controller, treasurer, attorney general, and insurance commissioner. This part of the primary ballot was dominated by state officials who were playing musical chairs in seeking to move from one executive branch office to another (e.g., Cruz Bustamante, John Garamendi, Bill Lockyer), or from legislative seats (e.g., Debra Bowen, Tom McClintock, Debra Ortiz, Chuck Poochigian, Keith Richman), or mayor's offices (e.g., Jerry Brown). There were relatively few new faces on the statewide party ballots.

With self-funded millionaires seeking their party's nomination for governor and so many current office holders running in the down-ticket races, California's June primary reinforced voters' perceptions that their state government was beholden to special interests, party politics, and career politicians. For many voters, their response was to skip the election altogether, resulting in the lowest primary turnout in state history.

TWIN DEFEATS OF PROPOSITIONS 81 AND 82

On the initiative front, after a 2005 special ballot that was crowded with eight ballot measures, the June primary was a relatively quiet affair. The two state propositions included a $600 million library bond (Proposition 81) placed on the ballot by the legislature and a citizen's initiative that would raise taxes on the wealthy to provide preschool for all four-year-olds in California (Proposition 82). The former was a fairly uncontroversial measure that drew little discussion or organized opposition, while the latter had all the features to attract public attention—Hollywood celebrity, money, a popular children's cause, and a tax that only impacted the state's wealthiest residents.

Movie actor and director Rob Reiner had burst onto the California political scene with Proposition 10 in 1998—an initiative that passed and provided funds for state and county children's programs through a dedicated tax on cigarette purchases. He had chosen as his next cause a citizen's initiative that would tax the income of the wealthiest Californians to pay for a public preschool program. A January 2006 poll conducted in anticipation of this

initiative found that 66 percent of likely voters were generally favorable toward raising income taxes on the state's wealthiest residents and 63 percent
supported taxing them for this particular purpose.

Early voter support for the preschool proposal was in the context of a recent
public education campaign for preschool access that was funded with public
dollars from Proposition 10. When critics alleged that the use of several million dollars in public funds for this purpose was improper in light of the upcoming initiative campaign, the political dynamics of the preschool initiative
were dramatically altered. Reiner, who had become the lightning rod for the allegations of misuse of funds, was forced to withdraw from the Proposition 82
campaign.[4] Meanwhile, business groups and others opposed to this latest effort
to tax the wealthy mounted an active and well-funded campaign against it.

The PPIC surveys in March, April, and May indicated that bare majorities
of Californians (between 50% and 52%) were supporting Propositions 81
and 82. While Democrats showed solid support for both measures, there was
considerable opposition among Republicans, and independents were divided.
The library bond and the preschool initiative failed to reach a majority in June
(see table 6.6). Proposition 81 was defeated by a narrow margin (47% yes)
while Proposition 82 lost by a wide margin (39% yes).

The Los Angeles Times Exit Poll of June primary voters indicated that Republicans and independents strongly opposed Proposition 82, the preschool
initiative, as did a majority of moderates and conservatives. While liberals
and Democrats were solidly in favor, they were outnumbered at the polls. No
postelection survey was available for Proposition 81, the library bond; however, while it won in Democratic-leaning Los Angeles County and the San
Francisco Bay Area, its margins were not large enough to overcome defeat
in Republican strongholds such as Orange County (California Secretary of
State, "Statement of the Vote: 2006 Primary Election," 2006).

In reality, both measures had fallen victim to the partisan divide. Proposition 82 also drew the opposition of special interests. Unlike Schwarzenegger's
efforts with his after-school initiative, supporters of the preschool initiative
failed to turn it into a populist cause. The defeat of both ballot measures in
June raised concerns about the $37 billion in infrastructure bonds going be-

Table 6.6: June 2006 Vote on Statewide Measures

Proposition 81: Library Bond	
Yes	47.3%
No	52.7
Proposition 82: Preschool Education Initiative	
Yes	39.2%
No	60.8
Registered voter turnout	33.6%

Source: California Secretary of State, "Statement of the Vote," June 2006.

fore voters in November. Their success would depend on how well the GOP governor and Democratic legislature could remain united in an election year and whether interest groups would mount an organized opposition.

THE GOVERNOR'S RACE: ARNOLD IS BACK

With no primary challenger, Schwarzenegger was in an enviable position of turning his full attention to a reelection campaign. While his Democratic opponent was recovering from a bruising and expensive primary race, relatively few attacks had been directed at the governor from either inside or outside his party. Indeed, a July survey showed that Schwarzenegger's ratings were heading back up, and he had already captured an early lead in the gubernatorial race. Nearly half of likely voters (49%) approved of the way the governor was handling his job—a seven-point increase since May.

As for the fall match-up, Schwarzenegger led Angelides by thirteen points (43% to 30%) in July. Equally important for a GOP governor, he led by eighteen points among independents (43% to 25%) and drew the support of one in six Democrats, while a solid eight in ten Republicans stood behind him in this race. Still, it was early in the contest, at a time when Angelides had not been actively campaigning, and one in four voters opted for other candidates or were undecided.

THE NOVEMBER BALLOT:
DIRECT DEMOCRACY IS ALSO BACK

In contrast to a quiet June ballot, thirteen state propositions were headed for the November 2006 election. Foremost on the governor's and legislature's agenda were the four infrastructure bond measures. Propositions 1B (the $19.9 billion transportation bond), 1C (the $2.9 billion affordable housing bond), 1D (the $10.4 billion education facilities bond), and 1E (the $4.1 billion water and flood control bond) were the backbone of Schwarzenegger's year of rebuilding endeavor. State lawmakers had also agreed to put up Proposition 1A, the transportation funding protection amendment, which would prevent the state from spending gas tax funds on anything other than transportation except in dire fiscal emergencies.

In addition to making decisions on more than $37 billion in bond measures, November general election voters would also face eight citizens' initiatives:

- Proposition 83, which proponents called "Jessica's Law" after a nine-year-old girl who was kidnapped and murdered by a sex offender in Florida, would increase prison terms and require lifetime electronic monitoring for violent or habitual sex offenders. The measure was endorsed by Schwarzenegger and was supported by Republicans and Democrats alike.

- Proposition 84, another bond, would direct $5.4 billion to a variety of water projects and natural resource preservation efforts, including state parks. This measure was put up by a coalition of environmental groups, after the governor and legislature dropped their own efforts on the issue because Republicans insisted on new reservoirs that Democrats opposed. It was endorsed by Schwarzenegger and legislative Democrats, but opposed by most Republicans.

- Proposition 85 was a virtual repeat of Proposition 73, the parental notification measure that failed in the November 2005 special election. The governor had endorsed Proposition 73 in 2005, but was not campaigning for Proposition 85.

- Proposition 86 sought to increase the state tax on cigarettes by $2.60. The proceeds would go to health programs, health insurance for low-income children, and medical research. The initiative was supported by the California Hospital Association and health groups. It was opposed by cigarette manufacturers. Schwarzenegger had come out against the measure.

- Proposition 87 would levy a new tax on oil producers and use the revenues to fund research on alternative sources of energy. The stated goal of the measure was to reduce gasoline consumption by 25 percent over the next ten years. Major proponents included Hollywood producer Steven Bing, who contributed $50 million to the campaign, as well as Silicon Valley investors. Siding with his party, the governor opposed this tax measure.

- Proposition 88 was a bid to generate about $450 million a year for schools with a statewide $50 parcel tax. The campaign was initially funded with a nearly $7 million donation from Netflix founder Reed Hastings and venture capitalist John Doerr. But it was opposed by Schwarzenegger, Democrats, and Republicans alike. Its founders and funders soon deserted it, and Proposition 88 became an "orphan initiative."

- Proposition 89 was a campaign finance reform measure sponsored by the California Nurses Association, which would raise the corporate income tax rate to provide public financing for state electoral campaigns. It would also place tight caps on contributions to candidates. The California Teachers Association joined up with the Chamber of Commerce in working to defeat Proposition 89. In an unusual display of unity, partisan and special interest groups, the perennial adversaries of labor and business, and Democratic and Republican officeholders including Schwarzenegger had found a common purpose in fighting this threat to their political clout.

- Proposition 90 would make it harder for state and local governments to use their power of eminent domain to obtain private property for private developments, such as shopping malls. It was being funded by New York real estate investor Howie Rich, a libertarian, who was supporting a host of efforts in direct democracy states throughout the nation aimed at limiting the size and power of government.[5]

As they contemplated the November ballot's bond total of about $43 billion across five measures (Propositions 1B, 1C, 1D, 1E, and 84), voters were generally approving of using state bonds to pay for infrastructure improvements. Nearly six in ten likely voters (59%) in an August survey thought it was a "good idea" in general to have the state issue bonds for projects such as roads, schools, and water facilities. However, faced with the upcoming ballot, voters' support for using state bonds for this purpose had declined from 69 percent in September 2002. In August, favor for using bonds was higher among Democrats (69%) and independents (58%) than Republicans (46%).

The size of the debt under consideration appeared daunting for many Californians. Among likely voters, 59 percent overall, 76 percent of Republicans, 56 percent of independents, and 48 percent of Democrats said the total of the five measures was "too much." Only 21 percent of voters in the August 2006 survey called it "the right amount." The individual bond measures drew mild to moderate support in the August survey. Fifty percent of likely voters said they planned to vote yes on Proposition 1B, the $19.9 billion transportation bond, including 60 percent of Democrats, 48 percent of independents, and 40 percent of Republicans. Proposition 1C, the $2.8 billion affordable housing bond, was favored by 57 percent of likely voters, with support at 71 percent among Democrats, 58 percent among independents, and 40 percent among Republicans. On Proposition 1D, the $10.4 billion education facilities bond, 51 percent of likely voters said they would vote yes, including 67 percent of Democrats and 50 percent of independents, but only 32 percent of Republicans. And Proposition 1E, the $4.1 billion bond for water and flood control projects, was favored by 56 percent of likely voters overall, 66 percent of Democrats, 56 percent of independents, and 46 percent of Republicans. About one in ten voters was undecided on each of these measures.

It appeared that voters were reacting primarily to the size of the bonds, with the smaller amounts (1C, $2.8 billion, and 1E, $4.1 billion) drawing the greatest number of yes votes. However, the relatively small size of Proposition 84, the $5.4 billion water and natural resources initiative, did not appear to help it. Only 40 percent of likely voters supported Proposition 84 in the August survey, while 45 percent planned to vote no and 15 percent were uncertain. That measure fell below a majority in all political groups, including Democrats (49%), independents (44%), and Republicans (28%).

Even though they faced a long roster of initiatives in what would be their fifth trip to the polls since the recall, Californians' support for their state's direct democracy provisions was actually on the rise. Nearly three in four likely voters (74%) in the August 2006 survey said it was a "good thing" that voters could make laws through initiatives, while 21 percent called it a "bad thing." The number expressing positive opinions about the initiative process had risen 6 points since October 2000. Now, more than two in three voters in all political groups approved of voters being able to make laws at the ballot box.

In addition, voters' confidence in the policy decisions made by initiatives had climbed during this era of the provision's unprecedented use. With the thirteen measures on the November ballot bringing the number of initiatives voters had contemplated since the beginning of the decade to eighty-six—seventeen more than the total for the entire decade of the 1990s (the state's previous high)—six in ten likely voters in the August 2006 survey said public policy decisions made through the initiative process were "probably better" than those made by the governor and state legislature. Only 24 percent said decisions made by initiatives were "probably worse" than those made by elected leaders and 6 percent said the two methods were about the same. Confidence in voters' decisions had risen seven points since October 2000. Majorities of Republicans (64%), independents (63%), and Democrats (57%) in August 2006 all believed that policy decisions made through the initiative process were better than those made by their state government.

Consistent with the increased emphasis on setting policy at the ballot box since the 2003 recall, voters' trust in government had fallen during the decade. Only 23 percent of likely voters in the August survey said they trusted the government in Sacramento to do what is right "just about always" or "most

Table 6.7: Trust in State Government

"How much of the time do you think you can trust the government in Sacramento to do what is right?"

	Likely Voters	Democrats	Republicans	Independents
Always/most of the time	23%	27%	23%	28%
Only some of the time	72	66	72	66
None of the time (volunteered)	5	5	5	4
Don't know	0	2	0	2

"Do you think the people in state government waste a lot of the money we pay in taxes, waste some of it, or don't waste very much of it?"

	Likely Voters	Democrats	Republicans	Independents
A lot	61%	53%	67%	59%
Some	34	40	31	32
Not very much	4	4	1	7
Don't know	1	3	1	2

Source: PPIC Statewide Survey, August 2006.

of the time," while 72 percent said "only some of the time" and 5 percent volunteered "never" (see table 6.7). In August 2005, a similar 24 percent of likely voters said they generally trusted their state government. Voters' trust in Sacramento had remained low since the recall campaign and was considerably lower than it had been in January 2001 (46%) and 2002 (44%). Trust in state government was equally low in all political groups in the August 2006 survey. Echoing this ongoing distrust of their state government, more than six in ten likely voters in August 2006 believed their elected leaders wasted "a lot" of the money Californians paid in taxes (61%). The events of the past few years had significantly increased this perception from what it had been before the recall (47% in January 2001; 41% in January 2002).

A DEMOCRAT'S REPUBLICAN

As the 2006 legislative session drew to a close, Schwarzenegger and the Democratic majority were basking in a balmy climate of cooperation. By the end of August, the governor and legislature had reached a deal to raise the state's minimum wage by $1.25 an hour, compromising with Democrats on the amount while getting them to give up their insistence on automatic annual adjustment for inflation. The two sides also agreed on a prescription drug deal with sanctions on pharmaceutical companies that failed to provide discounts for low-income Californians. This was a big concession for the governor, who had sided with the drug manufacturers in the 2005 special election. The bipartisan agreements were signed with much fanfare and photo opportunities of the governor and Democratic leaders smiling together.

What was widely seen as Schwarzenegger's boldest bipartisan move of the year was his cooperation on a bid to make California the first state in the nation to regulate greenhouse gas emissions. In a move aimed at combating global warming, lawmakers passed a law requiring the state to reduce its greenhouse gas emissions about 25 percent by the year 2020. While the new law left the details of just how to achieve that reduction up to the state Air Resources Board, it was called a major step for the environment and was expected to echo worldwide. On September 27, Schwarzenegger and Assembly speaker Fabian Núñez held twin ceremonies—one at Treasure Island in the middle of the San Francisco Bay and another at Pepperdine University overlooking Malibu Beach—celebrating the bill's signing. In doing so, the governor seemed to be turning his back on the business groups that had egged him on in his failed year of reform. He was also knocking the supports out from under the platform of his challenger, Phil Angelides.

The reformulated Schwarzenegger played well with voters. His approval ratings were rebounding and a September survey found that more voters approved (53%) than disapproved (39%) of his performance in office. This was a gain of fifteen points since the previous September (38%). His approval was basically unchanged in an October survey (52% approve, 41% disapprove) and he continued to be highly popular among Republicans (81%), but less so among independents (45%) and Democrats (31%). Nonetheless, his approval among Democrats had risen nineteen points since October 2005 (12%). Similar dramatic gains were made among all adults, with 47 percent in October 2006 approving and 45 percent disapproving of Schwarzenegger's performance in office, up from 33 percent approval and 58 percent disapproval one year earlier.

This put the governor in good standing for his reelection bid. In September, 48 percent of likely voters said they planned to vote for him, giving him a seventeen-point lead over Angelides (31%), while 6 percent backed other candidates and 15 percent were undecided. Despite a month of hard campaigning by both candidates, their standings had not changed much by October (48% Schwarzenegger, 30% Angelides). Schwarzenegger ran very strong among Republicans (86%), and independents also favored him over his challenger (43% to 24%).

Meanwhile, Angelides was capturing a much smaller majority within his own party (57%), while a significant one in five Democrats were supporting the governor in the October survey. Also spelling trouble for Angelides was the Republican's strength in Los Angeles (38% Schwarzenegger, 40% Angelides) and the San Francisco Bay Area (40% Schwarzenegger, 34% Angelides)—both typically Democratic strongholds. Elsewhere, the governor led his challenger by as much as forty-two points. The only demographic pocket where Angelides had an edge in October was among Latinos (52% Angelides, 25% Schwarzenegger), while white voters favored Schwarzenegger by more than thirty points (56% Schwarzenegger, 23% Angelides).

This "summer of love" with the governor did little to improve Californians' image of their legislature, however. Only 32 percent of likely voters in September 2006 approved of the way the state Assembly and Senate were performing, while 55 percent said they disapproved. By October, the legislature's ratings had fallen to 26 percent approval and 61 percent disapproval among likely voters. Still, this represented an improvement from the previous October, when 21 percent of likely voters gave the legislature a positive job evaluation and 65 percent disapproved. While Republicans (63%) were more likely than Democrats (51%) and independents (57%) to disapprove of the legislature's performance in October 2006, negative ratings outnumbered positive ratings in all political parties.

How had Schwarzenegger managed to pull out of his year of reform nosedive? Part of the boost to his image came from comparisons with Angelides. Elected to the state treasurer's office in 1986, Angelides had been a successful land developer before entering politics as chair of the California Democratic Party. The grandson of Greek immigrants, Angelides was seen as a champion of old-style liberal causes such as labor, poverty, and minority issues. But he was having trouble establishing his gubernatorial platform as anything other than anti-Arnold. One of his main campaign tactics was trying to link Schwarzenegger with the unpopular President Bush, of whom 64 percent of Californians in the September 2006 survey disapproved.

But the link wasn't holding. The Republican governor had carefully distanced himself from the conservative national administration, ignoring party line on issues such as stem cell research and being unavailable when Bush visited California for the GOP midterm election campaign in the fall. Schwarzenegger was instead putting his stamp on traditionally liberal issues, such as minimum wage and environmental protection. In addition to usurping Democratic turf, this approach helped reestablish the governor's populist credentials as a political maverick, rather than a partisan insider. What's more, he was seen as taking on the topics of most importance to ordinary Californians—allaying their long-standing mistrust of politicians who seemed out of touch with the people.

The governor's efforts appeared to be paying off. While a majority of voters in the September 2006 survey said they were dissatisfied with the amount of attention the candidates for governor were spending on important issues (54%) and only 32 percent were satisfied, unhappiness was ten points lower than it had been in a September 2002 survey taken during the previous governor's race (64% dissatisfied, 27% satisfied). Moreover, while four in ten voters now said they were less enthusiastic than usual about voting in the upcoming governor's election, this number was fifteen points lower than during the Davis-Simon contest (55% less enthusiastic).

Schwarzenegger's unique brand of fiscal populism also played well with California voters. Publicly vowing that he would never raise taxes, the governor had allowed the state's general fund expenditures to grow by 27 percent during his time in office (*San Jose Mercury News*, October 25, 2006). His original proposal to borrow $68 billion to repair the state's infrastructure was more than even Democrats could stomach, and the $37 billion plan agreed on was historic in its size and scope. This seemingly contradictory approach to budgeting echoed voters' own conflicted views on state fiscal issues. In the September survey, a majority of likely voters (51%) said their local government did not have the adequate funding for needed infrastructure projects in their area and only 39 percent thought the funding was sufficient. But when asked whether they would prefer to pay higher taxes and have the state spend more on infrastructure or whether they would rather pay lower taxes and have the government spend less for such projects, voters were conflicted. Half (47%) opted for lower taxes and less infrastructure spending, while a nearly equal proportion (45%) favored higher taxes and more money for state projects.

THE INFRASTRUCTURE BOND MEASURES

As the November election approached, the success of the infrastructure bond package was questionable. A majority of likely voters in the September 2006 survey favored the $2.9 billion affordable housing bond (Proposition 1C: 57% yes, 30% no), and the $4.1 billion water facilities bond (Proposition 1E: 55% yes, 30% no). But the project's backbone—the $19.9 billion transportation bond—drew support from just over half of likely voters (Proposition 1B: 51% yes, 36% no). And the $10.4 billion education facilities bond fell below a majority (Proposition 1D: 49% yes, 40% no). There had been little movement on any of these bond measures since the August survey.

Voters continued to give mixed reviews to the infrastructure bonds in the October survey, with only Proposition 1C leading by more than twenty points (56% yes, 34% no, 10% undecided). Proposition 1B (51% yes, 38% no, 11% undecided) and Proposition 1D (51% yes, 39% no, 10% undecided) were in precarious positions, with Proposition 1E faring only slightly better (53% yes, 36% no, 11% undecided). Although the Republican governor had made the infrastructure bonds the centerpiece of his year of reform, his endorsement did not appear to be swaying members of his own party, who were rejecting the education facilities bond (54% no, 37% yes, 9% undecided) and leaning toward turning down the affordable housing bond (48% no, 43% yes, 9% undecided). The transportation bond (46% no, 44% yes, 10% undecided) and the water facilities bond (44% yes, 43% no, 13% undecided) also fell short of a majority among Republican voters in October. Democrats and independent voters, on the other hand, favored all four bonds by sizeable margins.

GUBERNATORIAL ELECTION OUTCOME

"You know I love doing sequels," Schwarzenegger announced during his victory speech at the Beverly Hilton Hotel. "And this, without doubt, is my favorite sequel" (*Los Angeles Times*, November 8, 2006). He had just been reelected by a seventeen-point margin (see table 6.8). As had been the case in all of PPIC preelection surveys, the CNN Exit Poll conducted November 7 indicated that Schwarzenegger received an overwhelming endorsement from his party members and solid support from independents, while a significant number of Democratic voters crossed party lines and also voted for the incumbent GOP governor. The Democratic candidate, Phil Angelides, who had tried to rally voters through his partisan appeals, had alienated Republicans and independents in the process, thus receiving little support outside of his party. The exit poll also indicated that the governor drew significant support across most demographic groups and regions of the state, and among mod-

Table 6.8:   November 2006 Vote for Governor

Arnold Schwarzenegger	55.9%
Phil Angelides	39.0
Other	5.1
Registered voter turnout	56.2%

Source: California Secretary of State, "Statement of the Vote," November 2006.

erate as well as conservative voters. Many who were disapproving of GOP president George Bush and voted for Democratic candidates in the other races still cast their ballots for California's Republican governor. More than 56 percent of the state's registered voters turned out to cast ballots in the November 2006 election, in contrast to the scant 50.6 percent participation in the 2002 gubernatorial contest.

But Schwarzenegger did not provide "coattails" for fellow Republicans, as Californians chose Democrats for most of the other elected offices. Democratic U.S. senator Dianne Feinstein won reelection by a landslide margin. Five of the six executive branch offices also went to Democrats, including attorney general (won by former Democratic governor Jerry Brown) and state treasurer (won by former Democratic attorney general Bill Lockyer). In the state's fifty-three-member Congressional delegation, one Republican seat was lost, as voters sent a predominantly Democratic delegation to Washington. Voters also returned control of the state Assembly and Senate to the Democratic leadership that had worked with Schwarzenegger in 2006, limiting GOP gains to one Senate seat. In the end, Schwarzenegger's conciliatory approach in 2006 managed to convince a sizeable number of Democrats and independent voters that he had returned to the populist, nonpartisan path he had pledged to follow during the recall campaign. In eschewing the influence of special interests and promising to work cooperatively with the legislature to produce bipartisan legislation for voters' consideration, he offered Californians a solution for many of the problems they felt were plaguing representative democracy.

THE FATE OF THE "YEAR OF REBUILDING" PACKAGE

While Governor Schwarzenegger's immediate political future seemed to be settled by the early summer, his legacy remained in doubt, as his infrastructure bonds had been receiving only modest support. In the end, however, a bipartisan push moved the electorate in favor of the four bond measures placed on the ballot by the governor and legislature (Propositions 1B, 1C, 1D, 1E) (see table 6.9). A bond measure placed on the ballot by a citizens' initiative (Proposition 84) and endorsed by the governor and legislature also passed with a 54 percent vote in November. Clearly, the governor's choice of a nonpartisan topic that appealed to the people (infrastructure), a broad base of support from special interests as diverse as labor unions and business groups, and Schwarzenegger's campaign appearances with prominent Democrats such as U.S. senator Dianne Feinstein, convinced voters that this legislative action had the bipartisan approach they required.

Proposition 1A, another measure placed on the ballot by the governor and legislature, was designed to protect the existing transportation funding from other state budget uses. This measure won by the widest margin—garnering the support of three in four voters—perhaps most dramatically indicating the power of bipartisan compromise and the public's desire to control how tax monies are spent. But four citizens' initiatives dealing with tax and spending issues, as well as bids to restrict abortions and limit government's power of eminent domain, were rejected by voters. Some of these measures had taken on a partisan and special interest tone in the course of the election, specifically: the oil tax for alternative energy development (Proposition 87, defeated by 55%); the cigarette tax to fund health programs (Proposition 86, defeated by 52%); and a tax on corporations to provide public funding for political campaigns (Proposition 89, defeated by 74%). The bid to require parental notification for minors' abortions (Proposition 85) was defeated by 54 percent, nearly identical to the 53 percent who had rejected a similar measure the previous year. Proposition 88, a statewide property tax increase to fund schools that was abandoned by its author halfway through the campaign, went down to a 77 percent defeat. And Proposition 90, the measure sponsored by a New York libertarian seeking to restrict eminent domain, nearly squeaked by with 52 percent voting no (California Secretary of State, "Statement of the Vote: 2006 General Election," 2006).

Table 6.9:   November 2006 Vote on Statewide Measures

Proposition 1A: Transportation Funding Protection	
Yes	77.0%
No	23.0
Proposition 1B: Highway Safety, Traffic Reduction, Air Quality, and Port Security Bond	
Yes	61.4%
No	38.6
Proposition 1C: Housing and Emergency Shelter Trust Fund	
Yes	57.8%
No	42.2
Proposition 1D: Kindergarten–University Public Education Facilities Bond	
Yes	56.9%
No	43.1
Proposition 1E: Disaster Preparedness and Flood Prevention Bond	
Yes	64.2%
No	35.8

Source: California Secretary of State, "Statement of the Vote," November 2006.

In the end, voting on these propositions appeared to come down to which side had the bigger wallet. Proposition 87, the tax on oil production, set a new spending record—becoming the nation's first $150 million ballot measure (*Los Angeles Times*, November 9, 2006). But the $57 million spent promoting the plan to fund research on alternative energy sources (most of which was donated by Hollywood producer Stephen Bing) was drowned out by the $95 million the oil industry spent to oppose it. And tobacco firms spent more than $66 million fighting Proposition 86, the tax increase on cigarettes, while supporters raised a mere $14 million. Once again, the difficulty of using the initiative process to take on large, corporate interests was demonstrated.

When election voters were asked to reflect on the November ballot propositions in a November 2006 survey, the majority (56%) strongly agreed that too much money was spent by the initiative campaigns. Still, only about one in three strongly agreed that there were too many propositions on the ballot (35%) and that the wording of the propositions was too complicated or confusing (33%). While most voters were at least somewhat satisfied with the way that the initiative process was working, many said that at least minor changes are needed. The initiative reforms that voters believe will improve the workings of direct democracy and representative government are discussed in the final section of this book.

CONCLUSION

At the beginning of his reelection year, Arnold Schwarzenegger had lost his populist luster and had seemingly dim prospects for a second term. His job approval ratings had fallen dramatically and voters expressed little confidence in state government as the governor and legislature haggled over politics. Schwarzenegger responded by asking the voters for a second chance to fulfill his promise to work across party lines in solving the state's problems.

He presented a bold new policy agenda that included massive spending for infrastructure projects without raising taxes. Ironically, while the era of major state projects constructed largely during the tenure of governor Pat Brown in the 1960s served as Schwarzenegger's model for his plans to repair California's crumbling infrastructure, limits that voters had placed on state lawmakers' ability to finance public works since then made the governor highly dependent on direct democracy to accomplish the same goals. But this requirement played into his strengths.

The "year of rebuilding" agenda included other highly popular legislative efforts, ranging from raising the minimum wage to discounts for prescription drugs to reducing greenhouse gas emissions. Each one gave him an opportunity to rehabilitate his badly damaged populist image. These actions provided a chance to show that he could work toward bipartisan solutions and that he was not beholden to the special interest groups who opposed these legislative actions.

When Governor Schwarzenegger unveiled the state budget, he increased funding for public schools, thus defusing one of the biggest issues in his battle with Democrats and public employee unions in 2005. With a budget surplus from an expanded economy, the governor was able to increase funding for many popular public services without raising taxes. The governor and legislature reached an early agreement on the budget, freeing their attention for other policy issues in the summer. Not surprisingly, Schwarzenegger's approval ratings began to improve in the wake of bipartisan successes and after diffusing the past tensions with special interest groups.

The June primary showcased a mean-spirited Democratic gubernatorial race between state treasurer Phil Angelides and state controller Steve Westly that was a throwback to the unpopular 2002 election. These two candidates spent millions of dollars attacking each other, with little attention to the issues of interest to voters. The primary set a new record for low voter turnout, and did little to improve the Democratic challenger's chances in a matchup against an incumbent governor. Meanwhile, voters narrowly rejected a state library bond and strongly opposed a citizens' initiative to provide universal preschool with a tax increase on the wealthy. The rejection of the two spending measures was a wake-up call for the governor and legislature, reminding them of the importance of working across party lines and spurring them to reach agreement on the multibillion-dollar infrastructure bond package and place it on the November ballot.

The governor helped his reelection bid after the primary by signing a number of bills passed by the Democratic-controlled legislature. Other California governors had sought and received support for their policies from legislators across the aisle, but Schwarzenegger highlighted these bipartisan accomplishments like none before him. Most notably, he seemed to set aside the priorities of political parties and special interests by signing the prescription drug discount, minimum wage increase, and global warming bills while surrounded by Democratic legislators sharing the spotlight with a Republican governor. Schwarzenegger continued to gain in the polls, showing a steady rise in approval ratings as his image improved across party lines.

In the November election, Californians chose to reelect the GOP governor who had restored voter confidence in the legislative process after returning to his populist, centrist messages and bipartisan policies. They rejected his Democratic opponent, who had called on special interests to rally voters' party allegiances during a nationwide referendum on an unpopular Republican administration. Many who voted for the GOP governor still supported the Democratic candidates in statewide and legislative races. Voters passed all the infrastructure bond measures placed on the ballot through the bipartisan efforts of the governor and legislature, while defeating the initiatives that reflected partisan and special-interest agendas.

But while voters' faith in their governor was rebounding in the wake of his return to populism and bipartisan efforts, most continued to express distrust in their state government. And though Californians still praised the initiative process, a campaign season dominated by the large bankrolls of special interests pointed to the flaws of a provision that was designed to be a populist tool. As the year of rebuilding drew to a close, voters were developing ideas about the changes needed in this process and how to mesh the workings of representative government and direct democracy.

NOTES

1. See Elisa Barbour and Paul G. Lewis, "California Comes of Age: Governing Institutions, Planning and Public Investment," in *California 2025: Taking on the Future*, ed. Ellen Hanak and Mark Baldassare (San Francisco: Public Policy Institute of California, 2005), 157–91; Legislative Analyst's Office, "Overhauling the State's Infrastructure Planning and Financing Process" (Sacramento, Calif.: December 1998); California Business Roundtable, "Building a Legacy for the Next Generation" (Sacramento, Calif.: 1998); Center for the Continuing Study of the California Economy, "Smart Public Investments for the California Economy: Information and Analysis for Infrastructure Planning" (Palo Alto, Calif.: September 1999); California Commission on Building for the 21st Century, "Invest for California—Strategic Planning for California's Future Prosperity and Quality of Life" (Sacramento, Calif.: 2002).

2. See discussion in chapter 2.

3. For a detailed description, see Joe Mathews, *The People's Machine: Arnold Schwarzenegger and the Rise of Blockbuster Democracy* (New York: Public Affairs, 2006), 232–34.

4. Reiner and the California Children and Family Commission (generally known as the California First 5 Commission) were later cleared of wrongdoing, after investigations by the Sacramento district attorney and the Bureau of State Audits found that the commission's use of state funds for campaign advertising was legal. See article by Dan Morain, "No Wrongdoing Done on First Five," *Los Angeles Times*, November 22, 2006, B6.

5. See investigative article on Rich and efforts to pass initiatives in several states by Patrick Hoge, "Mogul's Network Bankrolls Proposition 90," *San Francisco Chronicle*, October 5, 2006, A1.

7

Epilogue: Toward a Hybrid Democracy

In this historic era of increasing use of initiatives and declining power of the legislative process in California, the strengths and weaknesses of both representative and direct democracy have been on full display. In the aftermath of the November 2006 election, the elements that propelled the state into a changing balance of power between the voters and their elected officials—a desire for populism coupled with distrust in government and heightened concerns about the effects of special interests and partisan gridlock—were all in evidence not only in California but also nationwide in the midterm elections. In California, there were signs that a breakthrough hybrid democracy—relying on a combined use of the legislative process and the ballot box to make public policy—was emerging. In this final chapter, we also discuss the public's support for changes that may increase their trust in government, and the need for both legislative and initiative reforms to improve coordination of the two systems of democracy.

A NEW DAY IN SACRAMENTO

Arnold Schwarzenegger hobbled to the stage on January 5, 2007, to take the oath of office for his second term as governor of California. It was a marked contrast to his appearance a little over three years earlier when he took office after the 2003 recall. Having broken his leg in a ski accident the previous month, the former action hero made his way slowly up to the podium on crutches. Instead of his ubiquitous image appearing on giant screens throughout the event, this time the governor did not emerge until just before the swearing in. The thousands of spectators, hundreds of media from around the world, and star-studded guest list that had attended his first inauguration were largely absent this time. Some commented that it seemed "like a small-town parade instead of an international event" (*Los Angeles Times*, January 6, 2007).

But in his second inaugural address, Schwarzenegger's message was every bit as ambitious as his first, once again invoking a vision of populism and fulfilling the "will of the people." This time, however, he was able to refer to his enlightening experiences with both the legislative process and direct democracy. "Three years ago when I was sworn in, I said that the recall election was not about replacing one man or one party. It was about changing the entire political climate in the state," the governor proclaimed. "In the 2005 special election, I took the wrong approach in trying to do these things. But in my failure, I rediscovered my original purpose" (Schwarzenegger, "Gov. Schwarzenegger's Second Inaugural Address," 2007).

Describing the experience as opening his eyes, "like Paul on the road to Damascus," Schwarzenegger said he "saw that people, not just in California, but across the nation, were hungry for a new kind of politics, a politics that looks beyond the old labels, the old ways, the old arguments." Pointing out that the numbers of independent voters were rising as Californians increasingly turned away from the major political parties, Schwarzenegger proposed that the state move "past partisanship . . . past bi-partisanship . . . to post-partisanship." This new era, he said, would promote centrism and trust in the political system, strengthening and reforming representative government so that elected leaders reflected the "views of the mainstream, not the fringes. In return, our citizens once again have trust and respect in their government." Postpartisanship, he urged, should become a model not just for California, but for the nation and the world.

With his characteristic plotting, Schwarzenegger had focused squarely on one of the enabling factors that had fueled the public's desire for direct democracy. This time, the enemy was characterized as partisanship—the polarizing influence that pulled elected leaders away from the center and toward the political extremes. As he reminded Californians in his January 5 address, the bipartisan approach was responsible for the legislative successes of the previous year, such as the minimum wage increase and the global warming initiative. And it would be needed to solve the issues that remained for the governor and legislature to tackle in the new session, such as reforming immigration policy and fixing the state's overburdened prison system.[1]

Bipartisan cooperation would soon be put to the test as the governor announced his intention to take on one of the most intractable problems facing the state: health care coverage for the more than 6 million Californians without medical insurance. The proposal he presented on January 8 would require all Californians to have insurance, either through an employer or by purchasing an individual policy. The plan, which Schwarzenegger estimated to cost $12 billion, would require employers with more than ten workers to offer health benefits or pay into a state coverage program. Medi-Cal, the state's Medicaid program, would be expanded and medical coverage would be extended to all children living in low-income homes, regardless of immigration status. The state would create a purchasing pool to help low-income residents who did not qualify for Medi-Cal to buy medical insurance. To help fund these programs, the plan would call on doctors to contribute 2 percent of their gross income and hospitals to pay 4 percent of gross revenues back to the state (Schwarzenegger, "Governor's Health Care Proposal," 2007).

Given the size and diversity of California's population, Schwarzenegger's proposal amounted to the nation's most ambitious attempt to provide near-universal health coverage (only Maine, Massachusetts, and Vermont had previously attempted it). It was also ambitious in challenging doctors and hospitals, some of the most powerful lobbies in the state, as well as businesses upset by the mandatory insurance requirement, conservatives opposed to providing benefits to illegal immigrants, and many other special interest groups. Moreover, voters had overturned a previous effort to require employers to provide health coverage, with the failure of Proposition 72, in 2004.[2] Schwarzenegger's plan, which needed approval by the legislature, drew an immediate partisan response, with Democrats praising the effort while Republicans opposed it (*Los Angeles Times*, January 9, 2007).

Schwarzenegger projected his postpartisan vision again the following day, when he delivered his annual "State of the State" address to the legislature. Reiterating his familiar populist theme of government being dysfunctional and out of touch with the people, the governor characterized the federal administration as "paralyzed by gridlock and games." He went on to praise the members of the California Senate and Assembly for having broken out of that mold and taken action on issues such as the infrastructure, prescription drug costs, and greenhouse gas emissions the previous year. "What this said to the people is that we are not waiting for politics. We are not waiting for our problems to get worse. We are not waiting for the federal government. We are not waiting—period. Because, the future does not wait" (Schwarzenegger, "State of the State Address," 2007).

The governor unveiled an agenda for 2007 so ambitious and broad-ranging that some analysts characterized it as a "Hollywood epic."[3] Setting goals as diverse as lowering the carbon content in motor fuels, expanding vocational education programs in public schools, and dramatically increasing the number of prison beds, Schwarzenegger outlined his plan to prepare the state for an anticipated increase in population he described as "the equivalent of adding three new cities the size of Los Angeles" over the next twenty years. Contained in the proposal were several political hot buttons, including building new dams, requiring oil companies to produce cleaner gasoline, and the already released plan for universal health care coverage. The proposal called for an amount of public construction—including building or renovating an additional 55,000 classrooms—that surpassed the $42.6 billion in infrastructure projects approved by the voters in 2006. To pay for it, the legislature and voters would be asked to pass a combined total of about $43.3 billion more in bond issues over the next three years.

As if that wasn't enough of a test of his new, postpartisan era, Schwarzenegger also revived his effort to divest legislators of the authority for drawing political districts—an idea that had been soundly rejected in his failed year of reform. This time, the plan called for power to be given to an independent Citizens Redistricting Commission, created "to fix a political system that has become petrified by self-interest." Describing California's failure to address its problems and plan for its future as the fault of a stagnant state government, he quipped, "There was more turnover in the Hapsburg monarchy than in the California legislature." In asking the legislature to revisit the issue of political reform, Schwarzenegger once again invoked the public's desire for populism, disapproval of partisanship, fear of special interest influence, and distrust of government that had enabled his successes in using the new, hybrid democracy during his first term in office.

Schwarzenegger completed the roll-out of his second-term agenda the following day, with the release of his proposed 2007 to 2008 state budget. "I'm very happy to announce today that in this new budget our new operating deficit has been reduced to zero," Schwarzenegger proclaimed January 10, in a press conference on the budget release. "You heard me right—we have reduced the operating deficit to zero. It was not easy, it was a lot of hard work, and it is by no means finished, but this is a great accomplishment" (Schwarzenegger, "Gov. Arnold Schwarzenegger's Remarks," 2007).

The $143.3 billion budget he proposed purported to eliminate the state's chronic deficits with the proceeds of increased state general fund revenues, savings from early repayment of the economic recovery bonds approved by voters in 2004, income from new Indian gaming compacts, and a windfall in state gasoline tax money resulting from price spikes the previous year (California Department of Finance, "Governor's Budget 2007–08: Proposed Budget Summary," 2007).

The proposed budget included benefits to please many key constituencies, including increases in funding for public schools and prisons, and substantial sums dedicated to environmental protection and the development of clean energy. But the budget also rankled Democrats with cuts in welfare payments and diversion of public transit funds, while Republicans were worried about the reliability of its revenue forecasts. The Indian gaming compacts, for instance—projected to add an annual $506 million to state coffers—had not yet been approved by the legislature.

And while the governor was crowing about having eliminated the state's red ink, he was also proposing more than $43 billion in new bond debt to fund the projects described in his State of the State address one day earlier. Moreover, although the budget was based on a projected 7.2 percent increase in revenues while raising expenditures by only 1 percent over the previous year, it still proposed spending about $1.8 billion more than the state was expected to take in. The Legislative Analyst's Office described the plan as based on unrealistic assumptions about both revenues and expenditures, and warned that "its key proposals also raise serious policy and legal issues" (Legislative Analyst's Office, "Overview of the Governor's Budget, 2007–08," 2007). But, true to Schwarzenegger's long-standing pledge, the budget did not raise taxes. Once again, the governor would rely on his popularity and populist message to voters, attempting to overcome the criticisms from government agencies, partisan leaders, and special interests.

And continuing his approach of calling voters to the ballot box with increasing frequency, in March 2007 the governor signed a bill changing the state's presidential primaries to February while keeping the state and congressional primaries in June—meaning that California will have three scheduled elections every presidential contest year. The goal, he said, was to give the state a bigger voice in the presidential selection process by making its primary earlier than most other states (*Los Angeles Times*, May 16, 2007). It would also give supporters of a bid to change the state's term limits law the opportunity to get an initiative on the ballot before legislative luminaries such as Assembly speaker Fabian Núñez and Senate president pro tem Don Perata were termed out of office (*Sacramento Bee*, March 7, 2007).

A POLITICAL JOURNEY
FILLED WITH HOPES AND IDEAS

Throughout this historic era of California's latest experiments with direct democracy, from the depths of voter despair around the November 2002 election to the highs of voter optimism in November 2006, Californians have been signaling that their governance and political system is in need of repair. We now look at the hopes and ideas about changing the legislative system and initiative process expressed by voters during the five consecutive fall elections. Taken together, these preferences offer a consistent message of the importance of populism, partisanship, special interests, and voter distrust in shaping the future agenda for governance and political change. The voters have offered a blueprint for reforms to help facilitate an integrated system of governance by elected representatives and direct democracy.

In 2002, California's elections for its statewide representatives appeared to suffer a major setback, when a gubernatorial race that set new records for campaign spending resulted in new records for low voter turnout in the primary and general elections. In the closing days of a bitter gubernatorial campaign, whose highlight reel was largely filled with the candidates' advertising smearing their opponent, the PPIC Statewide Survey in late October found that most voters were not satisfied with the choice of candidates and looked unfavorably at both the Democratic incumbent and Republican contender. As a result, many voters said that campaigns had gotten worse, and that the values and ethics displayed by the candidates had gone downhill in the past decade. No doubt, the 2002 campaign process leading up to the election left the electorate with a dislike of the political parties that sponsored such a slugfest and a distrust of the victor who was viewed as damaged goods. In response to this off-putting event, voters expressed some clear ideas for what was needed to improve the campaigns for state office.

More than three in four California voters said they would look more favorably upon candidates who signed a campaign code of ethics pledging to run a truthful, fair, and clean campaign. In place of reliance of negative commercials, two in three said they would have liked the 2002 election more if the gubernatorial candidates had held more debates. Moreover, large proportions signaled that they would have preferred to hear the candidates communicate their messages directly through speeches, call-in shows, and town hall meetings, depending less on mass mailings and commercials to reach the voters. Most expressed a preference for including volunteers, rather than relying solely on professional operatives in campaigns, and to include the use of public funding, not just money from wealthy candidates and donations from special interests. A majority also expressed regrets about a campaign system that tended to focus on "high propensity voters" rather than reaching out to all Californians and encouraging broader participation. Five years later, we see no evidence that the 2002 voters' wish list for campaign reforms has been implemented (see also Baldassare, Cain, and Cohen 2003a; Baldassare et al. 2004).

In 2003, Californians who had given up all hope in their representative government turned to a little-known provision in their ninety-two-year old direct democracy tool kit and mounted a recall to replace their unpopular governor. In the days leading up to the special election, the PPIC Statewide Survey in early October 2003 found that Californians overwhelmingly felt the ability of voters to recall their state elected officials was a good thing, yet they were deeply divided on whether or not the current recall was an appropriate use of this process. An electorate that knew little about the recall process at the start was highly familiar with its flaws by the end. Voters reacted to the 2003 recall in a manner eerily similar to the 2002 election—saying that the election made them feel worse about California politics—and expressing negative feelings about the candidates, the lack of substance in the campaigns, and the overreliance on paid advertising to communicate the candidates' positions. Other problems specific to the recall ballot—notably keeping the recalled official's name off the replacement ballot, while including scores of candidates who were little more than jokesters and publicity seekers, fueled perceptions of the need for changes in this part of the direct democracy process. Most voters wanted to raise the signature requirements for qualifying a recall election and replacement candidates. Majorities also believed that statewide officials should only be recalled in the event of illegal or unethical activity. Most voters favored requiring a majority vote for the election of a replacement and holding a runoff between the top two vote-getters if no single candidate drew more than 50 percent. Once again, voters voiced their desire for more public debates and their dissatisfaction with the lack of substance provided by the candidates' advertising. But legislators' calls for election reforms after the 2003 recall subsided soon after this historic event and none of the changes desired by voters have been enacted to date (see also Baldassare, Cain, and Cohen 2003b).

In 2004, the newly elected Governor Arnold Schwarzenegger enjoyed broad support as he stressed the popular themes of bipartisan compromise in the legislature and the need to include voters in decision making at the ballot box. Still, his popularity had little effect on the widespread dissatisfaction with state government and distrust in the legislative process that had been evident in all of the PPIC preelection surveys. Reforms proposed in efforts to improve governance, including loosening budget vote requirements and legislative term limits, were rejected by voters, who saw them as unneeded expansions of elected officials' powers. Proposed fixes for improving representative democracy, such as campaign finance reform and legislative redistricting, were met with skepticism and received lukewarm support. Only efforts to improve the efficiency of government operations appeared to resonate with voters, as the governor's plans for a "California Performance Review" raised their hopes of taming what they viewed as an unruly bureaucracy.

In the postelection survey in November 2004, voters overwhelmingly described the initiative process as a good thing, and most believed that they could make better public policy decisions than their elected leaders (see Baldassare, DeFever, and Michaud 2005). Yet most voters in the September 2004 preelection survey were quick to point out that changes in the state's direct democracy provisions were needed. Signaling the public's desire for populism and their negative feelings about partisanship, the October 2004 survey prior to the presidential election found that the vast majority of voters wanted to drop the electoral college system in favor of a popular vote. Half felt that the major parties did not adequately represent them and said a third party was needed in the September 2004 survey. In the end, the 2004 election year generated a great deal of interest in discussions of governance and fiscal reforms—but once again, few changes resulted.

Having grown impatient with the legislature and feeling confident in his ability to persuade voters to back his plans at the ballot box, Governor

Schwarzenegger in 2005 turned to the initiative process to make the policy changes he wanted and called a special election. The result was a decisive defeat, as voters rejected all eight measures on the ballot. In the postelection survey in November 2005, six in ten election voters called the initiative-only ballot a bad idea, yet most continued to express positive attitudes about voters' ability to make public policy through the citizens' initiative process. More than at any time in this five-year period, however, voters voiced dissatisfaction with the way the initiative process was working and expressed interest in making changes. Specifically, in light of a special election with roots in partisan disputes and fueled by special interest money, a majority of voters wanted ballot measures restricted to the November general election instead of appearing in primaries and special elections (53%). Moreover, most only wanted the governor to be able to call a special election if the legislature agreed that one was needed (54%). Signaling a desire for more legislative input into the initiative process, more than eight in ten voters wanted a system of reviews and efforts at legislative compromise before a measure went on the ballot. And as an expression of their disdain for special interest money and misleading campaign advertising, overwhelming majorities wanted public debates on the initiatives (77%) and more public disclosure of who was funding the signature-gathering and initiative campaign efforts (85%). To date, however, the highly unpopular use of the initiative process in the 2005 special election has not generated any reforms.

The 2006 election provided a stark contrast from the previous year. Legislative agreements were plentiful and the ballot measures submitted to voters reflected bipartisan consensus. The GOP governor was reelected, the Democrats' control of the legislature was unchanged, and voters endorsed a multi-billion-dollar bond package created jointly by the governor and legislature. This turn of events raised the approval ratings both of elected officials and the initiative process, but voters still perceived that fundamental changes were needed for the two systems to work together effectively. In the November 2006 postelection survey, voters continued to strongly favor greater legislative involvement in reviewing ballot measures and seeking compromises with initiative supporters, as well as finding ways to stem what appeared to be the growing influence of special interests in the direct democracy system. In PPIC preelection surveys, voters also favored changes to their representative government, including a majority now supporting the idea of independent legislative redistricting. But the public remained skeptical of the need for other governance changes, with majorities of voters in preelection surveys opposing reforms such as lengthening legislative term limits and lowering the two-thirds majorities needed for fiscal actions. In all, popular reforms of the legislative process still tended to focus on restricting the powers of elected officials. Importantly, against the backdrop of successful bipartisan legislation and ballot measures in 2006, the governor and legislature made no progress in efforts to improve the joint workings of representative and direct democracy. The mechanisms regulating California's governance system had changed very little since before the recall, even though voters expressed support for a variety of reforms.

TOWARD A HYBRID DEMOCRACY

A new system of governance has evolved in California over five elections in a half-decade of furious political activity. An era of a "hybrid democracy" is now underway, with elected representatives through the legislative process and voters at the ballot box jointly sharing responsibility for making public policy. The roots of this political change are found in four trends evident in recent California politics—the public's support for a populist approach to policy making and their basic distrust of government, along with widespread concerns about the influence of partisanship and special interests on decisions made by their elected representatives. Arnold Schwarzenegger has been the celebrity spokesperson for the growing voter demand for a power shift in the governance system. However, Schwarzenegger has also been the prime beneficiary of the rise in populist attitudes, government distrust, disillusionment with the major parties, and fears about special interest groups that were taking place during this time.

In California, the governor, the legislature, and the voters are now charged with the task of tackling important policy issues together. This hybrid democracy is not a temporary trend, as all indications point to permanent power sharing between representative government and direct democracy. But all the pieces are not yet in place for an effective and efficient governance structure that can respond to these policy demands. Voters and elected officials will need to focus together on making improvements in both the initiative process and the legislative system and meshing the joint workings of the two. In recent elections, voters pointed to some of the changes needed in both systems. Elected officials will now have to show leadership and reach bipartisan consensus on bringing reforms to the voters for approval. The recall and its aftermath highlight several areas of the governance system that need attention, including improvements in the legislative and initiative processes and the coordination of these two systems, reforms of campaigns and elections, and increasing voter participation.

One area for change that became obvious through the recent election cycle is the need for better coordination between the legislative system and the initiative process. While voters strongly favor the use of the ballot box for making policy, they would also like to see their elected representatives play a bigger role at the front end. Legislators could review measures to ensure that there are no legal issues or drafting errors, thus avoiding the frustrating experience of voters passing measures that will subsequently be voided by courts. They could also play an important role by holding hearings on proposed initiatives, allowing voters and interest groups to weigh in before the measures reach the ballot. In addition, legislators could seek compromises with initiative sponsors before the measures go on the ballot, thus avoiding the expense and effort of campaigns in some cases. Voters appear willing to give their elected officials more time to study the issues and lead public discussions on initiatives as a way to ensure that the proposed measures constitute sound policy.

While most voters are highly enthusiastic about possessing the tools of direct democracy, they readily admit that changes are needed in both the initiative and the recall provisions. Many are willing to slow down the process of qualifying initiatives, giving time for volunteers to gather signatures so that the system is less dependent on paid professionals. The experience of the 2005 election convinced many California voters that initiative-only special elections should be a last resort, to be used only if the governor and legislature both agree that the issues cannot wait until the next regular election. The 2003 recall raised questions about the relatively low requirements for signatures needed to qualify a recall effort and name a replacement candidate on the ballot. Voters would prefer to have a recall only in the event of serious wrongdoing by an elected official, not simply because a politician has fallen out of favor. And they want replacement candidates limited to those with a sincere interest in taking office. In all, voters would like to make sure that their prized system of direct democracy is not overused or put to the wrong purpose.

The most controversial elements of improving the system of hybrid democracy involve changes to representative government. Many voters believe this part of the system is broken beyond repair, while elected officials can find it difficult to reach a bipartisan consensus. Still, voters want their leaders to work together and make laws, and elected officials know they can improve their standing with legislative successes. Voters appear ready to support a redistricting process that would take politics out of the business of drawing legislative boundaries. This reform would add to the legitimacy of elections and elected officials. A by-product of independent redistricting could be creating competition in what are now gerrymandered districts, making elected officials more responsive to voters instead of to party leaders. Other changes that have been proposed include easing legislative term limits to increase the experience level among state lawmakers and reducing the two-thirds vote requirement to a simple majority so that legislators could more easily pass a state budget. While these changes are unpopular today because voters see them as politically motivated, they may eventually receive the support needed to pass if they were presented as bipartisan measures with backing by diverse interest groups.

Campaigns and elections are now such a major disappointment to voters that they are undermining confidence in both representative government and the initiative process. Voters are dissatisfied with the lack of substance, the reliance on television commercials and mass mailings for communication with the public, the misleading and demeaning messages of paid advertising, the dominant role of wealthy individuals and organized interests, and campaign strategies that target certain voters while excluding others. Candidate and initiative campaigns are setting new records for spending, while both are coming under harsh criticism from voters who find them uninformative. Voters want more public debates and open forums that provide an opportunity to learn more about the candidates. They also want to hear directly from the spokespersons of the "yes" and "no" sides of initiative campaigns. While the prospect of full government funding for political campaigns falls well short of majority support, there is a need for nonpartisan sources such as the media, nonprofit organizations, and public institutions to play a more active role in providing a constructive and informed dialogue for candidate and ballot measure contests.

Finally, the lack of broad public participation in elections raises questions about the legitimacy of using the ballot box to make public policy and in the elected officials that are chosen to represent the people. If current trends are not reversed in California, an increasingly "exclusive electorate" that is relatively small and highly unrepresentative of the state's adult population will be directly (i.e., through initiatives) or indirectly (i.e., through elected officials) making policy choices that affect a large group of residents who have had no say in the process. A move toward an "expanded electorate" will require bipartisan efforts and public and private support to increase voter registration and participation on election day. Moreover, since a large and growing number of voters are registering as independents, the primary election has become a meaningless exercise to the millions of voters outside the major parties. And because the primaries are drawing small numbers of voters, they are no longer the appropriate vehicles for making policies through the initiative process. For the time being, initiatives should only be placed on general election ballots, so that the largest numbers of voters are involved. In the long run, primary elections for state and national offices will need to include independent voters (as was the case after voters approved the "open primary" and before the parties opposed it in the courts), to encourage a larger and more diverse group of participants in the state's elections.

What is the relevance of California's governance trend for the national political scene? California has long been the testing ground for the use of the initiative process in making policy, and it has been in the spotlight since recalling Davis and electing Schwarzenegger. This may signal that a "hybrid democracy" will flourish in the other states that share a similar system of direct democracy. Also, California has accelerated the use of the ballot box in making policy over the past five years, and has recently had success in passing bipartisan legislation. Schwarzenegger's accomplishments occurred at a time when federal lawmakers seemed stymied by extreme partisanship and special-interest politics. American voters in the midterm election signaled a strong desire not just for changing party control, but also for their elected leaders on both sides of the aisle to find common ground on major national issues. The California experiment may offer guidance for making federal policy amid populism, partisanship, special interests, and voter distrust.

The future of hybrid democracy is in the hands of California voters and their elected officials, who have participated in the evolution of a governance system that is still less than perfect. While Schwarzenegger's continued efforts to achieve bipartisan legislative actions on major issues such as health care and his victories at the ballot box on rebuilding the state's infrastructure are likely to attract the most headlines, it is the willingness of elected officials and voters to improve this new form of governance that will be the important trend to watch in the long run. Will they make the reforms necessary to fuse their legislative and initiative processes into an effective system of combined governance, or will they allow the hybrid democracy to sputter and perhaps even fail? The future of this democratic experiment, its continued use in California, and its spread to other states and the nation may ultimately depend on how much its users are willing to adapt and change.

NOTES

1. Not everyone agreed that Schwarzenegger's "post-partisan" approach was working. Some Republicans claimed that the governor was giving in to Democrats and ignoring the opposition of his own party. Democrats countered that the measures that had been worked out in collaboration with the Republican governor were not as far-reaching as they would like. See Peter Nicholas, "Governor May Be Selling an Illusion of Unity," *Los Angeles Times*, March 11, 2007, A1.

2. Schwarzenegger had opposed Proposition 72, on the October 2004 ballot. See discussion in chapter 4.

3. See Carla Marinucci, "Schwarzenegger Pens Second-Term Script that Reads Like a Hollywood Epic," *San Francisco Chronicle*, January 10, 2007, A1.

Bibliography

Abrams, Elliott, ed. *Democracy: How Direct? Views from the Founding Era and the Polling Era.* Lanham, Md.: Rowman & Littlefield, 2002.

Allswang, John M. *The Initiative and Referendum in California, 1898–1998.* Stanford, Calif.: Stanford University Press, 2000.

American National Election Studies. "The ANES Guide to Public Opinion and Electoral Behavior." Ann Arbor: University of Michigan, Center for Political Studies, 2004.

Baldassare, Mark. *When Government Fails: The Orange County Bankruptcy.* Berkeley: University of California Press, 1998.

———. *California in the New Millennium: The Changing Social and Political Landscape.* Berkeley: University of California Press, 2000.

———. *A California State of Mind: The Conflicted Voter in a Changing World.* Berkeley: University of California Press, 2002.

———. *California's Exclusive Electorate.* San Francisco: Public Policy Institute of California, 2006.

Baldassare, Mark, Bruce E. Cain, D. E. Apollonio, and Jonathan Cohen. *The Season of Our Discontent: Voters' Views on California Elections.* San Francisco: Public Policy Institute of California, 2004.

Baldassare, Mark, Bruce Cain, and Jonathan Cohen. "Wanted: Retail Politics." *California Journal* 34, no. 1 (January 2003a): 22–25.

———. "California Voters Take Charge." *California Journal* 34, no. 11 (November 2003b): 14–18.

Baldassare, Mark, Renatta DeFever, and Kristy Michaud. "Making Health Policy at the Ballot Box: Californians and the November Election." San Francisco: Public Policy Institute of California, 2005.

Baldassare, Mark, Michael Shires, Christopher Hoene, and Aaron Koffman. *Risky Business: Providing Local Public Services in Los Angeles County.* San Francisco: Public Policy Institute of California, 2000.

Balz, Dan. "Schwarzenegger Prepares to Do Battle in Calif.: GOP Governor

Increasingly Partisan, Opponents Say." *Washington Post*, March 28, 2005, A1.

Barabak, Mark. "Negative Campaign Repelled Some Voters." *Los Angeles Times*, November 11, 2002, B1.

———. "The Republican Convention: Schwarzenegger Wraps His Life Story around GOP Themes." *Los Angeles Times*, September 1, 2004, A1.

Barabak, Mark Z., and Michael Finnegan. "The Recall Campaign: Rivals Use Debate to Go on Attack." *Los Angeles Times*, September 25, 2003, A1.

Barber, Bernard. *The Logic and Limits of Trust*. New Brunswick, N.J.: Rutgers University Press, 1983.

Barbour, Elisa, and Paul G. Lewis. "California Comes of Age: Governing Institutions, Planning and Public Investment." In *California 2025: Taking on the Future*, edited by Ellen Hanak and Mark Baldassare, 157–91. San Francisco: Public Policy Institute of California, 2005.

Berthelsen, Christian. "Governor Sets Money-Raising Record: $26.6 Million in His First Year—Most of It from Special Interests." *San Francisco Chronicle*, November 17, 2004, A1.

Blitz, Michael, and Louise Krasniewicz. *Why Arnold Matters: The Rise of a Cultural Icon*. New York: Basic Books, 2004.

Bluth, Alexa. "Revised Budget Backs off Cuts: $103 Billion Plan Mostly Spares Health Services." *Sacramento Bee*, May 14, 2004, A1.

———. "Group to Drop Pension Lawsuit, but State Would Have to Raise Workers' Contribution Share." *Sacramento Bee*, June 5, 2004, A1.

———. "Rift Puts Budget Pact at Risk." *Sacramento Bee*, June 11, 2004, A1.

Bowler, Shaun, Todd Donovan, and Caroline J. Tolbert, eds. *Citizens as Legislators: Direct Democracy in the United States*. Columbus: Ohio State University Press, 1998.

Bowler, Shaun, and Todd Donovan. *Demanding Choices: Opinion, Voting and Direct Democracy*. Ann Arbor: University of Michigan Press, 2000.

Bowler, Shaun, and Bruce E. Cain. *Clicker Politics: Essays on the California Recall*. Upper Saddle River, N.J.: Pearson-Prentice Hall, 2006.

Bradley, Bill. "Wrong Turn Right: Inside Arnold's Fateful 2004 Shift." *New West Notes* political blog, http://archive.newwestnotes.com/inside-arnolds-fateful-right-turn, December 23–29, 2005.

Brinkley, Alan. *The Unfinished Nation*. Vol. II. 4th ed. New York: McGraw-Hill, 2004.

Broder, David S. *Democracy Derailed*. San Diego: James H. Silberman/Harvest/Harcourt, 2000.

Broder, John, and Dean E. Murphy. "Rivals Mix Issues and Attacks in Free-for-All Recall Debate." *New York Times*, September 25, 2003, A1.

Bustillo, Miguel, and James Rainey. "Davis Concedes Mistakes, but Fights 'Power Grab.'" *Los Angeles Times*, August 20, 2003, A1.

Cain, Bruce E., and Thad Kousser. *Adapting to Term Limits: Recent Experiences and New Directions*. San Francisco: Public Policy Institute of California, 2004.

Cain, Bruce E., and Kenneth P. Miller. "The Populist Legacy: Initiatives and the Undermining of Representative Government." In *Dangerous Democracy? The Battle over Ballot Initiatives in America*, edited by Larry J. Sabato, Howard R. Ernst, and Bruce A. Larson, 33–62. Lanham, Md.: Rowman & Littlefield, 2001.

California Business Roundtable. "Building a Legacy for the Next Generation." Sacramento: California Business Roundtable, 1998.

California Commission on Building for the 21st Century. "Invest for California—Strategic Planning for California's Future Prosperity and Quality of Life." Sacramento: California Commission on Building for the 21st Century, 2002.

California Commission on Campaign Financing. "Democracy by Initiative: Shaping California's Fourth Branch of Government." Los Angeles: Center for Responsive Government, 1992.

California Department of Finance. "Historical Census Populations of California State, Counties, Cities, Places and Towns, 1850–1990." Sacramento, Calif.: 2001.

———. "Race/Ethnic Population Estimates: Components of Change for California Counties—July 1970 to July 1990." Sacramento, Calif.: 1999.

———. "Race/Ethnic Population with Age and Sex Detail, 1990–1999." Sacramento, Calif.: May 2004a.

———. "Race/Ethnic Population with Age and Sex Detail, 2000–2050." Sacramento, Calif.: May 2004b.

———. "Population Projections by Race/Ethnicity, Gender and Age for California and Its Counties, 2000–2050." Sacramento, Calif.: May 2004c.

———. "Race/Ethnic Population Estimates: Components of Change for California Counties—April 1990 to April 2000." Sacramento, Calif.: 2005.

———. "Estimated Race/Ethnic Population with Age and Sex Detail, 2000–2004." Sacramento, Calif.: April 2006.

———. "Population Estimates for Cities, Counties and the State with Annual Percent Change, January 1, 2005 and 2006." Sacramento, Calif.: May 2006.

———. "Governor's Budget Summary 2003–04." Sacramento, Calif.: January, 2003.

———. "Governor's Budget, 2004–05." Sacramento, Calif.: January 2004.

———. "Governor's Budget, May Revision 2005–06." Sacramento, Calif.: May 2005.

———. "Governor's Budget Summary 2006–07." Sacramento, Calif.: January 2006.

———. "Governor's Budget, May Revision 2006–07." Sacramento, Calif.: May 2006.

———. "California State Budget 2006–07." Sacramento, Calif.: June 2006.

———. "Governor's Budget 2007–08: Proposed Budget Summary." Sacramento, Calif.: January 2007.

California Environmental Quality Act (CEQA). *Statute and Guidelines*. Sacramento, Calif.: 2005.

California Performance Review. "Issues and Recommendations." Sacramento, Calif.: 2004.

California Secretary of State. "Financing California's Statewide Ballot Measures on the November 3, 1998 General Election Ballot: Campaign Receipts and Expenditures through December 31, 1998." Sacramento, Calif.: May 1999.

———. "Campaign Finance." Sacramento, Calif.: November 2002.

———. "Historical Registration Statistics." Sacramento, Calif.: October 2002.

————. "Initiative Update." Sacramento, Calif.: July 8, 2005.

————. "Official Voter Information Guide: California Statewide Special Election, October 7, 2003. Proponent's Grounds for Recall and the Governor's Response." Sacramento, Calif.: August 31, 2003.

————. "Report of Registration." Sacramento, Calif.: August 2003.

————. "Report of Registration." Sacramento, Calif.: April 2006.

————. "Report of Registration. Sacramento, Calif.: October 2006.

————. "Statement of the Vote: 2000 Primary Election." Sacramento, Calif.: March 7, 2000.

————. "Statement of the Vote: 2000 General Election." Sacramento, Calif.: November 7, 2000.

————. "Statement of the Vote: 2002 Primary Election." Sacramento, Calif.: March 5, 2002.

————. "Statement of the Vote: 2002 General Election." Sacramento, Calif.: November 5, 2002.

————. "Statement of the Vote: 2003 Statewide Special Election." Sacramento, Calif.: October 7, 2003.

————. "Statement of the Vote: 2004 Primary Election." Sacramento, Calif.: March 2, 2004.

————. "Statement of the Vote: 2004 General Election." Sacramento, Calif.: November 2, 2004.

————. "Statement of the Vote: 2005 Statewide Special Election." Sacramento, Calif.: November 8, 2005.

————. "Statement of the Vote: 2006 Primary Election." Sacramento, Calif.: June 6, 2006.

————. "Statement of the Vote: 2006 General Election." Sacramento, Calif.: November 7, 2006.

————. "Propositions That Are on the November 7, 2006 General Election Ballot." Sacramento, Calif.: 2006.

California State Auditor. *Energy Deregulation: The Benefits of Competition Were Undermined by Structural Flaws in the Market, Unsuccessful Oversight, and Uncontrollable Competitive Forces.* Sacramento, Calif.: 2001.

Cambridge Energy Research Associates. *Beyond California's Power Crisis: Impact, Solutions and Lessons.* Cambridge, Mass.: Cambridge Energy Research Associates, 2001.

Cannon, Lou. *Governor Reagan: His Rise to Power.* New York: Public Affairs, 2003.

Center for the Continuing Study of the California Economy. "Smart Public Investments for the California Economy: Information and Analysis for Infrastructure Planning." Palo Alto, Calif.: Center for the Continuing Study of the California Economy, September 1999.

Chong, Jia-Rui, and Eric Malnic. "In the Recall Candidates' Words." *Los Angeles Times*, September 25, 2003, A23.

Citrin, Jack. "The Political Relevance of Trust in Government." *American Political Science Review* 68 (1974): 973–88.

———. "Do People Want Something for Nothing?: Public Opinion on Taxes and Government Spending." *National Tax Journal* 32 (1979): 113–29.

———. "Who's the Boss? Direct Democracy and Popular Control of Government." In *Broken Contract? Changing Relationships between Americans and their Government*, edited by Stephen C. Craig, 268–93. Boulder, Colo.: Westview Press, 1996.

Citrin, Jack, and Christopher Muste. "Trust in Government." In *Measure of Political Attitudes*, edited by John Robinson, 465–532. New York: Academic Press, 1999.

Clark, Terry Nichols, and Lorna Crowley Ferguson. *City Money: Political Processes, Fiscal Strain and Retrenchment.* New York: Columbia University Press, 1983.

Clark, Terry Nichols, ed. *Urban Innovation: Creative Strategies for Turbulent Times.* Thousand Oaks, Calif.: Sage, 1994.

Clark, Terry, and Ronald Inglehart. "The New Political Culture." In *The New Political Culture*, edited by Terry Clark and Vincent Hoffman-Martinot, 9–72. Boulder, Colo.: Westview Press, 1998.

CNN Exit Poll. "America Votes 2006." www.cnn.com/ELECTION/2006. (November 7, 2006).

Cohn, Gary, Carla Hall, and Robert W. Welkos. "The Recall Campaign; Women Say Schwarzenegger Groped, Humiliated Them." *Los Angeles Times*, October 2, 2003, A1.

Cronin, Thomas E. *Direct Democracy: The Politics of Initiative, Referendum and Recall.* Cambridge, Mass.: Harvard University Press, 1999.

Crystal Cathedral. "About Hour of Power: Viewership." *Crystal Cathedral Hour of Power.* www.hourofpower.org/about/index.cfm (19 June 2006).

Davis, Aaron C., and Mark Gladstone. "Governor, Democrats Unable to Settle Ballot: Special Election to Decide Three Measures." *San Jose Mercury News*, August 19, 2005, A10.

Davis, Gray. "Governor's Inaugural Address," January 6, 2003. Text printed in the *Sacramento Bee*, January 7, 2003.

De Alth, Shelley, and Kim Rueben. "Understanding Infrastructure Financing for California." San Francisco: Public Policy Institute of California, 2005.

Delsohn, Gary. "Davis Is Told: No Trash Talk." *Sacramento Bee*, August 1, 2003, A1.

———. "Governor Calls Foes 'Girlie Men': Democrats are Outraged over the Remark Directed at Them, Calling It 'Sexist' and 'Anti-Gay.'" *Sacramento Bee*, July 18, 2004, A1.

———. "Governor: Starve State's 'Monster.'" *Sacramento Bee*, January 19, 2005, A1.

———. "Ambitious Initiative Effort Is On." *Sacramento Bee*, March 17, 2005, A1.

———. "Governor: No Political Aim in Border Remarks." *Sacramento Bee*, April 30, 2005, A1.

———. "Schwarzenegger Hands in First Petitions." *Sacramento Bee*, May 5, 2005, A3.

———. "Governor Heads to Florida, Texas and Illinois Seeking Cash for a Possible Special Election." *Sacramento Bee*, May 20, 2005, A3.

————. "Democrats Do Budget About-Face." *Sacramento Bee*, June 11, 2005, A1.

————. "No Tough-Talk as Measures Trail." *Sacramento Bee*, June 22, 2005, A3.

Dickerson, Marla, and Stuart Silverstein. "Job Loss in State Worst in a Decade." *Los Angeles Times*, December 16, 2001, A1.

Donovan, Todd, and Shaun Bowler. "Direct Democracy and Minority Rights: An Extension." *American Journal of Political Science* 43 (1998): 1020–25.

Donovan, Todd, Shaun Bowler, and David McCuan. "Political Consultants and the Initiative Industrial Complex." In *Dangerous Democracy? The Battle over Ballot Initiatives in America*, edited by Larry J. Sabato, Howard R. Ernst, and Bruce A. Larson, 101–34. Lanham, Md.: Rowman & Littlefield, 2001.

Epstein, Edward. "State GOP Strongly Endorses Recall." *San Francisco Chronicle*, July 10, 2003, A1.

Fields, Robin. "The Davis Enigma: Success Comes without Popularity." *Los Angeles Times*, March 19, 2002, A1.

Finnegan, Michael. "The Davis Recall Campaign: Davis Recall Qualifies for a Fall Ballot." *Los Angeles Times*, July 24, 2003, A1.

————. "Governor Backs Proposition 75." *Los Angeles Times*, September 18, 2005, B1.

————. "Unions Working a New Tactic against Governor." *Los Angeles Times*, October 3, 2005, A1.

————."Election 2006: California Races." *Los Angeles Times*, November 8, 2006, A1.

Fleishman, Jon. "FlashReport Meets with Gov's Staff in Advance of Big Speech." *FlashReport*. January 6, 2006. http://flashreport.org/ (January 6, 2006).

Folmar, Kate. "Governor's Supreme Motive: Success." *San Jose Mercury News*, October 25, 2006, A1.

————. "Governor Warns of 'Armageddon': Top Officials Campaign for $15 Billion Bond." *San Jose Mercury News*, January 21, 2004, A3.

Folmar, Kate, and Aaron C. Davis. "Fall Ballot Campaign Set Record for Expenses." *San Jose Mercury News*, February 1, 2006, B5.

Fox, Sue. "Deal Could End Siphoning of Local Taxes: The Governor Might Agree to Ban the Shifting of Property Levies from Cities and Counties to the State—After Two Years." *Los Angeles Times*, May 8, 2004, B6.

Furillo, Andy. "Initiatives Get a Shot in the Arm: Group Tied to Schwarzenegger Endorses Pension System Shift, Teacher Tenure Measures." *Sacramento Bee*, March 1, 2005, A1.

————. "For the Ballot, Money Matters: Special Election Was a Boon to Those Paid to Get the Word Out." *Sacramento Bee*, February 4, 2006, A1.

Gamble, Barbara. "Putting Civic Rights to a Popular Vote." *American Journal of Political Science* 41 (1997): 245–69.

Gerber, Elisabeth. *Interest Group Influence in the California Initiative Process*. San Francisco: Public Policy Institute of California, 1998.

————. *The Populist Paradox: Interest Group Influence and the Promise of Direct Legislation*. Princeton, N. J.: Princeton University Press, 1999.

Gerston, Larry N., and Terry Christensen. *Recall: California's Political Earthquake.*

Armonk, N.Y.: M. E. Sharpe, 2004.

Gledhill, Lynda. "Budget Deal Rests on Heavy Deficit, Heavy Borrowing." *San Francisco Chronicle*, July 28, 2004, A1.

Gledhill, Lynda, Christian Berthelsen, and Mark Martin. "Budget Countdown . . . Snacks, Sighs, GOP Surprise." *San Francisco Chronicle*, August 3, 2003, A22.

Gold, Matea, and Joe Mathews. "The Recall Campaign: Film Persona a 'Double-Edged Sword' for Schwarzenegger." *Los Angeles Times*, September 26, 2003, A19.

Halper, Evan. "State Republicans Calculate a Plan for Their Own Budget." *Los Angeles Times*, January 15, 2003, A1.

———. "Spending Plans Fall Victim to Politics." *Los Angeles Times*, May 31, 2005, A1.

———. "GOP Legislators Block State Budget." *Los Angeles Times*, June 16, 2005, B1.

———. "Gov. Uses Veto Pen in Signing Budget." *Los Angeles Times*, July 12, 2005, B1.

Halper, Evan, and Joe Mathews. "Hopes Dim for On-Time Delivery of State Budget." *Los Angeles Times*, June 27, 2004, A1.

Halper, Evan, and Peter Nicholas. "Governor's Allies Turn Budget Foes." *Los Angeles Times*, July 1, 2004, B1.

Halper, Evan, and Nancy Vogel. "The California Budget: 'Broken System' Budget Unveiled." *Los Angeles Times*, January 11, 2005, A1.

Halper, Evan, and Jenifer Warren. "State Senators Take On Guards." *Los Angeles Times*, May 19, 2004, A1.

Helfand, Duke, and Jean Merl. "The Governor's Budget: Schools Win, Lose in Governor's Proposal." *Los Angeles Times*, January 9, 2004, B14.

Hill, John. "Davis Quietly Approves Budget." *Sacramento Bee*, September 6, 2002, A1.

———. "Governor Retreats on Pensions." *Sacramento Bee*, April 8, 2005, A1.

———. "Revision Sets Stage for Fight." *Sacramento Bee*, May 14, 2005, A1.

Hofstadter, Richard. *The Age of Reform*. New York: Random House, 1955.

Hoge, Patrick. "Mogul's Network Bankrolls Proposition 90." *San Francisco Chronicle*, October 5, 2006, A1.

Hubbell, John. "Governor, Five Tribes Sign Gaming Pacts: Schwarzenegger Says Funds Will Go to Transportation." *San Francisco Chronicle*, June 22, 2004, B3.

Initiative and Referendum Institute. *Initiative and Referendum Institute at the University of Southern California*. www.iandrinstitute.org (January 15, 2007).

Initiative and Referendum Institute Europe. *The Initiative and Referendum Institute Europe*. www.iri-europe.org (January 15, 2007).

Johnson, Hans. "California's Population in 2025." In *California 2025: Taking on the Future*, edited by Ellen Hanak and Mark Baldassare, 23–49. San Francisco: Public Policy Institute of California, 2005.

Johnson, Hiram. "Inaugural Address, January 3, 1911." *Governors of California*. www.governor.ca.gov/govsite/govsgallery/h/documents/inaugural_23.html (January 15, 2007).

Kazin, Michael. *The Populist Persuasion: An American History*. New York: Basic Books, 1995.

LaGuardia, Alan. "Ballot Watch." *Sacramento Bee*, October 1, 2005, A3.

LaMar, Andrew, and Kate Folmar. "Democrat Is Drafted to Broker Ballot Talks: Many Issues Still Unresolved." *San Jose Mercury News*, August 18, 2005, A9.

Leamer, Laurence. *Fantastic: The Life of Arnold Schwarzenegger*. New York: St. Martin's Press, 2005.

Legislative Analyst's Office. "Overhauling the State's Infrastructure Planning and Financing Process." Sacramento, Calif.: December 1998.

———. "California Spending Plan 2000–01." Sacramento, Calif.: August 2000.

———. "California Spending Plan 2001–02." Sacramento, Calif.: September 2001.

———. "Overview of the 2003–04 Governor's Budget." Sacramento, Calif.: January 2003.

———. "An Initial Assessment of the California Performance Review." Sacramento, Calif.: August 2004.

———. "2005–06 Overview of the Governor's Budget." Sacramento, Calif.: January 2005.

———. "Overview of the 2005–06 May Revision." Sacramento, Calif.: May 2005.

———. "2006–07: Overview of the Governor's Budget." Sacramento, Calif.: January 2006.

———. "Analysis of the 2006–07 Budget Bill: After-School Programs and Proposition 49." Sacramento, Calif.: February 2006.

———. "Overview of the Governor's Budget, 2007–08." Sacramento, Calif.: January 2007.

Levi, Margaret, and Laura Stoker. "Political Trust and Trustworthiness." *Annual Review of Political Science* 3 (2000): 475–507.

Lo, Clarence. *Small Property vs. Big Government: Social Origins of the Property Tax Revolt*. Berkeley: University of California Press, 1990.

Lee, Eugene. "The Initiative Boom: An Excess of Democracy." In *Governing California: Politics, Government and Public Policy in the Golden State*, edited by Gerald C. Lubenow and Bruce E. Cain, 113–36. Berkeley, Calif.: Institute of Governmental Studies, 1997.

Lipset, Seymour Martin, and William Schneider. *The Confidence Gap: Business, Labor and Government in the Public Mind*. New York: Free Press, 1983.

Lochhead, Carolyn. "Gay Marriage: Did Issue Help Re-elect Bush?" *San Francisco Chronicle*, November 4, 2004, A1.

Los Angeles Times Exit Poll. March 5, 2002.

———. November 5, 2002.

———. October 7, 2003.

———. March 2, 2004.

———. June 6, 2006.

Los Angeles Times. "The Recall Campaign; Debate Viewed in 2.4 Million Homes." *Los Angeles Times*, September 26, 2003, A19.

Lubenow, Gerald C., ed. *California Votes: The 2002 Governor's Race and the Recall That Made History*. Berkeley: Berkeley Public Policy Press (University of California, Berkeley), 2003.

Lucas, Greg. "State Budget Signed, But Not Finished." *San Francisco Chronicle*,

September 6, 2002, A23.

Magleby, David B. *Direct Legislation: Voting on Ballot Propositions in the United States.* Baltimore, Md.: Johns Hopkins University Press, 1984.

Magleby, David B., and Kelly D. Patterson. "Campaign Consultants and Direct Democracy: The Politics of Citizen Control." In *Campaign Warriors: The Role of Political Consultants in Elections,* edited by James A. Thurber and Candace J. Nelson, 133–52. Washington, D.C.: Brookings, 2000.

Mariani, John. "Governor Puts Details off for Now." *Post-Standard* (Syracuse, N.Y.), January 6, 2005, A12.

Marimow, Ann E. "Capitol Gain: Schwarzenegger's First Year in Office." *San Jose Mercury News,* November 15, 2004, A1.

Marinucci, Carla. "On Politics." *San Francisco Chronicle,* October 14, 2002, A4.

———. "Beatty Kicks up Political Dust at Cal." *San Francisco Chronicle,* May 22, 2005, A1.

———. "Pressure for a Special Election: Conservatives Say Backing Off Now Is Not an Option." *San Francisco Chronicle,* June 7, 2005, B1.

———. "How Big Donors Aid Angelides' Candidacy." *San Francisco Chronicle,* June 1, 2006, A1.

———. "Schwarzenegger Pens Second-Term Script that Reads Like a Hollywood Epic." *San Francisco Chronicle,* January 10, 2007, A1.

Marinucci, Carla, and Mark Martin. "Governor Endorses Minutemen on Border." *San Francisco Chronicle,* April 29, 2005, A1.

Martelle, Scott, and Robert Salladay. "Glitterati, Gawkers Shrug off Second Inauguration." *Los Angeles Times,* January 6, 2007, A14.

Martin, Mark. "Governor Faces Test in GOP Contests." *San Francisco Chronicle,* October 18, 2004, B1.

———. "Governor Says He Will Call Special Election: Remark Counters Compromise Moves toward Legislature." *San Francisco Chronicle,* March 15, 2005, B8.

Martin, Mark, and Lynda Gledhill. "Schwarzenegger, Democrats Trade Charges of Lying: at Issue Are Alleged Vows on Education Funds, Ballot Issue." *San Francisco Chronicle,* May 18, 2005, B1.

Martin, Mark, and John M. Hubbell. "Governor, Democrats Prepared to Go to Voters with Hot Issues." *San Francisco Chronicle,* January 7, 2005, A12.

Mathews, Joe. *The People's Machine: Arnold Schwarzenegger and the Rise of Blockbuster Democracy.* New York: Public Affairs, 2006.

Matier, Phillip, and Andy Ross. "Big Money: Initiative Campaigns Hugely Costly." *San Francisco Chronicle,* November 9, 2005, B1.

Matsusaka, John. *For the Many or the Few: The Initiative, Public Policy, and American Democracy.* Chicago: University of Chicago Press, 2004.

May, Meredith. "Schwarzenegger in S.F. Pushing After-School Plan." *San Francisco Chronicle,* October 12, 2002, A17.

McCarthy, Bill. Assembly Constitutional Amendment 27. California Assembly, introduced January 25, 2006.

McCuan, David. "Can't Buy Me Love: Interest Group Status and the Role of Political Professionals in Direct Democracy." In *Initiative-Centered Politics: The New Politics of Direct Democracy*, edited by David McCuan and Steve Stambough, 51–75. Durham, N. C.: Carolina University Press, 2005.

McCuan, David, and Steve Stambough, eds. *Initiative-Centered Politics: The New Politics of Direct Democracy*. Durham, N. C.: Carolina University Press, 2005.

McCuan, David, Shaun Bowler, Todd Donovan, and Ken Fernandez. "California's Political Warriors: Campaign Professionals and the Initiative Process." In *Citizens as Legislators: Direct Democracy in the United States*, edited by Shaun Bowler, Todd Donovan, and Caroline J. Tolbert, 55–79. Columbus: Ohio State University Press, 1998.

Melley, Brian. "AG Sues to Remove Redistricting Initiative from Ballot." *Associated Press News Wire*, July 9, 2005.

Miller, Arthur. "Political Issues and Trust in Government." *American Political Science Review* 68, no. 3 (1974): 951–72.

Morain, Dan. "Schwarzenegger a Big Fund-Raiser in 2004: The Governor Generated More Than $23 Million in Political Donations, Finance Reports Show." *Los Angeles Times*, February 1, 2005, B1.

———. "Election 2006: The California Vote: Deep Pockets Carry the Day." *Los Angeles Times*, November 9, 2006, A28.

———. "No Wrongdoing Done on First Five." *Los Angeles Times*, November 22, 2006, B6.

Morrison, Patt. "Total Recall: Against Davis or For Republicans?" *Los Angeles Times*, February 10, 2003, B3.

Murphy, Dean E., and Charlie LeDuff. "Movie Star In, Senator Out for Recall Race in California." *New York Times*, August 7, 2003, A1.

National Conference of State Legislatures. "Recall of State Officials." March 21, 2006. www.ncsl.org/programs/legismgt/elect/recallprovision.htm (April 1, 2006).

———. "Ballot Measures Database." www.ncsl.org/programs/legismgt/elect/dbintro.htm (December 1, 2006).

———. "Initiative and Referendum in the 21st Century: Final Report and Recommendations of the NCSL I&R Task Force." Washington, D.C.: NCSL, July 2002.

———. "Joint Project on Term Limits." Results reported in Jennifer Drage Bowser, Keon S. Chi, and Thomas H. Little, "Coping with Term Limits: A Practical Guide." Denver: NCSL, August 2006.

———. "Term-Limited States." February 2006. www.ncsl.org/programs/legismgt/about/states.htm (April 1, 2006).

Nicholas, Peter. "Gov. Faces Widening Network of Opposition." *Los Angeles Times*, March 16, 2005, A1.

———. "Governor May Be Selling an Illusion of Unity." *Los Angeles Times*, March 11, 2007, A1.

Nicholas, Peter, and Evan Halper. "Governor Goes on the Road with His Threat to Unseat Democrats." *Los Angeles Times*, July 17, 2004, B1.

Nissenbaum, Dion. "Assertive Actor Selling Himself, Psyching Out Foes." *San Jose Mercury News*, August 10, 2003, A1.

———. "Reality Check: An Analysis of Campaign Commercials." *San Jose Mercury*

News, September 4, 2003, A17.

———. "Capitol Heats Up: Rhetoric Intensifies as Fall Vote Grows More Likely." *San Jose Mercury News*, May 26, 2005, A1.

Nissenbaum, Dion, and Ann E. Marimow. "Recall Free-for-All: Amid Bickering, Five Major Candidates Contrast Views." *San Jose Mercury News*, September 25, 2003, A1.

Planning and Conservation League. Action Alert, issued March 13, 2006.

Powers, Ashley. "A Good Day to Scare up Support." *Los Angeles Times*, November 1, 2005, B7.

Public Policy Institute of California. "Just the Facts: 2005 Special Election Voter Profiles." San Francisco: Public Policy Institute of California, November 2005.

———. PPIC Statewide Surveys 1998–2006. Questionnaires and results available online at www.ppic.org/main/series.asp?i=12. San Francisco: Public Policy Institute of California (accessed January 15, 2007).

Rainey, James. "The Recall Campaign; Riordan 'Stunned' by Friend, Aide Says." *Los Angeles Times*, August 7, 2003, A23.

Rau, Jordan. "Gov. Offers Bold Prescription." *Los Angeles Times*, January 9, 2007, A1.

Rau, Jordan, and Robert Salladay. "Legislature Wraps Up Difficult, Humbling Year." *Los Angeles Times*, August 29, 2004, A1.

———. "Special Election Ballot Taking Shape." *Los Angeles Times*, May 11, 2005, B1.

Rau, Jordan, and Nancy Vogel. "Governor Wields Heavy Veto Pen." *Los Angeles Times*, October 1, 2004, B1.

———. "Governor, Public Workers' Unions Square Off for a Battle over Clout." *Los Angeles Times*, May 6, 2005, B8.

Raymond, Valerie. *Surviving Proposition 13: Fiscal Crisis in California Counties*. Berkeley: Institute of Governmental Studies (University of California, Berkeley), 1988.

RecallGrayDavis.com. "Recall against California's Gov. Gray Davis Led by Former State Legislator." *Recall Gray Davis*, website for recall campaign headed by Howard Kaloogian. February 5, 2003. www.recallgraydavis.com/news.folder/pr20030204–1.asp (June 22, 2005).

Riches, Erin. "Proposition 53: Should California Earmark General Fund Revenue for Infrastructure?" In California Budget Project, Budget Brief, August 2003, 6–7.

Sabato, Larry J., Howard R. Ernst, and Bruce A. Larson, eds. *Dangerous Democracy: The Battle over Ballot Initiatives in America*. Lanham, Md.: Rowman & Littlefield, 2001.

Salladay, Robert. "Cheers and Jeers Greet Governor." *Los Angeles Times*, December 8, 2004, B1.

———. "Lockyer's Statement under Fire." *Los Angeles Times*, March 8, 2005, B3.

———. "Gov. Readies Special Election to Attack Legislature, Unions." *Los Angeles Times*, May 17, 2005, A1.

———. "Governor Hits Stump in Replay of Recall." *Los Angeles Times*, September 13, 2005, B1.

———. "State of the State: Governor Lays out Agenda of Concrete and Steel." *Los Angeles Times*, January 6, 2006, A1.

Salladay, Robert, and Dan Morain. "Governor Donates $1.25 Million." *Los Angeles*

Times, September 24, 2005, B3.

Sanchez, Renee. "Partisan Rancor over Budget Returns to California." *Washington Post*, July 10, 2004, A2.

Sanders, Jim. "No Change Back on Money Spent: The Same Parties Maintain Control of Legislative Seats after an Expensive Election." *Sacramento Bee*, November 4, 2004, A3.

———. "Prop. 89 Spot Draws on Governor's Quotes." *Sacramento Bee*, October 15, 2006, A3.

———. "Early Primary Plan Is Sent to Governor: February Presidential Vote Could Spur Drive to Alter Term Limits." *Sacramento Bee*, March 7, 2007, A1.

Schmidt, David D. *Citizen Lawmakers: The Ballot Initiative Revolution.* Philadelphia: Temple University Press, 1989.

Schrag, Peter. *Paradise Lost: California's Experience, America's Future.* New York: New Press, 1998.

———. "Meeting Your 'New Day in California' Governor." *Sacramento Bee*, November 17, 2004, B7.

———. *California: America's High-Stakes Experiment.* Berkeley: University of California Press, 2006.

Schultz, E. J., and Jim Sanders. "Speaker Puts a Dissenter in 'Doghouse.'" *Sacramento Bee*, May 6, 2006, A1.

Schwarzenegger, Arnold. "Governor Schwarzenegger's 2004 State of the State Address." Text of speech delivered on January 6, 2004, *Governor of California* website. www.governor.ca.gov/state/govsite/gov_speeches_index.jsp (January 10, 2004).

———. "Excerpts of Gov. Schwarzenegger's May Budget Revision Announcement." Text of speech delivered on May 13, 2004, *Governor of California* website. www.governor.ca.gov/state/govsite/gov_speeches_index.jsp (May 20, 2004).

———. "Governor Schwarzenegger's 2005 State of the State Address." Text of speech delivered on January 5, 2005. *Governor of California* website. www.governor.ca.gov/state/govsite/gov_speeches_index.jsp (January 20, 2005).

———. "Governor's Remarks at the Release of his 2005–06 State Budget." Text of speech delivered on January 10, 2005. *Governor of California* website. www.governor.ca.gov/state/govsite/gov_speeches_index.jsp (January 20, 2005).

———. "Governor's Remarks at the Sacramento Press Club Luncheon." Text of speech delivered on January 26, 2005. *Governor of California* website. www.governor.ca.gov/state/govsite/gov_speeches_index.jsp (March 1, 2005).

———. "Governor's Remarks at May Budget Revise." Text of speech delivered on May 13, 2005. *Governor of California* website. www.governor.ca.gov/state/govsite/gov_speeches_index.jsp (June 1, 2005).

———. "Governor Schwarzenegger's Address Calling a Special Election to Reform California." Text of speech delivered on June 13, 2005. *Governor of California* website. www.governor.ca.gov/state/govsite/gov_speeches_index.jsp (December 5, 2005).

———. "Governor Schwarzenegger's Press Conference." Text of speech delivered on November 10, 2005. *Governor of California* website. www.governor.ca.gov/

state/govsite/gov_speeches_index.jsp (February 15, 2006).

———. "Governor Schwarzenegger's 2006 State of the State Address." Text of speech delivered on January 5, 2006. *Governor of California* website. www.governor .ca.gov/state/govsite/gov_speeches_index.jsp (March 10, 2006).

———. "Governor Schwarzenegger's Remarks at Release of 2006–07 Budget Press Conference." Text of speech delivered on January 10, 2006. *Governor of California* website. www.governor.ca.gov/state/govsite/gov_speeches_index.jsp (March 15, 2006).

———. "Governor Arnold Schwarzenegger's Remarks at a Press Conference Detailing Bond Negotiations." Text of speech delivered on March 16, 2006. *Governor of California* website. www.governor.ca.gov/state/govsite/gov_speeches_index.jsp (May 23, 2006).

———. "Office of the Governor press release, June 30, 2006." *Governor of California* website. www.governor.ca.gov/state/govsite/gov_pressroom_index.jsp (June 30, 2006).

———. "Gov. Schwarzenegger's Second Inaugural Address." Text of speech delivered on January 5, 2007. *Office of the Governor* website. www.gov.ca.gov (January 6, 2007).

———. "Governor's Health Care Proposal." Text of proposal released on January 8, 2007. *Office of the Governor* website. www.gov.ca.gov (January 8, 2007).

———. "State of the State Address." Text of speech delivered on January 9, 2007. *Office of the Governor* website. www.gov.ca.gov (January 10, 2007).

———. "Gov. Arnold Schwarzenegger's Remarks at State Budget Release Press Conference." Text of speech delivered on January 10, 2007. *Office of the Governor* website. www.gov.ca.gov (January 11, 2007).

Sears, David O., and Jack Citrin. *Tax Revolt: Something for Nothing in California.* Cambridge, Mass.: Harvard University Press, 1982.

Shires, Michael. *Patterns in California Government Revenues since Proposition 13.* San Francisco: Public Policy Institute of California, 1999.

Shires, Michael, John Ellwood, and Mary Sprague. *Has Proposition 13 Delivered?: The Changing Tax Burden in California.* San Francisco: Public Policy Institute of California, 1998.

Silva, J. Fred, and Elisa Barbour. *The State-Local Fiscal Relationship in California: A Changing Balance of Power.* San Francisco: Public Policy Institute of California, 1999.

Skelton, George. "Star Power Drives a Dubious Plan." *Los Angeles Times*, October 4, 2002, B10.

———. "Capitol Journal: Student Governor Needs to Buckle Down and Work." *Los Angeles Times*, November 15, 2004, B4.

———. "A Victory for Old-Fashioned Lawmaking." *Los Angeles Times*, May 8, 2006, B3.

Smith, Daniel A., and Caroline J. Tolbert. *Educated by Initiative: The Effects of Direct Democracy on Citizens and Political Organizations in the American States.* Ann Arbor: University of Michigan Press, 2004.

Surrusco, Mike, Jon Goldin-Dubois, and Edwin Davis. "Designer Districts: Safe

Seats Tailor-Made for Incumbents." Washington, D.C.: Common Cause Educational Fund, April 2005.

Starr, Kevin. *Inventing the Dream: California through the Progressive Era.* New York: Oxford University Press, 1985.

Talev, Margaret. "Governor Lashes out at Recall Drive." *Sacramento Bee*, February 14, 2003, A3.

———. "Flair for Surprise Keeps Him in the Catbird Seat." *Sacramento Bee*, November 14, 2004, A1.

Tolbert, Caroline J. "Changing Rules for State Legislatures: Direct Democracy and Governance Policies." In *Citizens as Legislators: Direct Democracy in the United States*, edited by Shaun Bowler, Todd Donovan, and Caroline J. Tolbert, 171–90. Columbus: Ohio State University Press, 1998.

U.S. Census Bureau. *1910 U.S. Decennial Census.* "Historical Census Browser." University of Virginia, Geospatial and Statistical Data Center http://fisher.lib.virginia.edu/collections/stats/histcensus/index.html (March 8, 2006).

Vogel, Nancy. "Gov's Remap Bid Ruled Invalid." *Los Angeles Times*, July 22, 2005, A1.

Vogel, Nancy, and Mark Z. Barabak. "Earlier Primary Gives California a Major Voice." *Los Angeles Times*, March 16, 2007, A1.

Walters, Dan. "Is Schwarzenegger Muscling-up for 2006 Gubernatorial Campaign?" *Sacramento Bee*, September 30, 2002, A3.

———. "Schwarzenegger May Be Putting Himself into a Political Pitfall." *Sacramento Bee*, January 6, 2006, A3.

Waters, M. Dane. *Initiative and Referendum Almanac.* Durham, N.C.: Carolina Academic Press, 2003.

Weare, Christopher. *The California Electricity Crisis: Causes and Policy Options.* San Francisco: Public Policy Institute of California, 2003.

Weintraub, Dan. "Davis Recall Still Possible, Despite Dread of Poo-bahs." *Sacramento Bee*, March 9, 2003, E1.

———. "Arnold: Year One. Twelve Months in the Life of California's Celebrity Governor." *Sacramento Bee*, November 14, 2004, E1.

Wildermuth, John. "Governor Says Prop. 13 Is at Risk If His Ballot Measures Are Defeated." *San Francisco Chronicle*, June 15, 2005, A1.

———. "Drug Firms Arming for Battle at Ballot Box." *San Francisco Chronicle*, July 13, 2005, A1.

———. "$300 Million Price Tag on Initiative Battles." *San Francisco Chronicle*, November 2, 2005, A1.

Yankelovich, Daniel. *New Rules: Searching for Self-fulfillment in a World Turned Upside-Down.* New York: Random House, 1981.

Yost, Phil. "Davis Wants to Close the Budget Gap: His Foes Just Want His Head." *San Jose Mercury News*, February 9, 2003, OP1.

Index

Note: Page numbers followed by "t" indicate tables.

About the Authors

Mark Baldassare is president and CEO of the Public Policy Institute of California, where he holds the Arjay and Frances Fearing Miller Chair in Public Policy and directs the PPIC Statewide Survey. Before joining PPIC, he was a professor and held the Roger and Janice Johnson Chair in Civic Governance at the University of California, Irvine. His other recent books include: *A California State of Mind: The Conflicted Voter in a Changing World* (2002), *California in the New Millennium: The Changing Social and Political Landscape* (2000), and *When Government Fails: The Orange County Bankruptcy* (1998).

Cheryl Katz is an independent public opinion researcher and California journalist. She has directed public opinion polling for California newspapers, including the *Los Angeles Times, Sacramento Bee,* and *San Francisco Chronicle,* and radio and television stations. She is the author of numerous newspaper articles on California issues and scholarly publications in *Public Opinion Quarterly, International Journal of Public Opinion Research, Journalism Quarterly,* and *Journalism and Mass Communication Quarterly.*